Matched Pair

Matched Pair

THE ELYS OF EMBASSY ROW

By Jarvis Harriman

POOH STIX PRESS

Tucson, Arizona

Cover photo of the Elys by Luc de Montmollin,
March 1954, Livorno, Italy; cover photo of the Ely home by Jack Ely
Editorial services by Alice Chaffee
Cover and book design by Adine Maron
Pooh Stix Press logo design by Sandy Blake

Published in the United States of America by Pooh Stix Press,
PMB 318, 4725 Sunrise Drive, Tucson, AZ 85718
Printed by Haagen Printing, Santa Barbara, CA

First printing October 1999
ISBN 0-9634323-2-x
ISBN 0-9634323-1-1 (pbk.)
Library of Congress Catalog Card Number: 99-74083

Dedicated

to

the future

and to the descendants.

May they draw strength and inspiration

from the

faith,

courage,

humor,

and commitment

of those who went ahead.

CONTENTS

MAPS AND ILLUSTRATIONS

Photographs: Unless otherwise indicated, all photographs were taken by Jack Ely or members of the Ely family.

First Group: Primarily portraits of principal family members mentioned in text
Page 1:   Etchings taken from *Nathaniel Ely and His Descendants* by Heman Ely II, Ohio, 1885
Page 2:   Etchings taken from Albert Welles, *American Family Antiques*, vol. Jennings. New York: Society Library 1881
Page 3:   Four generations Ely family 1889, photo by unknown Elyria professional
Page 4:   1859 Jennings family photo by unknown San Francisco professional; 1908 Jennings family photo by unknown professional in Rome
Page 5:   Two Ely photos by unknown professionals; Maud Ely drawn by A. G. Learned
Page 6:   All photos by unknown professionals
Page 8:   Mary taken in England by unknown friend; Connie Ely and grandchildren taken by Olan Mills in Arizona, used by permission

Second Group: Primarily homes, family and friends 1895-1930
Page 1:   Walter Jennings gate taken by Jarvis Harriman 1995; Elyston and Burrwood by Jack Ely; aerial of Fort Hill by unknown professional
Page 2:   Dr. Southworth painted by Ellen Emmet Rand, used by permission of the Southworth family
Page 3:   Jack Ely and Cornelius Vanderbilt clipped from unknown paper by Maud Merchant Ely; Jack Ely in uniform, by unknown U.S. Navy photographer, 1918
Page 4:   All photos by Jean Brown Jennings, 1908 and 1925
Page 5:   William Avery Rockefeller and Walter Jennings by Jean Brown Jennings; Jennings at Jekyll Island Club by Tebbs and Knell, © Jekyll Club Launching photo by Standard Oil Company photographer
Page 6:   Wedding photos by professional photographer

Third Group: Primarily Connie and Jack with children, 1930-1948
Page 1:   Sketch by R.B. Hale, used by permission of Mrs. Hale
Page 2:   *Town & Country* magazine cover by: ©1999 Archives of Milton H. Greene, LLC. All rights reserved. www.archivesmhg.com
Page 3:   Sketch by Eric Parfit, used by permission
Page 4:   Frank Buchman and Jack Ely by Arthur Strong; Harry Truman and James Wadsworth by Arthur Strong
Page 5:   Connie Ely as "Mrs. Citizen" by Arthur Strong

Fourth Group: Primarily family around the world, 1948-1990
Page 2:   Jack as "Mr. Diehard," courtesy of MRA
Page 4:   Japanese delegation,1950, by R.J. Fleming
Page 6:   Group being received by Gamal Abdel Nasser in Cairo by R.J. Fleming
Page 7:   P.Q. Vundla and Nico Ferreira, courtesy of New World News

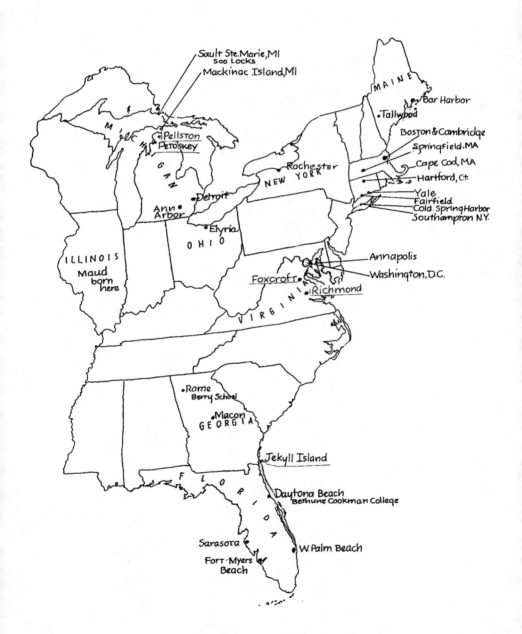

Montauk Point

Southampton

Shinnecock Bay

Great Peconic Bay

Fort Hill

Huntington Town

Cold Spring Harbor Village

Oyster Bay

Jones Beach

Manhattan

M. Harriman

x

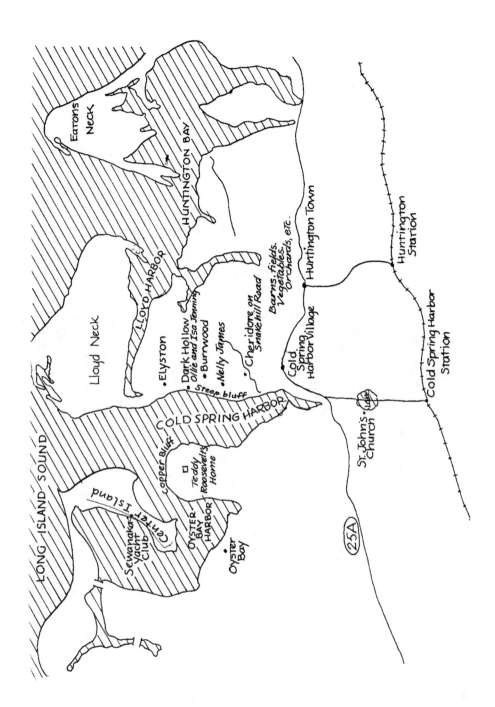

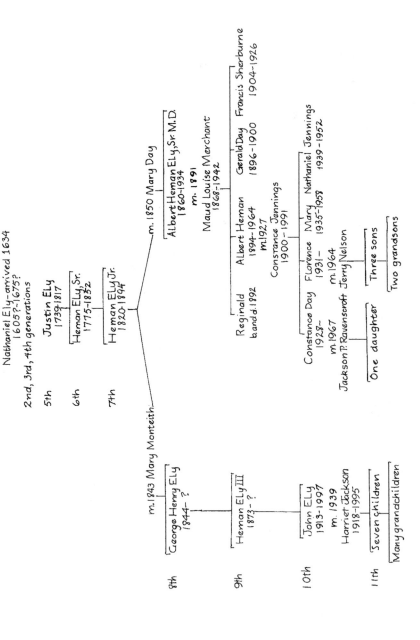

ELY

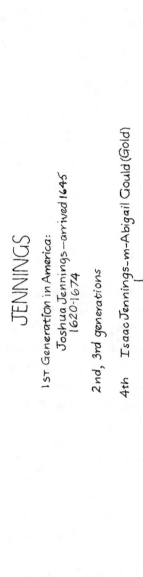
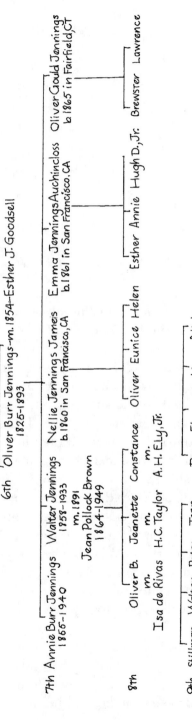

JENNINGS

1st Generation in America:
Joshua Jennings—arrived 1645
1620-1674

2nd, 3rd generations

4th Isaac Jennings—m—Abigail Gould (Gold)

5th Abraham Gould Jennings—m—Anna Burr
1781-1852 (born in "Old Homestead")

6th Oliver Burr Jennings—m.1854—Esther J. Goodsell
1825-1893

7th Annie Burr Jennings Walter Jennings Nellie Jennings James Emma Jennings Auchincloss Oliver Gould Jennings
1865-1940 1858-1933 b.1860 in San Francisco, CA b.1861 in San Francisco, CA b.1865 in Fairfield, CT
m.1891
Jean Pollock Brown
1864-1949

8th Oliver B. Jeanette Constance Oliver Eunice Helen Esther Annie Hugh D.,Jr. Brewster Lawrence
m. m.
Isa de Rivas H.C. Taylor A.H. Ely, Jr.

9th Stillman Walter Peter Jean Day Florence Mary Niel
m. m.
Jackson P. Ravenscroft Jerry Nelson

Preface

For an amazing unfolding adventure, I recommend writing the biography of someone, as I have here of Albert H. "Jack" Ely Jr. and Constance Jennings, his wife.

Jack Ely was twenty-eight years older than I, and Connie twenty-two years older. I knew them and their family well enough to know that here were two people worth knowing much, much more about. We did share, however, many experiences together. I participated in much that they lived through from 1946 onward. But not in the way I later did by immersing myself in their diaries, their correspondence and their earlier years.

Inevitably I came to certain conjectures and conclusions that seem to fit better into a preface than into the story itself. Here are three of them.

In recounting Jack's adventures in his South American trip in 1914, it seemed to me that Jack wrote, especially about the development opportunities and growth potential that he saw, as if someone had commissioned him to make a study of the possibilities for South America's future; someone who wanted to know the investment possibilities; someone who provided him with entrées to key people. That is simple conjecture, and I'll never know.

Then there is Jack's family. We have no record of what he felt about the difficulties between his mother and father. Jack was a sensitive man; he must have felt a great deal about that, especially in his later years when he entertained them in his home, when he went to see his father where he was recuperating, and when he watched his mother stonewall him. And his brothers: Reginald, who died ten days after birth; Gerald, who died at four; and especially Francis, who lived to be twenty-two. Jack's schooling, boarding school and college, was the American equivalent of the British training for the "stiff upper lip." Before that really set in, we have several childhood letters where he asks his mother, "How is Francis?" Jack would see Francis on vacations when he was at home, and especially when he was studying law and living with the family.

We have just two documented occasions when Jack talked about his family in later life; one when he was having to rest in bed during his 1959 trip around the world, the other when he was close to death and talking with his nurse. But in neither case do we know what he said.

Ah well, we know his family was on his mind.

And the third conclusion: When Day Ely Ravenscroft asked me to undertake this book, she lent me her copy of *The Wise Men*, by Walter Isaacson and Evan Thomas. This book, published in 1994, tells the story of W. Averill Harriman, Dean Acheson, John J. McCloy, George Kennan, Charles Bohlen and Robert Lovett, and their work over the years to win World War II and to create a strategy to contain the Soviet Union's expansionist ambitions. "They are my father's peers," Day told me. "These are the men who shared his background, his education, and his culture. He belongs among them."

I took that seriously. The more I have thought about it and studied it, the more I have realized the truth of it, but also a further thing—those six men created policy. Jack and Connie and the men and women they worked with (the story of much of this book), helped to create, under Divine Providence, the living that made those policies work. If the aim in the Cold War was to stop Communism, then work done by the men and women whose efforts Jack and Connie shared helped to assure a positive alternative to Communism . . . that a better future would evolve for Western Europe, and ultimately for Eastern Europe as well.

Communism set out to capture the means of production of England, France, Germany and Italy. This effort did not succeed. Instead, the spirit of working together, capital and labor, continent-wide, did succeed. From the beginnings in post-war Europe of the European Coal and Steel Community, to the advent of a common currency in 1999, it has grown. There is much to be done, but now we have the freedom to do it.

I have sketched out what this work was like, the human element essential to producing these results. I say here with great emphasis that the

Elys, and those whom I mention, were only a fraction of those who were vital to this work. Had space permitted, I would have mentioned several hundred people, most of whom I knew personally, whose lives were invested in this process—French, British, Dutch, Norwegian, Danish, Swiss, American, Canadian and German. It is almost criminal to write this story, for instance, without including Irène and Victor Laure and their children. The dramatic change that took place in the heart of Irène, a fiery French Socialist leader, and how she poured out her life to build a hate-free relationship between Germany and France, is one of the great stories of postwar Europe.

The skills that grew out of Frank Buchman's work, for example the sensitivity to deal with people, using your own shortcomings and needs to help the other person find a fuller life, and to be receptive to the power of God to work through you and beyond you—these were the skills, put to work across Europe in the late 1940s and 1950s, that were indispensable to building the Europe we have today. They were the same skills and tools that Jack and Connie Ely, and countless others, carried with them as they moved across Asia and Africa and through those many years that unfold in this story.

While Jack never held any post in government, in choosing to commit his life to God's direction he was following his own star, and that star was as surely focused on the destiny of the world as were any careers in or out of the federal government.

Jack and Connie were a delightful pair of human beings. As in any good marriage, their lives were reinforced by each other—what they were together, what they were able to do together, was much greater than the sum of two lives. They were a matched pair.

*   *   *

To put together all the facts needed for this book has required all sorts of help, from individuals and from institutions. I interviewed approximately 120 individuals, some of whom have since died. Some interviews were only telephone conversations, some were by correspondence, and some through visits in such lovely places as a garden in springtime Lisbon, an alcove high above the Lake of Geneva, a cottage on the shore of Loch Lomond, and a cabin at the Chalet Club in western North Carolina. I believe all of those individuals are acknowledged in the text. They are a wonderful group of people!

Many institutions aided me in this endeavor. I studied for a week in the manuscript division of the Library of Congress, for a number of days in the New York Public Library, and in the Elyria Public Library in Elyria, Ohio, the Hill School, the Sterling Library at Yale, the New York Historical Society, the University of Arizona. By telephone I had most courteous and helpful talks with Bethune-Cookman College, the Cold Spring Harbor Library, Columbia University Library, Columbia University Teachers' College Library, and the Connecticut Historical Society.

I received help from Peter Dervis, a New York historian specializing in uniforms such as those of Squadron A, and from Squadron A historian Kenyon Fitzgerald; from the General Theological Seminary; the Harding House and Museum in Ohio; and from the Huntington Historical Society, the Huntington Library, and the Huntington Town Clerk's office, in particular the Huntington Township historian, Dr. Klein. Others providing assistance were the Joint Free Public Library of Morristown and Morris County, New Jersey; Robert Keene, historian of Southampton; Kent School; Lake Superior State College; Lloyd Harbor Historical Society; the Lorain County Historical Society; the Louisiana State Museum; the Metropolitan Museum of Art; the Morristown-Beard School; the Museum of the City of New York; Mystic Seaport Museum; the National Personnel Records Center; the National Rowing Foundation; the New York Court of Appeals; and the New York Yacht Club historian.

I am also indebted to Northern Illinois University; Porter Sargent Publishers Inc. and Mrs. Jane Culver Sargent; the Mudd Library at Princeton University; Riverdale Country School; the Franklin Delano Roosevelt Library and Museum; St. John's Church, Cold Spring Harbor; Seventh Regimental Armory New York Army National Guard; the Society for the Preservation of Long Island Antiquities; Southampton Hospital, Southampton Town Hall, the Squadron A Association, Tulane University archivist Dr. Bill Memerey; the U.S. Coast Guard Academy Museum and O.W. "Sonny" Martin, Coast Guard National Historian; the U.S. Navy Naval Historical Center; the U.S. Naval Academy Library; the University of Oregon; the University of Washington; the Washington D.C. Public Library; Wittenberg University; The Woodlawn Cemetery, the archives of the Boeing Company, Seattle, and the *Yale Daily News*.

I was especially grateful to be able to talk things over with two of the Ely-Merchant family, and feel out different ideas—John Merchant of Rochester, son of Maud Merchant Ely's brother, and John Ely, Dr. Albert H. Ely's nephew. John Ely has since died.

Others who were always available to discuss ideas with were the late Arthur Meigs of Washington and George Vondermuhll of Connecticut. Also helpful were John and Denise Wood, Jerry and Barbara von Teuber, Jim and Ellie Newton, Philippe Mottu, Hans von Herwarth, Dr. Morris Martin, and Arthur Strong.

The Tucson Public Library Info Line comes in for special mention as they have dug up facts for me, for example the specifications of the Pan American Clipper and the years Franklin Roosevelt's children were born.

I had access to the inexhaustible resources of the Ravenscroft basement where all sorts of things are stored—including a suitcase full of letters dating to the 1880s, and a set of electric trains that I would have dearly loved to linger and play with!

Day Ely Ravenscroft and Florence Ely Nelson have answered unimaginable questions; and this book is really written for their offspring: Virginia Constance Ravenscroft, Nicolas Jennings Nelson, Thomas Burr Nelson and James Pollock "JP" Nelson.

Alice Blake Chaffee has been an inspired and encouraging editor—thanks, Alice!

It has been fun. Jack Ely's personal papers are still missing; a good many of my phone calls were to institutions where they might be hiding. Detective work has also failed to produce the name of Maud Ely's favorite gossip columnist or even the publication from which her column was clipped .

Nancy, my wife, shared this adventure with me as she has so many others.

And now we'll see whether what I have written will interest anyone but me!

Prologue

The tall young man stood at the edge of the crowd, watching. The mass of reporters, relatives and onlookers was pressed against the barricades that the police had erected in the great open shed on Pier 54, along the Hudson River, to keep the crowd back from the gangplank.

The young man studied the situation. This was the moment everyone was waiting for. The S.S. *Carpathian* had steamed under full power to the site of the sinking of the greatest passenger liner ever built, the S.S. *Titanic*, and had been able to pick up what survivors there were from the worst disaster in maritime history. Now, three days later, The *Carpathian* had docked and the survivors were to disembark and be taken to hotels to recuperate and meet their families.

On her maiden voyage, the ship which The White Star Line and the British shipbuilding industry had hailed as the latest in marine technology—a mammoth, unsinkable, luxury passenger liner—had struck an iceberg in the North Atlantic, and carried 1600 passengers and crew to the bottom.

Jack Ely watched the proceedings over the heads of the others. If he could get a story, perhaps even the first story into print, it would make his career with the *Yale Daily News*. He had caught the train from New Haven when he heard that the *Carpathian* was nearing New York Harbor. To prove his mettle with the *Daily News* would mean all the difference in his battle to earn his way through Yale.

His eye was caught by a gentleman who walked quietly off the ship. The man seemed to melt into the crowd. Jack kept his eye on the figure who was slipping away from the focus of attention, and followed him out to the taxi rank. The gentleman entered a taxi and sped off. Jack hailed another cab and was pleased to use the immortal line, "Follow that car!" He followed the cab to an apartment building and managed to get into the same elevator with the tall man.

What happened next we may never know precisely, but early the next morning the *Yale Daily News* carried this front-page headline: "TITANIC DISASTER BY EYE WITNESS." The eyewitness account is a gripping one, full of detail, and one that captures the best sentiments of courageous people in a life and death situation.

Did Jack write that story? Family lore places Jack in New York, in the crowd at Pier 54, and following the man in the cab. According to the legend, a New York paper picked up and published Jack's story, but no stories in the New York press have come to light that give Karl Behr's account of the sinking of the *Titanic*.

The man in the cab turned out to be Karl H. Behr, Yale Class of 1906, who was in the midst of a distinguished career as an internationally ranked tennis player. Jack Ely was at home on the tennis court and in the high society of the tennis world. Whether he recognized Karl Behr or not before he followed him will remain a mystery.

Ely went on to earn his way through Yale by selling advertising for the *Daily News*. The *Titanic* sank in the spring of his Freshman year, April 15, 1912.

Who was this Jack Ely?

1

Nation-builders: The Elys

ALBERT H. ELY JR. WAS A STRANGER. A stranger? He could walk into countless salons and be instantly recognized—first of all, for almost his entire life, because of his appearance. He was tall—six feet two inches—trim, and distinguished looking. His balding head made his looks even more striking. He dressed beautifully. He was an aristocrat and he looked every inch of one.

People knew him for his congeniality, his capacity as an almost unparalleled host, his gracious way that was infinitely considerate of other people, of rich and poor, celebrity or unknown, of their feelings and of their needs.

But almost no one really knew him.

Albert Heman Ely Jr. was always called Jack. Few knew why. His mother, Maud Merchant Ely, having given birth to a boy who died when he was ten days old, now desired to have a girl; and being a great lover of things French, she had decided upon the name of Jacqueline. When, on March 21, 1894, her delivery was accomplished and her newborn turned out to be a boy, "Jack" it was and Jack it continued to be until he died on September 28, 1964.

The first of Jack's ancestors to come to America was Nathaniel Ely, born around 1605 in the town of Tenterden, in Kent, England. Nathaniel's grandfather had been vicar of the "established church," or the Church of England, in that town.

In the family genealogy Nathaniel is called "the emigrant." He is first heard of on this continent in 1634. He came with a group from Tenterden and settled in what is now Cambridge, in the Massachusetts Bay Colony. In the next few years Nathaniel moved on with some of his fellow colonists to settle Hartford in Connecticut, and his name is on the founders' monument in the Center Church burying ground, Main Street, in that city. He then moved with others down to the shore to Norwalk, and finally migrated to Springfield in western Massachusetts, where the next several generations of the family lived. Nathaniel farmed and developed property, held office as a selectman from time to time, built roads under contract with the authorities, and eventually obtained a license to operate an inn. At one point he got into trouble with his license because he didn't keep enough beer in stock!

Following the successful conclusion of the American Revolution, a number of the states had to reevaluate what they considered to be their rightful boundaries. Seven of the original colonies—Massachusetts, Connecticut, New York, Virginia, North and South Carolina and Georgia—had claimed that their royal patents from the English monarch gave them the land running west from their grants clear to the Mississippi River or even, as some of their charters stated, to "the South Seas." After the Revolution, the states went through a process of relinquishing these claims one way or another, so that the lands beyond the thirteen original colonies became the property of the whole, the United States of America.

The State of Connecticut was somewhat different. The Congress recognized Connecticut's right to what was called its Western Reserve. This was land running along the same lines of latitude of the original royal colony, and lying west of the western boundary of the state of Pennsylvania and for 120 miles west.

Connecticut used some of this Reserve to settle claims arising out of the Revolution—primarily to compensate the people living in the inland settlements at Danbury and Groton, in the shore towns of New London, New Haven, Fairfield, Norwalk, and others who had been burned out by the British in their version of a scorched-earth campaign toward the end of the war. Because of this, these lands were called "the Firelands," and the name persists in history books. Connecticut then put what was left, some 3.2 million acres, up for sale, the proceeds of which were invested to benefit the state's educational system. A group of investors known as the Connecticut Land Company purchased most of this land, for about thirty-seven cents an acre. Enter Justin Ely, great-great grandson of Nathaniel, "the emigrant."

Justin was a merchant of West Springfield, Massachusetts, close by where Nathaniel had settled. Justin's forebears had done well as landowners. He graduated from Harvard College in 1759, and became successful by buying and selling property in his home state and in Vermont and New York. As a concerned citizen he served in the General Court of Massachusetts. When the American Revolution began he was thirty-seven years old, and he seems to have played his part in the Revolution by working with those who were drafted into the Continental Army and seeing that they had what they needed.

Justin had a lot of confidence in the future of the country, and by 1816 had acquired some 12,500 acres of the former Western Reserve. He and his wife had four children—Theodore, Anna, Justin and Heman. He put his son Heman to work making something of the Western Reserve property.

Heman named the town he founded on those Western Reserve acres Elyria, from the family surname. Elyria is a thriving modern town today, lying just west of Cleveland. Heman indicates in one document that he liked the name not only because it honored his family but also because it reminded him of the classical land of Illyria (now Albania) of which he had read when he was in France.

In the Elyria Public Library, itself made possible to some extent by Heman's son Charles Arthur Ely, one can read the extensive correspondence between Justin and Heman. Their letters, hand-written but conveniently transcribed into typescript by modern-day researchers, went back and forth between western Massachusetts and the Ohio frontier by various means. How such an extensive and immediate correspondence was maintained in such primitive conditions is a wonder. When Heman began to develop the land there were no roads to speak of. Horseback and pack animals did much of the work. The barge canal was not yet built; there were no large boats on the lakes. It was not until later that the railroad served this territory.

Previously Heman and his elder brother Theodore had gone into some overseas trading ventures together in the early years of the nineteenth century. The T. and H. Ely Company, of New York City, faced some interesting problems.

In Heman Ely's day, Europe was in constant turmoil. England, France, The Netherlands, Spain, Austria were warring, jostling for place, with alliances forming and breaking up. In the young United States, men like the Ely brothers were coping with a host of issues that they knew very little about. Entering into diplomatic and trade relations was not a simple business. Trading upon the seas was not a matter of just loading a sailing ship with goods and heading out for the other shore.

To understand these complexities and to try to break some bottlenecks, Heman Ely set out for England in 1809. The story is told in his letters—how he decided the better climate for trade agreements might be in France and so made his way to Paris. Because of the state of hostility between the nations he had to pay someone to smuggle him into the country. Once there, he witnessed some history-in-the-making. He was present at a "grand fête" of Napoleon and Josephine and attended the ball where a cotillion was danced by kings and queens; he was present in 1810 when Emperor Napoleon and Empress Maria Louise of Austria were married at the chapel of the Tuilleries. He was also thrown into jail at least once because someone thought he was disrespectful of the Emperor!

Theodore and Heman Ely had a rocky time of it in their commercial ventures, largely because they had relied on international trade in this uncertain and volatile period. Finally their father Justin persuaded Theodore to wind up the business in New York, and encouraged Heman to develop the Western Reserve property.

The War of 1812 between the United States and England—which had a very lively component in the Great Lakes region lying between the United States and Canada—caused the Elys to put off developing their land near Lake Erie until the war was over. In 1816 Heman Ely journeyed out from western Massachusetts as far as Buffalo with a horse and sulky, and from Buffalo rode horseback to the Black River, which ran north through their land to the lake. The trip from West Springfield to the Black River was about 600 miles.

The whole area was stirring with settlers moving in. Treaties for land acquisition had been made with the Indian tribes over the years, by the French, British and Americans, and during the time the Elys created the town of Elyria there were no particular troubles with the Indians.

The Black River has two branches, which come together where Heman Ely decided to lay out his town. On each branch there was a forty-foot waterfall, and he determined to put a grist mill at one of these falls and a saw mill at the other. He contracted with two men of the region to build these, and to build him a log house. He then returned to Massachusetts.

Heman came out the next year with two wagons, one pulled by a team of horses and the other by oxen. He brought with him his step-brother, Ebenezer Lane (who later became Chief Justice of the Supreme Court of

Ohio); a housekeeper; a young black boy as his servant, and two workmen. The trip took twenty-six days. Travelers either camped along the way or found someone to take them in. Sometimes they had to stop and cut their way through the forest, and they had to ford the frequent streams or float across them.

From these beginnings grew the town of Elyria and the other towns of Ohio. It was rough work, felling trees by hand with an axe to clear the land; but this was the way the country was built. The journals of Justin and Heman (and those who worked with them) itemized every plot they cleared, every lot they sold, every keg of nails they brought in or bolt of cloth or plow or axe. Most of the workmen they hired were competent craftsmen. The second house Heman built, in 1818, was a thoroughly Eastern-style home that lasted into modern times and was lived in by his descendants—a beautiful big home that was one of the showplaces of the town.

Heman went east the next year and married Celia Belden. He brought her out to the new town, where she gave birth to three children—Heman II, Albert, and Mary. But Celia and the baby Mary died in childbirth. Heman went back east a year later and married Harriet Salter, and they had a son, Charles Arthur, he who gave the beginnings of the public library. After Harriet's death some years later, Heman brought out a third wife, Cynthia West Sargeant, a widow who survived him.

The journals are full of town-building—how a Masonic lodge was formed; starting a school, and a church; the progress of the first store-keeper; who lent money to whom, who paid it back; who succeeded, who failed. Heman's son Heman Ely II helped to organize the first bank in Elyria, worked with Uncle Ebenezer Lane to bring the railroad to town in about 1848, was a member of the State Legislature, and worked to expand the infrastructure of business and a thriving community. He married Mary Monteith, born in the west, and they had two daughters, Celia Belden Ely and Mary Monteith Ely, and a son, George Henry Ely. His wife Mary died, and he took a second wife in Hartford, Mary Frances Day, daughter of the Honorable Thomas Day and Sarah Coit Day. Mary Day's life in Elyria had such an impact on the community that when she died, forty-five years later, her friends published a book of appreciation about her.

Two hundred years earlier, Nathaniel "the emigrant" had had a close friend and next-door neighbor, Robert Day. Nathaniel's son Sam had married a daughter of Robert Day, and the Days of Hartford, of whom Mary Frances was one, had gone down the years as close friends of the Elys.

Mary Frances Day and Heman had two more daughters, Edith Day

Ely and Harriet Putnam Ely, and two sons, Charles Theodore and Albert Heman Ely. Albert was born in 1860, in the big house built by his grandfather in 1818.

Albert spent his childhood in the town in which he was the grandson of the founder. The Elys were secure in their place as builders of America, in Ohio, Massachusetts, and Connecticut. Neither Albert's father nor his grandfather had taken time for a college education, although great-grandfather Justin had gone to Harvard.

On his mother's side, however, there was a rich tradition of education. Her father had graduated from Yale in 1797 and had been granted a Yale doctorate later in life. Her uncle, Jeremiah Day, had graduated from Yale and served as its president from 1817 to 1846. Albert Heman's half-brother, George Henry Ely, had his degree from Yale in the class of 1865.

Mary Day Ely took great care of the family she married into. She saw to it that Albert, who started his schooling in Elyria, was prepared for college at Phillips Academy in Andover, Massachusetts.

Albert entered Yale with the class of 1884, but for some reason graduated with the class of 1885. He was a success there, a member of the senior promenade committee, of the Yale chapter of the national fraternity Delta Kappa Epsilon, and of the senior society, Wolf's Head. He was also a member of Hé Boulé, an exclusive sophomore fraternity, secret in character at least in later years, and somewhat disparaged by the authorities. He was a handsome young man, and a very lively one socially.

A clipping from a New Haven newspaper in a column headed "Select Society Circles" reports: "One of the finest and most select germans [dance parties] that has ever occurred in New Haven took place at Loomis' Temple of Music. . . . It was what is termed a very swell affair, and was given by Messrs. Herbert L. Daggett and Albert H. Ely of the senior class in the academic department of Yale, in consideration of the fact that they had both recently attained their 21st year. The hall was neatly decorated, and Robinson's orchestra, assisted by a number of New York musicians, furnished the music. The favors were particularly fine (they consisted of various silver objects). . . . The guests of Messrs. Ely and Daggett were principally students, although a few well known New Haven society gentlemen participated in the joy of the occasion. The ladies were principally from out of town. . . . The supper was served by a New York caterer and the menu was very elaborate."

There is a note in the family scrapbook from a young lady in Hartford inviting Al, as he was called, for an evening there, and there are dance cards of the Hartford High School. According to another newspaper clipping, "The students in the first entry of Durfee held a reception. Among those noted was Mrs. Huntington Denton, well known in the highest plane of New Haven society, received in the rooms of Wilson Catherwood and A.H. Ely . . . the affair was the most brilliant of its kind that has ever been given in the college buildings."

Wilson Catherwood, of Philadelphia society, gave Al several guest cards to prominent Philadelphia clubs, including the Union League, the Social Art Club, and the University Club.

Albert studied medicine at the College of Physicians and Surgeons in New York City, now known as Columbia Medical School, graduating in 1888. Before graduation he won an appointment to the surgical staff of St. Luke's Hospital. He studied and worked at the hospital at the same time.

During Albert's studies at medical school he formed a friendship which was to last the rest of his life. Thomas Shepard Southworth, of West Springfield, Massachusetts (where Ely's forbears came from) took his degree from Yale in 1883. He traveled and studied for a year in Göttingen, Germany, as German was an important language in science and medicine, and German medical practice was admired in the United States. He entered the College of Physicians and Surgeons the year before Albert. It appears that Thomas Southworth gave Albert a sense of the value of experience abroad, because after Albert got his M.D., he and Southworth spent some months together in Europe.

Albert Heman Ely Sr. wrote of this experience for the twenty-fifth anniversary yearbook of his class at Yale:

> In July '90, in company with Dr. T.S. Southworth ('83), I sailed for Europe. That summer was passed in traveling; coaching about the Isle of Wight, a canoe trip down the Thames from Oxford to Richmond, Paris and the Exposition, a month in Switzerland, etc., ending with a month trying to cram up German in the old university town of Goettingen. Late in the fall we arrived in Vienna, and for seven months averaged ten hours of work each day in the various clinics of the immense Government Hospital of over 3,000 beds. At the end of this period, I traveled slowly westward to the Emerald Isle, where in dear, dirty Dublin I became an intern in the old Rotunda Maternity Hospital, and at the close of three months there received a certificate from the institution.

Back in New York, with a position in the outpatient department of the Roosevelt Hospital, Dr. Ely began to build a private practice. He made occasional trips home to Elyria, and on one of them he stopped off in Rochester, New York, to see a classmate. While there he attended a social event, and met Maud Merchant.

Maud was petite, an extraordinarily beautiful young woman, and possessed of a flirtatious nature.[1] Even late in life she was considered very attractive. Her father, George E. Merchant, was a highly successful railroad man who was much in demand in his field. He had been with various railroads in Iowa, the Dakotas and Illinois, where Maud and her sister, Elinor, and her younger brother, Gerald Eugene, were born. In 1881 Merchant was asked to take on the management of the Rochester and Pittsburgh Railroad. In the next few years he extended the railroad to Buffalo and developed its major business of hauling coal.

There is a story in the family that when Maud was a mischievous youngster, she and a pal stole a railway handcar and sped off on it. Thanks to very quick action by one switchman, they were shunted off the main track before the inbound express could kill them.

George Merchant was an excellent customer of one James Buchanan Brady. Brady was a salesman, and he took a gamble on an invention by an Englishman: a steel railroad truck to replace the standard truck built of timbers and iron wheels in the fast-growing American railroad industry. George Merchant saw the potential of this invention and gave Brady an order for steel railway trucks for the entire Buffalo, Rochester & Pittsburgh system, a tremendous feather in Brady's cap.

Brady was, in the overall picture of the age, a minor figure, a salesman, but he was flamboyant and extravagant, and was known as "Diamond Jim" because of the many diamonds he wore about his person. He lived a gossip-column lifestyle. Ladies flocked around him; one of his favorites was the famous actress Lillian Russell.

Diamond Jim Brady is alleged to have said of Maud Merchant, "She is the most beautiful woman I have ever seen."

In gratitude for the Buffalo, Rochester and Pittsburgh deal, Brady took young Gerald Merchant, George's son and Maud's brother, into his select circle of friends, which meant becoming a part of the social scene in New York and Saratoga and other fashionable places. In the summer of 1898 Brady invited Gerald to join his party for his Grand Tour of Europe. Brady, Edna McCauley, the real love of his life, and Gerald were established in the captain's suite on the French liner S.S. *Normandie*. The expedition was described as "the grandest of the Grand Tours Europe had seen up to that time."

Gerald's son, John Merchant, states that this friendship foundered on the return voyage. The cause apparently was that in their shipboard suite,

Gerald at one moment bent over the writing desk to see something the lovely Edna was writing, and at that moment Diamond Jim entered. He misconstrued the meaning of what he saw, and decided the handsome young Gerald was a competitor for Edna's affections rather than a trusted friend.

In contrast to the petite Maud, her sister Elinor was a large woman. She married Francis French of the French family of Rochester, whose key product, French's Mustard, is in every grocery today across the country.

According to family lore, at the age of eighteen Maud was engaged to three men at the same time. When Albert Ely met her she was engaged to a young man whose family owned a Rochester clothing store. Apparently the sparks flew between the handsome New York physician and the Rochester belle.

Here are her own words scribbled in her scrapbook, during a visit she made to New York City in 1889:

> March 21st - Met Dr Ely at Mrs. Pool's.
> Engaged to F.H. McFarlin of Rochester and in love with Dr Ely.
> March 24th - Dined at Mrs. Pool's with Dr Ely.
> March 31 - Dr Ely called.
> April 1st - note from Dr Ely.
> April 2nd - Dr Ely, Dr Cutler, Elinor & I went to the play.
> April 8 - Fred McFarlin came down from Rochester, thought something was wrong, remained until the 12th. Went to the theatre every night with him & said nothing.
> April 27th - Dr Ely called.
> April 28th - Dr Ely called.
> April 29th - dined with Dr Ely.
> May 2nd - Dr Ely called.
> May 4th - Dr Ely called.
> May 12th - Dr Ely called twice.
> May 15th - Engaged. Tore up Fred's letters - perhaps 1000.

A note in a memory-book states that Maud and Al's engagement took place at the Caemi Theatre in New York City.[2] A few weeks later, they visited Elyria to introduce Maud to the family. The whole family gathered on the steps of the new house (built in 1885) and a photo was taken.

The wedding of Maud Merchant and Albert Ely in October 1891 was a major social event for Rochester. "Old St. Paul's was redolent with the perfume of roses just at dusk last evening," wrote the Rochester Morning Herald, "and bright with the light of many chandeliers. It was filled, crowded indeed, with representatives of the wealth and beauty and fashion of the city and there, just as the day merged into night, the marriage of Miss Maud

Louise Merchant, of this city, and Dr. Albert Herman [*sic*] Ely of New York, was solemnized by Rev. Louis C. Washburn, rector of the church." Dr. Southworth was one of Al's ushers, and Maud's sister Elinor was one of her attendants. There was a good contingent from the Ely family of Elyria, along with flower girls from both families. The party reassembled at the Genesee Valley Club for a reception and dancing, and then Dr. and Mrs. Ely left on the train "for the West." The family has a collection of souvenir teaspoons that Maud brought home from this trip.

The newlyweds were "at home" to friends and well-wishers after November 10, at 19 West 46th Street, in New York.

This building, unlike the home in Elyria where Dr. Ely was born, still stands on West 46th Street. It is an attractive four-story structure set today tightly between two much taller buildings. Like many dwellings in New York City, it is only twelve and a half feet wide. The New York Social Register gives the same 19 West 46th Street as the address of Dr. Thomas S. Southworth.

It is hard to tell whether this was the residence or the professional addresses of the two physicians. It may well have been both. The neighborhood was nicer in those days than in the late 1990s, and the structure is attractive. Studies of the prominent families in the period in which the Elys lived there show that this was a fashionable location for the well-to-do.[3]

Dr. Southworth did not marry until 1903. By 1897 he and the Elys had moved to 47 West 56th Street, and apparently Dr. Southworth lived with them there until he married.

Within a year Albert and Maud had a baby boy named Reginald Merchant Ely, whose little life lasted just ten days. He was buried in Hartford, Connecticut, in the plot of his grandparents, the Honorable Thomas Day and his wife Sarah Coit, in the Old North Cemetery. In 1894 Albert Heman Ely Jr. was born—he who had been destined to be a girl and so was called Jack.

Shortly after Jack's birth, Dr. Ely received a letter from his father, Heman Ely II, written on May 22. "My dear Albert," Heman wrote, and began with details concerning his wife, Mary Day Ely, Al's mother. She was about to have an operation in New York, under Al's supervision, to relieve a problem with her ear. "Kiss my dear wife one, two, three times, and tell her I love her dearly and will write. . . . Albert Heman Ely Jr. shall be duly entered in my book. With love to Maud and Carrie, I am very affectionately, Heman Ely."

"My book" is presumably the impressive volume of the family genealogy: "Records of the Descendants of Nathaniel Ely the Emigrant, who Settled first in Newtown, now Cambridge, Mass., was one of the First Settlers of Hartford, also of Norwalk, Conn., and a Resident of Springfield, Mass, from 1659 until his death in 1675." It was published in Cleveland in 1885. Heman Ely must have meant he would enter the name of his grandson in his master copy by hand.

Two years later Jack was joined in the family by a little baby brother, Gerald Day. Day was Al's mother's maiden name, and perhaps Al also had in mind the long connection with the name dating back to the time of Nathaniel, "the emigrant."

Al wrote an item for his class at Yale which included this reference to the celebration of Yale's 200th year (1701 to 1901): "Of course I attended the Bicentennial celebration, and there was with me a manly little fellow who bore with much pride a class banner inscribed Yale 1916." He then wrote, "It is necessary to change the class record I recently sent you. Since writing it my little boy has died, and is now in his last resting-place. . . . I would like, however, to say to my classmates, that through this dispensation we have come to *know absolutely* that the little boy lives and is with God. This is not merely trust and faith, it is not that we so hope in order to comfort our hearts, it is a convincing knowledge that not only sustains but lifts us up in a wonderful way, and I would have them all believe it and take the Truth into their souls in order that they may attain as nearly as may be to the purity of the sweet child that has led the way for many. His span of life here was six years, five months, and twelve days; his new and better life began last Thursday, and will never end."[4]

Gerald Day was buried in the Ely family graveyard in Elyria.

All of these children had their births and baptisms recorded in the register of St. Thomas Church, Fifth Avenue, New York, one of the most socially prominent churches in Manhattan.

A few weeks later Dr. Ely, his little son Jack, and Eugene Edgel embarked for England on the S.S. *Olympia*. There is no indication in the records that Maud accompanied her husband and son on this voyage.

Edgel was the Elys' coachman and man-of-all-work. He was part Shinnecock Indian and part black, and he worked for the family for over forty years. The Shinnecocks had a reservation on the outskirts of Southampton, Long Island, where the Elys had built a summer residence that they named "Elyria."[5] They must have engaged Edgel when they first built that home. While they were in Europe, Edgel probably served as groom as Al, Jack and he coached their way across England, Ireland, France and back to the Isle of Wight before returning to the United States. At other times they rented a motor car and Edgel served as chauffeur. The family lore has it that as they entered one Irish village, the cry went up "Here comes the Devil's fiery chariot, and the Devil himself is driving!" Automobiles and dark-skinned faces were not common in rural Ireland at the turn of the century.

For Southampton, the first years of the twentieth century were what the historian of the town calls "the golden years" of the resort. The town itself is some eighty miles from Manhattan out on Long Island. The year-round population was small, and since the late 1870s it had begun to be a favorite place of an elite group of New Yorkers, for summer homes. Elyria was on Ox Pasture Road.

Dr. Ely very early became active in the community. In about 1904 he and a colleague, Dr. Joseph Wheelwright, consulted a town official known as "the overseer of the poor" about the plight of an African-American woman named Mrs. Moses Solomon, and her infant daughter. There were few persons of color living in Southampton, and most of the black servants for the elegant summer places left with their employers for the winter. Mrs. Solomon and her child, the doctors felt, would not survive the winter if not cared for. So they arranged to rent two rooms in the Goodale Boarding House. One room was for Mrs. Solomon. The other was for a nurse to begin to give care to the community—care that had not been available before this. This was the start of what became a dispensary for the town, and Dr. Ely was quoted in the local paper as saying a dispensary was urgently needed.

Three or four other summer-resident doctors took up Ely's and Wheelwright's concern, and the next summer they rented a house and put up a sign, "Southampton Hospital." The following year there were tents on the lawn around the house, and the next year they bought an additional house. Soon a fund-raising campaign was held among the locals and summer residents, and in 1913 a proper building was opened. Today the hospital is a thriving modern affair, and its 1995 annual report with expenditures of over $58,000,000 showed a modest surplus.

Dr. Ely served for fourteen years as president of the Village Improvement Association, turning his professional eye to such things as public health, the safety of the water supply, and to campaigning for pasteurized milk with the local dairy industry.

In 1904, Francis Sherburne Ely was born. Frances Sherburne was the name of Maud's mother.

Justin Ely
1739-1817

Heman Ely I
1775-1852

The first frame house in Elyria, Ohio, built by Heman Ely in 1818

Captain Abraham Gould Jennings

The Jennings coat of arms, awarded to an ancestral feather merchant. It incorporates the plumb-bob, chosen by the Royal Heralds as a representation of the merchant's upright character.

"The Old Homestead," built by Isaac Jennings in 1780 on the site of his home burned by the British in 1779. The address is 156 Round Hill Road, Fairfield, Connecticut.

1889 – Dr. Albert Ely takes his fiancée, Maud Merchant, to meet his family in Elyria, Ohio. Top row, from left: Harriet Putnam Ely Marshall, Heman Ely II, Mary Day Ely, George Ely, Frederic Ely Williamson

Second row: William A. Ely, Charles Ely, Maud Merchant Ely, Arthur Ely, Mary Louise Ely, Mrs. George Ely, Albert H. Ely, MD, Max Ely

Front row: Heman Ely III, Theodore Ely, Edith Ely Williamson, Robert Ely, James D. Williamson, Arthur Williamson

Mr. and Mrs. Oliver Burr Jennings with their oldest son, Walter Jennings, circa 1859, in San Francisco

The Jennings family in Rome, 1908. From left: Constance, Walter, Annie Burr, Jean, Miss Gallaudet, Oliver, and Jeanette

Dr. Albert Ely and Jack in 1900, just after Gerald Ely's death

Maud Louise Merchant Ely, from a drawing by A.G. Learned

Gerald and his older brother Jack with their father, Dr. Albert Ely, in Southampton

Walter and Jean Jennings on their honeymoon, 1891

Connie holding Florence, Jack holding Day. This was originally one picture, taken at Florence's baptism in 1931.

Ely Christmas card, 1937, taken in Washington: Jack, Connie, Day, Florence, and Mary

Ely Christmas card, 1950, taken at Caux, Switzerland. From left: Beryl Evans, Day, Niel, Jack, Mary, Connie, Anna Hale, Florence

Mary Ely
1935-1958

Niel Ely
1939-1952

Connie Ely in 1983, with her four grandchildren. From left: Virginia Ravenscroft (12)
and Nic (15), J.P. (10), and Tom Nelson (12)

Two years later little Gerald Day's body was moved from the Ely plot in Elyria to the Merchant family plot at Mt. Hope Cemetery in Rochester. There was a quiet family ceremony attended by Maud's father, mother, her sister Elinor and her brother Gerald Eugene. This move of the baby's body from the Ely plot to Maud's family's plot may have been linked to a growing coolness between Maud and her husband. Maud is said to have accused her husband of being attentive to his patients and their childbearing, but unable to see two of their own sons through successfully. Al and Maud continued to live together, but according to clippings that Maud saved in her scrapbook, they were frequently an item in the gossip columns for their separate ways of life. Apparently, the storybook romance began to crumble.

Dr. Ely became established as family physician and obstetrician to the fashionable families of the city. One of his most important clients was the Franklin Delano Roosevelt family, and he brought several of their five children into the world.[6] He wrote to Franklin Roosevelt in March of 1908:

> My dear Mr. Roosevelt—I doubt if you know how much your thoughtful note meant to me and I assure you that we physicians appreciate more than anything else in our trying lives the expression of gratitude for such efforts we can make for the welfare of our patients. To your family I have always felt especial interest because of the privilege of knowing your honored father and mother and their kind consideration of me in my early career. Naturally, therefore, I wish you to feel I have obligations to Mrs. Roosevelt and your children as also to yourself which can never be repaid.
> Yours very sincerely, Albert H. Ely.

This exchange of letters followed the birth of James Roosevelt, whose birth certificate Dr. Ely signed just before Christmas.

There is a sense in the present-day Ely family that the life of social position and glamour was more important to Maud than her children were. There is even a sense that this was ruthless. Certainly Maud developed a persona far grander than her life in Rochester had made possible. She had a penchant for French culture; in particular she had busts and prints and other images of Napoleon Bonaparte around her home, so much so that, as her life went on, this was seen as almost eccentric. Apparently she spoke French well. And she had many admirers—men friends, more intimate than convention smiled upon. At the same time it appears that as her husband's practice grew, some of his patients were more grateful for his attentions than even a conscientious medical practice would deserve.

One of Jack's daughters years later asked him how, if his parents were far from any role model for a young boy, he had found a firm moral grounding for his life. His reply: "My godfather." When Jack was christened in St. Thomas's Church, his godmother was Maud's sister Elinor Merchant French, and his godfather was Dr. Thomas S. Southworth.

Dr. Southworth has been described by his family as gracious, dignified, a man of integrity and honor and of high moral standards who demanded the best of himself and others, and as a man of faith. He shared the household with the Elys for the first ten years of young Jack's life, and may well have been the major influence in shaping the growing boy's character.

Whatever Dr. Ely's own morals may have been, he established a fine reputation for himself professionally. There is a note to Maud's father, George Merchant of Rochester, from a friend, saying "I have been talking this morning with friend Edward Bell, a prominent Wall Street banker, who has just had a severe surgical operation performed by your son-in-law, Dr. Ely. Mr. Bell thinks that Dr. Ely is the finest fellow in the land, professionally, socially and every other way."

Dr. Ely's granddaughters tell several anecdotes of his shrewdness as a physician when involved in exposing fraud connected with insurance cases. A woman was claiming that because of an accident on a trolley car, her leg was permanently contracted. Dr. Ely visited her in her hospital bed, hands behind his back in his customary manner; then at his signal the nurse drew back the sheets for his examination. He whipped out a seltzer siphon and squirted her with its icy contents. She left the bed on two good legs, screaming. In another case, he examined a plaintiff in a court proceeding, who claimed one arm was permanently unable to extend above the shoulder. In his confidence-building manner, Dr. Ely asked how high the arm had been able to reach before the accident, and the plaintiff extended the arm fully, thus causing the case to be thrown out of court.

One of the stories of Jack as a small boy concerns his maternal grandmother, Mrs. Merchant. She wrote a full account of it to her son Gerald, Jack's uncle, he who had been a friend of Diamond Jim Brady. It was late January of 1902, when Jack would have been just under eight years old. He and his mother left their home on West 56th Street to call upon Mrs. Merchant, who was visiting from Rochester and staying at the Murray Hill Hotel Park Avenue. Mrs. Merchant had just left the dining room to greet her daughter and Jack. They went up to her room on the floor above the lobby and were preparing to take a carriage over to the Ely home when a tremendous explosion shook the whole neighborhood.

The *New York Times* reported the explosion took place at "the noon hour." Dynamite had been stored in a tool shed almost at the door of the hotel, at the head of a shaft that ran into the subway system below Park Avenue at 41st Street.

"The whole house seemed to be coming down on us," Mrs. Merchant wrote. "Big pieces of glass falling all around us, great chunks of flashing chandeliers and windows falling, so much dust the house looked to be on fire." They went down the main staircase. She put her sealskin wrap over Jack's head and took him by the hand with Maud running after them. "We got out of it the cleanest of anyone in the building. Not a scratch or any dirt, only a little dust on our faces. But there at the door we saw the dreadful sights. Two or three women fainting covered with blood. One, her face covered with dirt—blood flowing from cuts in her head . . . another woman with blood running from her back through a flannel wrapper."

The waiter in the dining room she had just left was killed.

Firemen were already on the scene. The family was able to share a carriage with another woman, and drove to the house on 56th Street. "Jack was so brave," Mrs. Merchant wrote. "He never cried when we got into the coupe and came home. . . . Through all of it I only thought of Maude and Jack being killed."

Mrs. Merchant had asked for a room on the lower floor of the hotel because she had been ill and was recuperating. Later, the porter told her that the room he would have given her was destroyed.

The story was carried on the front page of the next day's *New York Times*, January 28, 1902, occupying four of the seven columns. The dining room waiter was one of four people killed, and some hundred and twenty-five were treated for injuries. Apparently nearly 600 pounds of dynamite had been stored in a shed at the construction site, where law prescribed that not more that 62 pounds be stored in that manner. A fire of unknown origin broke out in the shed and a worker nearby sounded the alarm. The loss of life was not greater because it was the lunch hour for the workers. The hotel was practically destroyed, and there was damage to many nearby buildings, including Grand Central Station.

Young Jack attended the Craigie School from the age of nine, in the fall of 1903, to the following June; the Morristown School, a boarding school in Morristown, New Jersey, in the next year; and the Craigie School again in the school year 1905-1906.[7]

The Morristown School is some forty miles due west of Manhattan. The Elys were giving Jack a fine education, but also they were sending him away from home, which was unusual for someone so young.

In Maud's collection is a lined Yale composition book (possibly something his father had given Jack) labeled "Greek History." Inside is an outline map of Greece, with lines drawn showing the civilizations of Corcyra, Aegospotami, Delos, Syracuse and Pilataea. The title page is inscribed in Jack's boyish hand, "Albert H. Ely, Jr., Greek History, Mr. Butler, Morristown School, Morristown, N.J., U.S.A., city residence 47 West 56th Street, NYC." In the back are cited Meyer's *Ancient History*, Botsford's *History of Greece*, Oman's *History of Greece*, and Longman's *Ancient Atlas*.

Jack became a member of The Knickerbocker Greys. This was an organization for boys, founded in 1881 by a society matron and her friends, to give some training in discipline as well as comradeship to their sons. Their uniform, whose design was borrowed from England, consisted of a gray jacket and knickerbockers, or knee-pants, with a round cap, and black braid trimming. At the time Jack belonged to the Greys they drilled at the 7th Regiment Armory on Park Avenue at 67th Street. A gossip columnist compared the Knickerbocker Greys to the social status of the Union Club, "decidedly social in tone, and membership is greatly sought after, mothers pulling as many wires to gain entrée . . . as for their debutante daughters . . . the roster of 'veterans' reads like a veritable Who's Who of American Society."

By the fall of 1906, Jack, aged twelve, was sent off to The Hill School, a boys' boarding and preparatory school in Pottstown, Pennsylvania. Founded in 1851, The Hill School is a place of great tradition. When Jack was at the school, John Meigs, son of the founder Matthew Meigs, was in his last years as headmaster of the school, the finale of a thirty-five year career.

Jack was a member of the Class of 1911. As his years there went by, he was involved in the editorial boards of *The Dial*, The Hill's annual yearbook; *The Record*, their literary magazine; and *The News*, the student-edited newspaper which, when he was chairman, was published on Tuesdays and Fridays.

In 1907 Dr. and Mrs. Ely took Jack with them to Ireland.

Although no records have been located of Jack's involvement in sports, family lore holds that he was a member of the track team. On one occasion, he is said to have been in the infirmary with a streptococcus infection—a strep throat—when the coach, who badly needed him for a track meet, persuaded the nurse to let him run. This apparently was the genesis of the heart trouble that appears later in Jack's adult life. The implication was that this illness was rheumatic fever.

Maud kept some of Jack's letters to her, which frequently mention the need for money to rent a bicycle or to subscribe to something. He also mentioned his eyes several times during his school years, and medicine that was prescribed for them. There are references to getting A's in French. One letter to his father, which Maud saved, says simply, in very early-childhood writing: "My dear father mother left for elyria this morning i am loanly [*sic*] without her, with love Jack." Jack often mentions his brother: "Are you well and is Francis?" or "Dear Mother, I am having a bully time. . . . I don't think I led the form this month. . . . Sorry Francis is sick. P.S. my eyes hurt quite badly."

Dr. Ely received a letter from John Meigs, written in March of 1908, thanking him for his letter of two days previous "and to assure you of the pleasure with which I anticipate the return of Albert to The Hill next autumn. I need hardly assure you that it is our desire to serve Albert more wisely and helpfully as we have come to know him better and to recognize more adequately his claim upon our personal regard and interest."

On his father's letterhead Jack wrote to Messers Bertron, Storrs and Griscom, 40 Wall Street: "Gentlemen: This is the copy of *The Dial* which I promised to send you. It has seen hard usage and is in a rather disreputable condition but nevertheless I think it will give you some idea. . . . Enclosed is an advertisement blank. . . . trusting that some day I may prove to you that I am worthy of your confidence, I remain, Very truly yours, Albert H. Ely Jr." There is no indication of whether he sold them an ad, but it was good training for his future career on the *Yale Daily News*.

Jack was a member of the Q.E.D. Debating Club. In 1909 he was one of the organizers of The Civic Club, the purpose of which was "to give the 4th, 5th and 6th formers the opportunity of learning something concerning the politics of our country." (In the boarding school tradition, 6th form is the senior class; the students are then ready to go on to college.)

One family story of Jack's school years concerns his ingenuity. It seems that he had an alarm clock, which he rigged so that when it went off, the winder would wind in a bit of string tied to a prop under the open window and yank the prop out so the window would close. This would add that extra touch of comfort to getting out of bed on a cold morning.

The Hill School *Record* for January 1910 includes half a dozen literary efforts by boys in the upper forms, including a short story by A.H. Ely Jr., '11, entitled "The Sixth Dance." It is a realistic tale told in the first person, of "Forbes," American Minister to Nicaragua, who has just succeeded in arranging for the proper candidate for president of the country to win the election and for the defeat of the dastardly candidate. At a state function

Forbes and the charming American girl, "the one girl who had ever aroused more than a passing interest in me," are taken hostage by the dastard for ransom, but they manage to defeat the rascal. Intimations of experiences to come, perhaps.

Jack spent his childhood at 47 West 56th Street, until sent away to boarding school. As of the late 1990s, this address is in the middle of a skyscraper whose front entrance is on 57th Street and which occupies the entire mid-section of that block, from 56th to 57th Street, and is some thirty-two stories tall.

At 2 West 56th Street, across the street and down a few doors, was the family of one Walter Jennings. And by 1909, the Walter Jennings family had moved to 43 West 56th, just two doors east of the Ely family.

. . . .

NOTES

1. "Maud" was the legal spelling of Jack's mother's first name. She herself often wrote "Maude," and so did her father, and the gossip columnists and others.

2. The author can find no trace of a "Caemi Theatre" in 1889 in New York or New Jersey, or advertisements for it, despite extensive inquiry.

3. The 19 West 46th Street address today is in a seedy commercial neighborhood. As of the late 1990s it houses a restaurant, El Pollo Latino, on the ground floor, with a Coca-Cola sign swinging from the wall, and a hair salon on the next floor.

4. Al's calculation of six years, five months is incompatible with the records, which show that Gerald was born in 1896 and died in 1900.

5. The Elys had owned at least one other home in Southampton before they built "Elyria."

6. Although in a number of references Dr. Ely is described as Mrs. Roosevelt's obstetrician, it is not clear how many of the Roosevelt children he actually brought into the world. The author has a copy of the birth certificate of James Roosevelt. In his published letters, FDR states that the family expected Dr. Ely at Campo Bello Island in the Canadian Maritimes in time for the delivery of Franklin Delano Roosevelt Jr., but that he did not arrive and a local physician assisted at that birth. Concerning FDR's other children, the New York bureau of records would not release information to the author, and the Roosevelt Library in Hyde Park has no information.

7. No reference has been found to a Craigie School in New York or New Jersey, despite a search in the New York Public Library, Library of Columbia University Teachers' College, New Jersey and New York historical societies, and the Porter Sargent Publishing Company. The reference is from Jack's entry in the Yale Class of 1915 Yearbook.

Franklin D. Roosevelt
Vice President
FIDELITY AND DEPOSIT COMPANY OF MARYLAND
55 Liberty Street   New York City
September 17, 1927.

Dr. Albert H. Ely,
Southampton, L. I.

My dear Dr. Ely:

I have always known that you were an angel, but now I am doubly certain and I cannot tell you how very grateful I am for all that you have done to help the Georgia Warm Springs Foundation, and also for your kindness to my cousin, Forbes Amory.

My chief hope is that some time this winter, if you are anywhere in the south, you will come to Warm Springs and visit us, and see with your own eyes the work which we are doing. At the present time we have forty patients and a great many applications, especially since the present rather serious epidemic not only in the east, but in many parts of the west. I am going gaily ahead borrowing money to increase the accommodations with the trust and confidence that some day, we shall be able to pay it back.

In addition to the polio cases, we have also, during the past few months, been experimenting with several cases of hemoplegia (not being in your profession I don't know how to spell it, but we laymen would call it partial paralysis as a result of a stroke). These cases have shown extraordinary improvement through the use of the warm pools. Also, we have had one interesting case of arthritis of the spine, to which relief has been given, though Dr. Hubbard does not, of course, anticipate any permanent cure.

From the medical point of view, the thing which interests me most is the undoubted fact that this warm pool has the chemical properties which enable patients to remain in it for an hour and a half or more without debilitation, and the location, climate, etc. are such that it can be used all the year round.

Probably also, this winter, we shall have a number of post-operative and recuperation cases in the hotel which will add to our problems.

When you get back to New York, I shall hope to see you and thank you again in person for all that you have done. I am very grateful.

Faithfully yours,

Franklin D Roosevelt

A particularly warm sample of the correspondence between Franklin Delano Roosevelt and Albert Ely, trimmed and saved in Maud's crowded scrapbook.

2

Nation-builders:
The Jennings Family

WALTER JENNINGS AND HIS SIBLINGS were the children of Oliver Burr Jennings and his wife Esther Judson Goodsell.

The Jennings were woven into the fabric of the developing American nation in very much the same way as were the Elys. Joshua Jennings, the first of the line on this continent, came from England in 1645 and two years later was in Hartford, Connecticut. While there he almost certainly met Nathaniel Ely, "the emigrant." We don't know the precise date that Ely moved on to help settle Norwalk, but it appears to be in 1649. Both men took responsibility for the growth and well-being of the town of Hartford. Joshua Jennings in due course moved on from Hartford to Fairfield, married and raised a family.

Joshua's son and grandson were both named Isaac. His great-grandson, Isaac Jennings the Third, served in several battles of the American Revolution. He married Abigail Gould, and the Gould name became prominent among their descendants. Gould had been changed from Gold; this change was a mark of the pervasive anti-Semitism of the time. Isaac and Abigail's grandson was the Oliver Burr Jennings of this story. In the generation between, Oliver's father, Abraham Gould Jennings, was a ship captain engaged in merchant trade overseas.[1] Abraham married Anna Burr, a descendant of Jehu Burr, who came to Boston in 1630 with Governor Winthrop.

Oliver Burr Jennings was born in 1825. His brother Abraham Gould Jennings (the same name as their father) became a prominent lace manufacturer in New York City. Oliver, after several years of schooling, went to work at the age of sixteen in nearby Bridgeport, Connecticut. Two years later he was hired as a clerk by a dry-goods firm in New York City. When the gold fever of 1849 hit the country, Oliver, then a young man of twenty-four, decided to try his luck in far-off California. His employer, Browning & Hull (which later became the well-known firm Browning, King & Co.) offered to stake him to a supply of goods for trade in the gold fields. As it turned out for Oliver and for a good many others, it was far more profitable and secure to be in the business of supplying the feverish gold-digging crowd than to prospect for gold yourself.

Getting to California in 1849 involved a hazardous journey. Many people took a ship to the Isthmus of Panama, or to Vera Cruz in Mexico, crossed to the Pacific Ocean on foot or mule-back or in whatever way they could afford, and found a ship that would take them up the coast to San Francisco. Oliver arrived in San Francisco a good six weeks before his supply of goods, which went by ship around Cape Horn and up the coast. While he was waiting for the goods, he went into the gold fields with a few tools and panned for gold. He returned to San Francisco some $1200 richer, collected his shipment and opened up shop.

Another fellow from Browning & Hull, Benjamin Brewster, had done the same thing. In 1853 both men were burned out in a fire, and subsequently decided to go into business together. The firm of Jennings & Brewster prospered. Oliver went home to Connecticut the following year and married his sweetheart, Esther Judson Goodsell. Esther followed Oliver back to San Francisco, sailing to Panama and riding a donkey across the isthmus. On Oliver's instructions, she first sold the Jennings family home in Fairfield to finance the move. The family tells of Oliver standing on Telegraph Hill, watching for the arrival of Esther's ship. They lived in San Francisco for the next eight years, and four children, Annie Burr, Walter, Helen and Emma Goodsell, were born there.

In 1862 Oliver Jennings and his partner Benjamin Brewster sold their business and returned to the East. Each of the partners came home with some $150,000, which was real money in those days.

At that point the Jennings family story links up with the story of another legendary American family. For Oliver Jennings' wife had a sister,

Almira Goodsell, who married a man named William Avery Rockefeller. William was the younger brother of John Davison Rockefeller.

Many of the books written about John D. Rockefeller have branded him as an unscrupulous, greedy man. A two-volume biography by Alan Nevins, written in 1940, is different in that Nevins weighs the evidence, not the myths and the bias, and comes up with a fascinating picture of a man and his era.[2]

Rockefeller was a bright, observant, meticulous young man, reading the signs of the times, sensing the tremendous engine of energy matching the resources of this young nation, seeing the successes and the mistakes of others. He gauged his capacity for precise action, which would be well thought out in a burgeoning economy and an industrial revolution. He decided that what others were doing he could do, and found that in many ways he had the patience, the clear thinking, the exacting habits to do it better.

By this time Oliver Jennings and his friend Benjamin Brewster were back in the East, taking the measure of what might come next. The Civil War was on; grain was being grown in huge quantities in the Midwest; iron and steel were being produced on a growing scale; railroads were making a huge difference in the capacity to move resources across the country. In western Pennsylvania, oil had come out of the ground in quantity. John Rockefeller and two partners had formed a company for dealing in commodities. In 1862 or '63 they began to refine petroleum, and shortly, after buying out one partner who did not agree, John Rockefeller and Sam Andrews set up the firm of Rockefeller & Andrews and went into the refining of crude oil in a big way.

The chief product, kerosene, was revolutionizing life across the world by providing a cheap and relatively safe source of lighting—for business, for the home, for schools. Within ten years kerosene became the indispensable item in every home in the U.S. and Europe, and from there to Asia and Africa and the rest of the world. It provided good enough lighting to enable people to make full use of their energies day and night rather than leading a dawn-to-dusk existence.

In 1859 the United States produced 2,000 barrels of crude oil. In 1869 she produced 4,250,000 barrels. John and his friends grasped the moment. They decided that refining petroleum was a more reliable business than digging for it, and that refining and transporting it to markets would be good business. Furthermore, they decided that by careful, accurate technical and business methods they could succeed and even become dominant, whereas the slam-bang attitudes of others were causing havoc in the industry. They took in three more partners: the wealthy Stephen Harkness, who preferred to remain in the background; his vigorous and capable nephew-in-law, Henry Flagler; and John's brother William.

By 1870 the firm of Rockefeller, Andrews & Flagler decided to expand further. They needed capital. They looked around to discover men with whom they could comfortably associate. In January of that year they announced the firm of Standard Oil Company of Ohio, with 10,000 shares of $100 each. The participants were:

John D. Rockefeller	2,667 shares
Stephen V. Harkness	1,334 shares
Henry A. Flagler	1,333 shares
Samuel Andrews	1,333 shares
William A. Rockefeller	1,333 shares
The firm of Rockefeller, Andrews & Flagler	1,000 shares
Oliver Burr Jennings	1,000 shares

The firm was well on its way. It owned one-tenth of the petroleum business in the United States with sixty acres in Cleveland, Ohio, and two great refineries there (the most modern and well-run in the industry) as well as a huge barrel-making plant, for oil was shipped in oaken barrels in those days. Standard Oil had timberland contracts to harvest white oak for their own barrels; lake shipping and warehousing facilities; a fleet of tank cars, great oak vats mounted on cars, rather like tubs instead of horizontal steel tanks as is done today. The firm owned sidings, warehouses and tanks in the New York area and lighters in New York harbor.

This was twenty-five years or more before the advent of the gasoline-driven internal combustion engine and the great revolution brought about by the motor car!

The owners of Standard Oil were a close-knit group of hand-picked men who could move decisively and quickly together, responsible only to themselves, under the leadership of John D. Rockefeller. The next man offered the opportunity to invest was Oliver's friend Benjamin Brewster. He bought into the company later that same year.

Oliver and his wife repurchased the property she had sold in Connecticut to finance their venture in California. It became a much-loved family place. They also kept an apartment at 48 Park Avenue in New York.

As time went on, Oliver took a silent part in the corporation, and held directorship positions from time to time. He had come from a family that well understood the value of education, although he himself had gone to work at age sixteen. Now, with wealth backing them, Oliver and Esther took care to send their children to the best schools available. Walter was sent to the Hopkins School in New Haven, and from there to Yale University.

Walter followed this with a law degree from Columbia Law School. Being the son of a wealthy family he took time from studies to travel, including an ascent of Mont Blanc in France, of which he wrote an account for his class at Yale. He entered employment with the oil transportation side of the business and worked his way to an understanding of it. This included a year and a half spent in Oil City in the heart of the Pennsylvania country that had given birth to the U.S. oil industry. In 1903 Walter became a director of Standard Oil of New Jersey, and five years later was elected secretary of the corporation.

Walter Jennings married Jean Pollock Brown, of New York, in 1891.

The family patriarch, Oliver Burr Jennings, died in 1893. Walter and his siblings—his older sister Annie Burr Jennings, Helen Goodsell James, Emma Brewster Auchincloss and Oliver Gould Jennings—inherited great wealth.

Walter and his wife, like many well-to-do New Yorkers, had a summer home on Long Island. Their first home there was "Tranquility" at Oyster Bay. In 1897 they bought an estate at nearby Cold Spring Harbor, some thirty-five miles from downtown Manhattan. This estate, of approximately 400 wooded acres stretching down to the beach on the north shore of Long Island Sound, was a superb spot. They named it "Burrwood." In many ways this property came to define the family. Walter and Jean built a large house of brick, with brick gateposts and a high wrought-iron fence with "WJ" in the center of each gate.

The orders that Walter and Jean gave to the architect described some lovely, unpretentious large homes they had seen in the Cotswolds in England, with gray stone and long, low lines fitting the land. Their architect, however, was interested in his own fame and made a showplace out of massive red brick, marble facings and "Beaux Arts" details. The result was grandiose and ugly. However, Jean had a matchless homemaking touch, and the inside was comfortable and welcoming for children, grandchildren and friends. Anticipating that none of the family would choose to live in this house after she and Walter were gone, Jean had a professional photographer take pictures of all the rooms and had a book made for the grandchildren showing details of her elegant home. She herself was interested in photography; beginning in the 1880s, she had a darkroom and developed her own pictures.

The stables were fully half a mile from the main house. The estate superintendent wore jacket and tie. He oversaw all the operations, which included crops for feed, a pedigreed dairy herd, sheep, and numerous workmen. From early days, Walter had a taste for fine horses and carriages. He assembled a notable collection of carriages and coaches, well known in the harness-driving world. He could often be seen driving his own horses, sometimes the elegant tandem rig for a pair of spirited animals, or the four-in-hand with coach, around Cold Spring Harbor. He passed on to his daughter Connie an appreciation and understanding of the art of carriage driving.[3]

Jean Brown Jennings was interested in gardening, farming, and the arts of homemaking. She had sheep on the property, and had blankets made for all the family from her own wool. The Jennings developed what amounted to a plantation style with houses and cottages for their employees. Many were recent immigrants who settled in and made a new life. When guests were at Burrwood, Jean loved to walk with them through the fields, the forest, and the gardens where there were marble sculptures.

Walter commuted daily to his offices at 26 Broadway, going by carriage to the railway station and thence by train to Manhattan. The estate had a stone wharf at the beach. Walter had a fine, if unassuming, motor yacht, the *Jock Scott*, named for one of his favorite salmon-fishing flies, and he employed a boatman.

Walter and Jean had three children: Oliver Burr, Jeannette, and Constance. The children grew up dividing their time between their house on West 56th Street and Burrwood.

Walter set aside a parcel of the Burrwood estate for a home for his sister Helen, who had married Walter Belknap James. He also designated a five-acre plot of Burrwood for each of his three children.

His third sister, Emma, had married Hugh D. Auchincloss. Their lovely estate, "Hammersmith Farm," at Newport, Rhode Island, was a favorite place to visit in the summer. Their son, Hugh D. Auchincloss Jr, later married Mrs. Janet Bouvier. Her daughter, Jacqueline Bouvier, married John Fitzgerald Kennedy, and became America's First Lady.

By 1915, the Walter Jennings family had moved to 9 East 70th Street. On the corner of Fifth Avenue, at 1 East 70th Street, was the Frick mansion. Henry Frick, who had helped Andrew Carnegie to make his millions in the steel industry, later bequeathed his home to house the Frick Collection, one of America's great private collections of art. At 7 East 70th lived the Arthur Curtiss Jameses, close friends of the Jennings and among America's most wealthy private citizens. James had large interests in Phelps Dodge & Company and was one of the largest holders of railroad stocks in the United States. He was, quietly, a philanthropist who gave many millions to charities.

On the other side of the Jennings lived an executive of Tiffany & Co. He loved fire engines and had in his home an alarm bell wired into the city fire department. Every time a fire bell rang anywhere in Manhattan, the Tiffany executive's bell would ring and the whole Jennings family could hear it. The Jennings kept up their home at 9 East 70th Street until Walter Jennings died in 1933. This home was staffed year-round and used by them, or by members of their family, regardless of where Walter and Jean Jennings themselves might be.

The Jennings' life was truly lived in the grand manner. Connie told years later of trips to the Adirondack Mountains or to Saratoga when she was very young. Her father would drive them in one of his collection of carriages, with a groom to assist him; behind them would come a dray from Burrwood loaded with their trunks and boxes.

One such trip held Connie's very first memory: "I had been given a lovely white tam-o'-shanter, one of the great big kind that come down over your ears, for our trip to the Adirondack Mountains for the summer [to Camp Tahawas, where they spent several summers]. Being only three years old, I fell asleep in the carriage on the second day of traveling. My nurse was holding me and my head was toward the outside of the carriage. Apparently she didn't notice that my white tam-o'-shanter had fallen off, and when I woke up it was gone. I was absolutely distressed, and I remember being so upset that I wanted to turn the carriage around and go back for it. But Father, who was driving, said that was impossible, the horses were just going to make it to the camp. So hopefully the man coming with the dray would see it and pick it up. I remember when it was delivered to me again, I was so excited that I put it on and wouldn't take it off."

Connie had been born at Burrwood. Her mother had sensed in the night that she was coming and her father had a groom saddle up and ride into town to bring the doctor, who kept a buggy all ready for just such occasions.

Walter's older sister, Annie Burr Jennings, had invested her life in taking care of her parents and their home. After their deaths Walter, feeling that Annie Burr needed a complete change, took her and a good friend of hers with his own family to Egypt and Italy for a year, in 1908. The friend was Miss Elizabeth Gallaudet, of the family that had founded Gallaudet School for the Deaf in Washington, D.C. The party included Walter's valet, a lady's maid for Jean and one for Annie Burr and Miss Gallaudet, a tutor for Ollie, a French governess for Jeannette and Connie, and a maid for them.

At one point the adults in the party, with Ollie and his tutor, took a steamer further up the Nile, while Jeannette and Constance were left in Thebes with the French governess. An archaeologist whom the party had met developed a crush on the pretty governess. Since she would not leave the little girls to go out with him, he took them all across the Nile to see the opening of the tomb of Queen Hatshepsut. They were able to enter the tomb. Jeannette picked up a scarab and the archaeologist allowed her to keep it.

Jean Brown Jennings took photos all through this trip. The family still has her three by five inch glass-mounted transparencies, which back at home were professionally hand-tinted. Several of them are reproduced in this book.

In Italy the party based in Rome. When they returned to New York, they had their guidebooks rebound in fine tooled leather with their diaries and photos carefully inserted at appropriate points. Walter and Jean Jennings bought a number of objects of art for Burrwood. One was a marble sarcophagus of the early Christian era, probably early fourth-century work. When it was received on Long Island it was installed as the centerpiece of a fountain in their beautifully landscaped and terraced garden. The sarcophagus eventually was given to the Metropolitan Museum of Art in New York City, and has been the subject of much study.[4]

It was also in 1908 that Annie Burr Jennings built her lovely home, "Sunnie Holme," in Fairfield. Two years earlier, her younger brother Oliver Gould Jennings had built his home, "Mailands." Mailands was a showplace, on the estate the family had owned since the 1600s. Annie Burr now created one of the most truly gracious homes imaginable. It was a simple clapboard country house, but huge, with nineteen or twenty bedrooms and fourteen bathrooms. The rooms on the main floor had twelve-foot ceilings. Florence Ely Nelson, Jack Ely's second daughter, remembers that Sunnie Holme had a glass-encased elevator to the upper floors. Annie Burr had the most charming gardens around the spacious property, stretching down with an unobstructed view to the shore. The gardens were open to the public much of the time. She also kept an apartment on Park Avenue.

Oliver and Annie Burr Jennings and several others created The Country Club of Fairfield in 1914, because they found the other local golf course, Brooklawn, too crowded.

In 1942, six years after Oliver's death, Mailands was sold to the Society of Jesus who made it the first building of the new Fairfield University. It is known today as McAuliffe Hall.

On a trip to the Holy Land, Oliver and Polly Brewster Jennings had ridden donkeys to the Jordan River from where they brought home a bottle of its waters, so that future family baptisms could take place with Jordan's waters. Jeannette Jennings Taylor had it boiled before she would use it for her four children. Connie inherited a liter of it. All of Connie's children and grandchildren were baptized with that water.

Annie Burr's life was full of good works. She was one of Connecticut's two representatives in the Mount Vernon Ladies' Association, that stalwart group who saved (and still own and maintain) Mount Vernon, the home of George Washington on the Potomac River. She also was famous in the family for her Christmas dinner parties. These were costume affairs, and the family went to great lengths to appear in exotic costumes. And Annie Burr was a fan of everything to do with Yale; she attended every football game, every crew race. Often she and her brother Oliver would take a crowd to a game or race by private railway car.

Both Walter and Oliver Gould Jennings were good businessmen and their respective fortunes improved under their management. The basis of the Jennings family wealth was the investment in Standard Oil made by their father when he joined the Rockefeller brothers in 1870. Walter was president of the National Fuel Gas Company, a subsidiary of Standard Oil, from 1908 to1919; he was a director of the Bank of the Manhattan Company, and a trustee of the New York Trust Company for forty years. He also served as a governor of the New York Hospital and of the Lying-In Hospital; was a trustee of his old school, Hopkins, and a member of the Society of Colonial Wars, of Delta Kappa Epsilon, and of the Yale senior society Skull & Bones. He belonged to a number of country clubs, and other clubs such as the University and the Metropolitan in New York. Like his brother, he was interested in scientific farming and managed a herd of prizewinning Jersey cows. Like others in his family he collected art treasures.

Walter Jennings' youngest child, Constance, known for most of her life as Connie, was a pupil at Miss Chapin's School in New York City. She spent the year1910, when she was ten years old, largely in Paris, as her father was working in the European branch of Standard Oil.

When Connie died in 1991, she left a beautiful red leather suitcase filled with letters, mostly to her. Those letters reveal that her aunts and uncles and family had a very rich affection for her, as a little girl and later in life. Typical is a letter from her Aunt Annie Burr Jennings in 1909, when Connie was nine years old, from the Tyrol. "Dear Connie," her aunt wrote, "You must think I am a most [illegible] creature, not to have written you all these many days since that good interesting letter you wrote me. . . . I have sent you and Jeannette some of the postal cards of the costumes . . . I bought a tiny doll for you and Jeannette to keep as a sample of a Tyrolese girl. . . . Yours most affectionately, Aunt Annie."

Connie's brother Ollie wrote her frequently. In August 1916 he wrote from what sounds like an army camp. (Europe was embroiled in World War I and the United States was dealing with Pancho Villa's incursions on the Mexican border of Texas and New Mexico.) This was most likely a training group from Yale, because later Ollie's father offered three horses to Yale for their student program. "Henry Farnum says [Battery] 'B' is going to Fort Sill for a month. . . . & we and 'E' are to come too for firing . . . . Yesterday we took the guns out for a drive, I being on a lead team. I certainly respect Father for managing a four from the box when we couldn't even from the saddle. It is great fun however making them all pull together."

In 1916 Connie went to Foxcroft, a fine girls' school in Middleburg, Virginia, some forty miles northwest of Washington. The school had been founded by Miss Charlotte Noland two years before. Foxcroft gave Connie opportunity for so many of the things that she loved—horseback riding and jumping in particular. She formed a personal friendship with the head-mistress, Miss Charlotte.

Jean Jennings came down several times a year to visit her daughter and there were occasional letters from brother Ollie, and once in a while from her father. Her mother's letters were always warm and affectionate: "I miss you dreadfully, my dear, & could not stand it if I did not know you were having a good time," ending almost always, "Any amount of love, yr loving Mother."

Her mother often wrote about something she was sending to Connie, some item of clothing, or jodhpurs, or some food treat. And she often referred to invitations Connie had received, asked what engagements she had, and would she like to invite a boy to a party they were giving or a weekend, "and if there are enough of them we can have a little dance, by way of variety!"

Her father wrote to Connie from his office, early in her time at the school: "I enjoyed your letter very much and especially because you make no reference to being homesick. . . . You evidently have entered into the spirit of the place. . . . I suppose later on you will begin to study a little although your letters at present tell only of riding, driving, plays & a few other diversions. . . . Have you seen any saddle horses worth buying? Much love from Father."

Walter Jennings sent the following to his daughter early in December of 1916: "Yesterday I stopped at Scribner's and bought eighteen books for children in accordance with request in your letter to Mother. . . . I bought a nice chestnut horse the other day ostensibly for Jeannette but I haven't given him to her yet and may keep him for myself. Do you think you will find a suitable horse down there for yourself? I want to get rid of some of the horses in the stable. . . . With much love, Your affectionate father Walter Jennings."

A few days later her mother wrote from their home on East 70th Street, "Well, the reception is over and J [Jeannette] is launched as a young lady, and in two years, I suppose, we'll be doing the same thing for you. It was great fun, about 400 people came during the p.m. We had some men from the Balalaika orchestra, and they played delightfully during the afternoon until 8 PM when we went to see the 'Century Girl' and then we went to the Ritz—Crystal Room—and danced and had supper, returning about 1:30, tired but having had a fine time."

Connie's elder sister Jeannette was a beauty—petite, blonde, blue-eyed, poised. Jeannette fitted comfortably into the life of privilege, of parties, dates, boyfriends, country clubs, being presented to society. Jeannette often called her sister Connie "Bam," short for "Bambina" (the baby) and signed letters "Jin."

Aunt Molly (Mrs. Richard Brown), Connie's godmother and a lifelong friend of her mother, wrote from Bar Harbor, Maine: "Dearest Connie, How do you like your new school? You ride to hounds and do samplers and learn deportment in good old XVIII Century fashion, don't you? Heartily approve . . . Dearest love to you, my dearest little girl."

A look at the lively Jennings parents comes in this note to Connie from her father in early 1917: "Mother and I are still undecided about going to White Sulphur Springs. We have forty young lambs and four hundred young chicks at Burrwood. Oliver comes down tonight for the Glee Club concert and the opera tomorrow afternoon, afterward back to New Haven. We saw the hockey game Wednesday night. Terribly close and exciting. The team came to our house after the game and had supper and dancing and returned to New Haven at midnight."

Brother Oliver wrote on May 2, 1917: "Dear Connie, thank you ever so much for the [birthday] telegram which I appreciate very much and hope to do likewise on May 16. You're having quite a party over the weekend with all the family, aren't you? I wish I could go but can't. I am on a boat with Adolph Dick and Henry Taylor in the naval reserve and will be in Great South Bay instead of Newport, so I guess I can get home occasionally. Much love from Oliver."

Henry Taylor, who had graduated from Yale, asked Jeannette to marry him. Because of the uncertainty of the war situation they picked a date with less than three weeks' notice, at St. James's Church in Manhattan, where the Jennings family were members. Connie was the maid of honor. The bridesmaids' dresses were in various shades of red, from dark red to Connie's, which was pale pink. Mrs. Jennings described herself as "loving but distracted" with the rush of things. Henry was ordered to Annapolis, and Jeannette joined him at Carvel Hall, a popular hotel in the town. He was assigned to a cruiser; Ollie, nearby at Norfolk, Virginia, was on an old battleship, the U.S.S. *Louisiana.*

The war—World War I, which the United States entered in 1917—was on all of their minds. Connie's great-aunt wrote, "The paper has just come which says that our war ships are fighting in the North Sea with the Allied ships. I don't know what is coming to the world." Jean Jennings' sister Florence Lentilhon, whose home was in Paris, knitted more than eighty pairs of socks for service men. Large amounts of woolen clothing were collected for the American troops in France. Walter Jennings decided to help the nation save coal by closing the greenhouses on the farm. Liberty Bonds were being sold in the streets. Jeannette wrote to Connie that she had sold $12,500 worth in one day. "Farmerettes" in blue overalls came to work the Burrwood fields in the absence of farm hands who had gone into the war effort. Walter Jennings told Connie that he and the Walter Jameses would try keeping both their horses in one stable under one groom.

Connie got letters from her aunts telling her how "beautiful" Ollie and Henry looked in their uniforms. Ollie was assigned to the staff of Admiral Albert Gleaves, who directed U.S. Atlantic convoys, and he resided at home on East 70th Street; Henry's ship, the U.S.S. *Olympia*, put out to sea under cover of wartime secrecy. Henry wrote to his new sister-in-law, "By the time I see you again you will have become quite a big girl. Take care of JJ [a nickname for Jeannette]. I don't suppose you will hear from me again in some time. So good-bye, and best love."

Before Connie graduated from Foxcroft in the spring of 1918 she received this letter from her mother. "Dearest Connie, Thank you for your letter telling of all the honors which have come to you. It is fine and I know you must be very glad to think you won them on 'your own'. Father and I are enormously proud of you & so are Oliver & Jeannette. I am overjoyed to think you received the prize for being the best rider, because there is so much more to it than just sitting on a horse, it means good judgement, & lots of other qualities." Her father wrote also, from his office on Broadway: "Please accept my congratulations on your winning Miss Charlotte's prize for the best rider. It is fine and you must be the envy of all the girls."

When Connie graduated, she stayed on to work closely with Miss Charlotte at the school. She would help with the parents of prospective students, showing them and their daughters around the campus and helping Miss Charlotte to introduce them to the school. After a year or so of this the headmistress decided she ought to be paying Connie, and she gave her a salary of $100 a month. "She paid me," Connie reminisced many years later, "to come down and be her assistant. This made me feel very official and quite marvelous to be earning money. It was more than my sister or cousins could do."

She helped to plan and build a number of improvements there, including a building, "The Spur & Spoon," to house the Alumnae Club. She taught riding and the care of horses. Eventually she had a little office near Miss Charlotte's in "Brick House." Her daughters remember Connie speaking of her concern for Miss Charlotte, and that when the lady was talking on the telephone Connie would lift her extension so that she could hear and interrupt, if necessary, when she heard Miss Charlotte accept an appointment that conflicted with one she already had made. She accompanied Miss Charlotte frequently in fox hunting, which the older woman loved.

Connie's interest in Foxcroft lasted all her life. After she was married to Jack she frequently went there, at first from their home in New York and later from their home in Washington. She would go whenever she felt the need to visit Miss Charlotte or to take part in school events—or simply to get away for a few days.

By the time Connie was nineteen Walter Jennings discussed with her plans for their estate and the care of their stables and horses. He often went salmon fishing on the Ristigouche River in Quebec, and in 1919 he wrote to her at Burrwood from the fishing lodge: "You are a very good girl to write me such a long interesting letter telling me so much about affairs at Fairfield and at home. I know that I am missing a treat which the laurel &

roses are furnishing. . . . sad for me to think of it because I am getting no fish. I'm feeling a bit better this noon because I got two this morning. . . Your report about my horse is most gratifying. By all means get a new bridle and suitable bit. I dread the idea of breaking in a new saddle but order new ones for all the horses & have Knoud's man go down & measure them. I told Mike to go to town some day with Richard & get a riding suit at Rogers Peet. Evidently he has forgotten about it. He can go in any time & get any color you prefer. I have no objection to erecting a few hurdles in the Woods. Talk with Mother as to the location or wait until I get home. We could do a little cutting of trees at certain places parallel to the main road. I see we beat Princeton at baseball down at Princeton & the papers said there were 20,000 people there. I never heard of such a crowd at a ball game. . . . Your affectionate Father."

In 1921 the Jennings family journeyed to New Jersey for the ceremonial launching of a Standard Oil tanker to be christened the *Walter Jennings*. Connie was selected to swing the champagne bottle at its prow; Jeannette had had this honor a year or so before, when the *Oliver B. Jennings* was launched. Connie enjoyed the launching, and her fur coat was soaked in champagne.

Connie was a frequent guest at the Auchincloss home at Newport. Aunt Emma, her father's sister, seemed to love having her there and seemed only concerned about whether there were enough young men around for a visit to be interesting for her. At least one young Yale man, Guy S. Rock, maintained an interest in her. He wrote warm chatty letters with news about mutual friends and about football and rowing and parties, and how much fun it was to visit at Cold Spring Harbor, ending, "very affectionately, Guy Rock."

Life was full. Her father shipped Freedom, a favorite horse of hers, by rail car to Middleburg for her, with James to look after him. There were unlimited parties at the holidays to choose from and constant invitations to be with her aunts, or with the Arthur Curtiss Jameses on their yacht, or at their place at Coconut Grove in Florida, or their home in Newport. In 1922 Aunt Emma Auchincloss took Connie to Paris and to Spain for several months. Ollie inquired in a note if she were playing polo with the King of Spain. Her cousin Guyfy wrote, "What a foolish thought that my Mother should ever be bored at having you near her, Connie. She likes nothing better than having those our age about her."

Her mother wrote that she and Mr. Jennings would be dining with the Prince of Wales. Her sister Jeannette wrote about the hunting around

Cold Spring Harbor—"pretty fair," and asking whether "Bam" could get some of her friends to "take a box seating nine at $100 or seats at $5 for the Babies Hospital Hockey match in the new Madison Square Garden—Harvard vs. McGill of Canada. Please help me sell my 120 boxes and 2000 seats. Next week I expect to expire, as I will have a new nurse, chamber maid, laundress and waitress. Last Sunday at Arden, Henry got a buck and several ducks and I got a German prince." Arden was the Harriman family estate up the Hudson River from New York. The E. Roland Harrimans, of the railroad and banking family, were among Walter and Jean Jennings' good friends.

Not far away from Burrwood lived Henry L. Stimson, who was called Colonel Stimson in those days. He was a warm friend of the family, and Connie sometimes went hunting with him up in the west hills.

The numerous cousins seem to have been devoted to Connie. Her cousin Brewster Jennings, son of her father's brother Oliver, sent her a note from his honeymoon, in June 1923. She was staying at the time at Knebworth House in England with her friend the Honorable Hermione Lytton. "Dear Connie," he wrote, "This letter you may notice is written on the first matrimonial morning, so to speak, and as I doubt whether a newly married couple often think of letters at such a time it may be an interesting souvenir to you. We missed you ever so much yesterday. . . . We plan to go Wednesday to Montreal and thence to Japan. Kate joins me, your affectionate cousin Brewster."

Connie's brother Oliver loved fine cars. Before World War I he owned a Biddle. In 1922 he had a Lancia. And he told his sister at one point that he "had made the family order a Rolls for next summer." Connie was no slouch where cars were concerned. She had a Lincoln; her father wrote her about a new body for it, and was negotiating with a representative of Fleetwood, the body builder, for some custom touches that she wanted.

Connie kept up her work at Foxcroft through 1926, mixing her duties with fox hunting and horse shows. She also took up volunteer work at the New York Hospital, where she found herself making decisions about indigent patients. She was conscientious about this responsibility and worked closely with people who had the training to do it properly. Because their family friend Mrs. Arthur Curtiss James was deeply devoted to Christodora House, a mid-town Manhattan "settlement" house providing services to the poor, Connie also served as its secretary for several years.

Connie had absorbed a great deal from her father who, while a responsible member of the Standard Oil inner circle, was also the privileged son of a large fortune. One of the dictums she had learned from her father was that she must work to be worthy of what she had but that she must not hold a paying job that some needy person could fill. Dona Nicholas, who worked for the Ely family in the 1930s, came to know "Miss Con," as she still calls her, very well, and recounted some of the things Connie had confided to her: "Miss Con ached to be 'average.' 'I would give anything in the world to swap places with you,' she told me. Why, I asked, would you swap places with me? You've got everything, and I'm struggling. She said. 'I would love to be married to a man who left home at nine in the morning for the office and came home at five to a supper I had made.' I asked, 'Miss Con, why can't you do that?' And she said, 'I am saddled with all of my responsibilities that were left to me.'"

. . . .

NOTES

1. Captain Jennings, in 1812, loaded a cargo in Britain and sailed for home. That same day news was received that the U.S. had declared war against Britain. An English warship was sent to capture him. Captain Jennings outsailed the warship in a chase that continued for more than a week and brought ashore a cargo worth more than a half-million dollars, which the U.S. desperately needed.

2. Alan Nevins, *John D. Rockefeller: The Heroic Age of American Enterprise*, 2 vols. (New York: Charles Scribner's Sons, 1940). Nevins in his introduction describes the book as an attempt to be objective and impartial, and intent on "understanding Rockefeller rather than either defending or indicting him. . . . If the author brought any bias to his work, it was that of a convinced believer in a free competitive economy."

3. In 1971 Connie, living in Scottsdale, Arizona, had an exchange of letters with Paul Downing, editor of the *Carriage Journal*. She had loaned Mr. Downing a volume of bound correspondence between her father and a Mr. Burton Mansfield on the subject of carriages and his own collection. The correspondence was so interesting to Mr. Downing that he asked if she would allow him to enter it into the archives of the New York Historical Society. This letter was followed by another, acknowledging her comment on "the untraditional appointments of a Surrey which appeared on the cover of a *Carriage Journal*." He wrote about the lack of know-how and good taste in the revival of interest in carriage driving, "that there are so many people these days who have money enough . . . but have not had sufficient cultural education to do these things in good taste. In my day," he continued, "a person who drove a carriage with a Buggy whip or a Buggy with a carriage whip would have been placed in the same class as a hostess who had her table set with the knife on the left and the forks on the right. You, having been brought up in the school to which all 'nice' people aspired, could write a most inspiring article for the *Carriage Journal* which, with your vast area of experience with one of the finest of all private stables, would be conducive to opening the brains of many of our constituents whose brains need opening."

4. An extensive article on this sarcophagus appeared in the *Metropolitan Museum Journal* of 1993, Volume 28.

3

Young Jack on His Way

B
Y THE FALL OF 1910, WHEN JACK'S CLASSMATES at The Hill were
entering their senior year, Jack had already qualified to enter Yale
University. But being then only sixteen and a half years old, appar-
ently both his family and the school felt he was a bit young to go on to Yale.
He was signed into Sargent's Travel School for Boys.

Porter E. Sargent and his wife Margaret, of Boston, would take a group
of boys to Europe for the school year. These were mainly boys of privilege
who were not well prepared for entering the college of their choice and
needed additional work and training. This meant that they were a year or
so older than Jack. There were fourteen boys, from New York, New Jersey,
Colorado, Missouri, West Virginia, Indiana, Florida and Massachusetts.
There were also two women, cousins of Margaret Sargent. Jack made no
mention of the women in his journal.

The journal each student was required to keep was really the heart of
the school year. It was a record of what they saw and learned, and apparently was to be recorded day by day as an exercise in history, geography, the
classics, and composition. Jack's four volumes total 685 hand-written pages,
often illustrated with photos cut from guidebooks, brochures or postcards.
As the journey progressed he used illuminated letters to begin chapters.
This exercise in journal writing became a hallmark of Jack's life—the recording of day-to-day activities, what he saw, what he felt was important. It

marked his emergence as a cultivated young man, at home with the world of the classics, at ease with the landmarks of history, and thoroughly at ease in Europe.

Jack, age sixteen, took his trunk, in the company of his father and mother, to Charlestown harbor in Boston. They used the occasion for him to climb the Bunker Hill Monument, and to see Lexington, Concord, and the Harvard area. The next morning, September 30, 1910, they said their good-byes and he boarded the S.S. *Romanic* of the White Star Lines and sailed for Europe.

They crossed the ocean with mixed weather, all of them seasick during one storm; they called at Ponta Delgada in the Azores, and at Gibraltar, and on to Naples which they reached on October 14. Not lost on them, as they began their immersion into the classical history of Western Civilization, was the fall of the King of Portugal three days before they touched the Azores, and the establishment of a new republic.

Also not lost upon Jack were the Blumer sisters of Providence, Rhode Island, fellow passengers on the *Romanic*, whose company he enjoyed.

At Naples they transferred from the *Romanic* to the *Athena*, a coal-fired steam yacht built for the Mediterranean trade, 200 feet long, with a crew of sixteen. The Travel School party were the only passengers. They spent some six weeks on the *Athena*. As they pulled away from the pier in Naples a boatload of Italian musicians serenaded them with "Santa Lucia" and "Marguerita."

Early in the trip on the *Athena*, some of the yacht's stokers went ashore to find out how their families had weathered a bad storm; Jack and Gerrard Kelly volunteered to take their places. Hot work, but a good interlude.

They visited Sicily, Tunis, Malta, Syracuse, Istanbul, Mt. Athos, Delphi, and Athens, as well as many tiny out-of-the-way spots, ending on December 1 at Ravenna and Ancona in Italy.

Young Jack had his favorite sights, and made frequent comparisons to places he had seen on previous trips with his family. He wrote of seeing the Pillars of Hercules, at the Straits of Gibraltar, in the sun, and compared that sight to the sunrise at Chamonix in France. He compared Sicilian peasant houses to Irish shanties. There were pranks—at the Palazzo Real in Palermo, they were shown Garibaldi's hairbrush: "and when the guide's back was turned I took the opportunity of using it myself."

At sixteen, he writes somewhat disparagingly of "the natives" all the way through the trip, and writes with disdain of poverty. In one town he notes: "Immoral and dirty to a degree of filthiness, one cannot help but admire them for their haughty dignity."

Much of Jack's journal displays a keen sense of observation and an appreciation for the local scene: "White robed Moslems sitting cross-legged in their narrow booths would call their wares in the guttural Arabic dialect; hurrying merchants would hasten through the crowd carrying their produce for the most part in the great wicker baskets which they skillfully balanced on their flat-topped turbans. Here and there a beggar would totter in our footsteps pleading pitifully until in compassion we had tossed him a copper."

Here he describes Sicilian scenes:

> Like the majority of Sicilian towns the bare white houses of Castellamara rise almost perpendicularly from the waterfront leaving but a narrow quay which extends around the beautiful land-locked harbor. High cliffs shelter the sturdy fishing boats of the inhabitants on one side; a small breakwater furnishes protection on the other. In former times the town acted as the seaport of the Segestans and as such assumed considerable importance. The dignitaries of Athens, Rome, and Carthage undoubtedly walked its streets after disembarking from their stately triremes. Now, however, it has lost all the resemblance of prosperity and is content to play the role of a dirty, picturesque, Sicilian town. . . .
>
> An example of the ignorance and semi-barbarity of the natives was brought to our notice as we passed through the main square of the town, for we perceived a savage encounter raging around the village pump—fierce, unkempt men pushing women and children aside, who in their turn added to the turmoil by screeching and shouting Italian execrations at the top of their husky lungs.
>
> Soon, however, the uproar and squalid poverty of the quaint little town was exchanged for the beauty and peace of the gently rolling country. On all sides the purple hills—shining brown when the rays of the sun kissed them through a fleecy cloud—stood in a great semi-circle, the southern arc of which our straining little horses were doing their best to reach.

At Alexander's sarcophagus in the imperial museum in Istanbul, Jack refers to "our narrow-minded Western intellects" as responsible for our disposition to un-tinted sculpture, whereas here there is carefully tinted stone.

The daily school routine was a fairly unrelenting round, with careful study of the places they saw and their background and history. There were lighter moments, however. In Athens a place that became their daily rendezvous after the day's study was completed was the Maison d'Orée patisserie, at which they would relax with hot chocolate and a variety of cakes. On their last day in Athens they went roller-skating in an indoor rink. And there was the moment when their *Athena* tied up to a wharf and they raced to get onto donkeys for a trip up a mountain—Jack's donkey was in the charge of "a charming little shepherdess."

At Delphi, "with clever foresight I managed to choose the most forlorn and shaggy old carthorse out of the spirited assortment of fast little ponies which had been assembled. It is best to draw the veil in the beginning over my mingled feelings of self-reproach and pity for the beast. In fact my own consolation, when I saw our gay cavalcade dash ahead through the orange groves in defiance to my vigorous use of spurs and crop, was that in lonely solitude I could better admire the beauty of the landscape."

At one point Jack and his companions, spending a quiet Sunday, realize it is more than a month since they have been in church. They look up an English church and attend "an impressive" service. This conviction to attend Sunday service became a hallmark of Jack's later life.

The journals give no hint that Jack was younger than the rest of the group. He occasionally mentions a charming or pretty girl, with no further comment. Jack served as postmaster for the group, which meant he would get their mail from prearranged stops and distribute it to the party.

The years 1910 and 1911 were a bridging time all over the world between the old ways and the oncoming dominance of the internal-combustion engine. In the journals we find the party using donkeys, horses, carriages, rowboats, sailboats, and the steam yacht; but as they get to Austria, Germany, France and England they spend more and more time in automobiles, with buses, trolleys, and trucks around them.

When the boys left the *Athena* at Ravenna, Italy, they were obliged to undergo a medical examination. "Penned up in a small enclosure at the base of a towering lighthouse, we waited patiently, while Sumner and myself broke the monotony by performing as monkeys to the edification of an inquisitive Italian crowd."

Then on to spend a month in Rome: a pontifical mass at St. Peter's on Christmas Day; horseback riding on the Via Veneto; a party where Jack sat at dinner with a beautiful Chicago girl whom he felt did not match his intellect; occasional theatre parties or concerts. A visit to the Keats-Shelley Memorial House on the Piazza di Spagna: "Here, in the very room where Keats breathed his last and Shelley wrote his immortal verses, we read the works of these inspired young poets and countless letters written in their correspondence. It was delightful to dream in these quiet rooms on the lives of these two men, so totally different in character and yet so closely associated. Shelley with his unpardonable atheism; Keats and his susceptible nature praising the infinite in every line which flowed from his pen."

Siena, Florence, Pisa, Venice, then on to Austria. At Innsbruck Jack, in great physical shape and cosmopolitan in his experience, takes them all bobsledding. In Munich they watch celebrations of the Bavarian regent Leopold's ninetieth birthday, and sit through six hours of *Die Meistersinger*. Then Strasburg. In Paris, a whiff of the jaded attitude: "The same old Paris, degraded and beautiful as usual, welcomed us when we set out from our hotel on the Rue Balzac this afternoon for our first walk down the Champs-Elysées. The famous thoroughfare was just as crowded, the taxi-cabs and automobiles were just as numerous, and the display of powder and paint was even more dazzling than on any day I can recollect here-to-fore."

Among the fourteen young men, Jack is often in a group of three or four, and the members of such groups vary—not a permanent clique. At one point he and one other retreat to an alley where they engage in fisticuffs to settle some argument, until separated by some locals who happen by. On a tramway ride from Paris to St. Germain, he writes, it was "hot, dirty and disagreeable but we managed to fight off 'ennui' by a continually [*sic*] 'rough-house,' more appreciated by us perhaps than by our fellow-travelers."

At the Louvre, Jack adds his own words to the volumes written about Leonardo da Vinci's Mona Lisa: "In those eyes, deep wells of human nature, we look and see the passing currents of humor, pathos, fidelity, suspicion and all the counter-emotions which surge with such rapidity through the female mind." And in Paris they find themselves often in the company of several girls "of Miss Payan's school."

Jack writes on what one feels in a church such as they have been seeing in Italy, as compared to one of the French Gothic design: "In a church of the Italian Renaissance one experiences none of the spiritual enthusiasm and devotion which attends one's entrance into a Gothic structure. The former building is usually flat roofed, necessitated by the great width of the nave, but in the northern cathedral an ethereal scope is given to the worshipper's soul and his thoughts are instinctively turned upward by the perpendicular and towering lines of the architecture itself. And in the cathedral at Strasburg this psychological fact is even more pronounced."

On to Canterbury, England, and here as they turn toward London an aeroplane flies directly overhead. They learned later that it was the first London to Paris flight, made by Perier in a Bleriot plane. They rent a car or two and see Hampton Court, Windsor Castle, and the Thames lively with picturesque boating parties in punts, shells and rowboats. They go to

The Follies at the Apollo Theatre, "one of the saddest, cheap-wit productions I ever hope to see. The audience, however, felt differently, for as each antiquated chestnut was cracked, they would go into convulsions; one poor imbecile behind me was forever exclaiming, a jolly fine one, a jolly fine one!! until I was tempted to wring his silly head."

Jack spends almost ten pages on his tour of the Inns of Court. Mr. Collins, apparently an assistant to Mr. Sargent, goes with Jack and they spend an afternoon studying the way the legal system works, which Jack feels is inferior to the U.S. system. In Harrod's department store, Jack recounts the inevitable differences in the use of the English language: "'Which is the elevator to the trunk department?' asks an American visitor. 'The silly ass!' mumbles a bystander. 'He means which is the lift to the boxes!'"

As the school year came to a close they had a pleasant dinner at the Savoy with the mother and aunt of one of the group, ending with "a big after-dinner-cigar and bottles of sparkling Apollinaris." On May 4 Jack made his final journal entry, as he and several others left London in a rented Riley motorcar to tour a bit in the countryside.

According to a biography of Jack in his file at The Hill School, Jack went on from England to join his parents in Berlin in June. They traveled from there into Switzerland and the Tyrol, and returned to New York in time for Jack to enter Yale in the fall of 1911.

Jack's father had graduated from Yale in 1885; his great-grandfather, Thomas Day (father of his father's mother) was in the class of 1797 and later earned a law degree from Yale. Jeremiah Day, the uncle of his father's mother, had graduated in 1795 and was president of Yale from 1817 to 1846. Jeremiah Day was not a high-profile president like the two Timothy Dwights; however, Brooks Mather Kelley, author of *Yale: a History*, published by the Yale University Press in 1974, credits him with making solid advances in the Yale of his day and concludes that his presidency is much underrated. George Henry Ely, the elder brother of Jack's father, graduated from Yale in 1865, and Jack's cousin, Frederick Ely Williamson, was of the class of 1898.

The biography that Jack wrote of himself for the class yearbook in 1915 lists many activities but does not mention the years in which he was involved in them. It is clear, however, that he was working for the *Yale Daily News* almost from his entrance into college, and served as business manager of the *News* in 1914. What is unwritten, according to his daughters, is that the life-style of Jack's parents was expensive to the point of their being unable to support him in college and thereafter. That was apparently the point of his efforts to earn money by selling advertising for the *Yale Daily News*, and to his own choice of careers later on.

A letter which his mother saved, written to his father in May of Jack's freshman year, gives a picture not only of his life at Yale but of his relationship to his father. He writes: "Dear Father, Two letters in two consecutive days must come as quite a surprise to you, but I am taking my monthly vacation now so that I have lots of time to write." He discusses the ferment on the campus, which was the result of an effort to bring the various components of the university into greater contact with each other. It was part of the historic development of the institution into a mature university, as detailed in Kelley's history of Yale.

"Couldn't you hunt up some influential alumnus," Jack asks his father, to write to the paper in an effort "to promote a closer spirit of unity in the university?" An article of about 450 words, he added, would be a great help to the cause and to him: "I suppose you think that I am suffering from a delusion that you haven't anything to do except to hunt up articles for the *News*. But I have to make the paper if I want to do anything in college, and confidentially if I make it now I have a very good chance for the Chairmanship in Senior Year."

Jack went on in this letter to tell his father what was happening in the university world regarding the trials for the Olympic teams, for the games which were to be held that summer in Stockholm. As there were established athletes in the many disciplines, many college men saw no point in trying out. "Couldn't you get Col. Thompson, who is the President of the American Olympic Commission, to write a short article on this . . . in the hope that the college athletes will all compete? . . . If it would be more convenient for him I will write an article and send it to him to sign." Then, conscious that he might be overloading his dad, Jack urged him to tend to the first matter first "and don't bother about this until you have fixed that up. With lots of love, affectionately, Jack."

Yale's history records that the movement to better integrate the university was successful at least to the degree that Yale has become one of the world's great universities, in part due to the extraordinary program of building residential "colleges" which greatly affected the campus during the 1920s and 30s. Whatever the outcome may have been of Jack's attempt to inspire university men to try out for the Olympics, that summer he traveled with the family to Sweden and the Olympics at Stockholm, to Finland and to Russia.

At Yale Jack was Secretary and Treasurer of the International Polity

Club; Class Secretary; a member of the Civic Government Club, the Cosmopolitan Club, the Wagner Club and the Elizabethan Club. He belonged to the Psi Upsilon Fraternity, and he was elected for his Senior year to Wolf's Head, one of the prestigious secret senior societies, to which his father had also belonged.

In his sophomore, junior and senior years, Jack lived with three classmates—H.S. Lynch, C.J. Coe and W.J. Burns (with the exception that Burns did not live with them in the Junior year) at three different New Haven addresses. Colles Coe was best man at Jack's wedding. Thereafter he remained a good friend for the rest of Jack's life, although he was not mentioned either in diaries or such letters of Jack's as are available.

After a busy Junior year, Jack and a friend, Charley Mallory, set out on an adventure. They booked passage to South America on the S.S. *Byron*, of the Lamport & Holt Line. Maud Ely bade her son goodbye in the park at the Brooklyn City Hall, and went on to their summer home at Southampton. Al Ely and Jack drove to the Fremont Street dock of the steamship line, where they met the Mallorys.

The *Byron* sailed on June 13, 1914. Jack had been to Europe on several different ships; by comparison, the *Byron* was diminutive. While the ship was clearing the harbor, Jack wrote a letter to "Miss Brown" (perhaps his father's secretary), with instructions for the summer, and gave the letter to the pilot to take back and be posted. There were thirty-eight passengers, more than half of them Brazilian students returning from schools and colleges in the States for their summer vacations. Others on board included a Mr. Taylor, coffee merchant and Jack's companion at the Captain's table, whom Jack found unattractive, and Patrick Wiley, on his way with wife and baby son to take up residence in the American Consulate in Paraguay.

Jack's training in writing a journal, from the Sargent School days, came into its own on this trip. He produced 251 pages—a mature and priceless look at the continent through the eyes of a young American. Jack and Charley had connections that gave them entrée to important segments of the business world of South America. These connections could have come from friends of his father and mother, or from Charley's parents. Considering that in this period Jack's father was obstetrician to Mrs. Franklin Delano Roosevelt, whose husband was by this time a prominent New York State politician and was serving as Assistant Secretary of the Navy, high-level connections were quite probable.

Jack and Charley had decided to do a lot of reading on the trip. They found a secluded spot behind a lifeboat and in the lee of the captain's cabin.

Their reading list included Walton's *The Compleat Angler*, Oscar Wilde, James Bryce's *South America: Observations & Impressions*, which had been published just two years before, Ibsen's plays, and Dana's *Two Years Before the Mast*. Jack writes, "During the morning I finished the *Compleat Angler* and passed it on to Charley. . . . I could not help reflecting as I read Sir Izaak and looked at the comfortable bulk of Charley stretched out in his steamer chair what a delectable bait he would make for a haddock."

Jack loved literature: "I will never forget my first thrill at reading *Swiss Family Robinson*, and my keen pleasure in following Darwin as we cruised together in the *Beagle*." He goes on: "Just as those books quicken our appreciation of the wonders and diversity of natural phenomena, so Bryce's book awakens us to the stupendous problems of human relations. South America beyond a doubt is the land of promise and such men as Bryce are forcing the world to acknowledge the vast power, the great resources, the high degree of civilization, the art treasures and the crying needs of that continent. And the remarkable and scarcely believable fact to me, one that I can scarcely realize, is that I am fortunate enough to live in this age of transition and of great movements before these great countries have been exploited and while the opportunity to develop them is open to all. Initiative and knowledge of actual conditions is sufficient capital for any man. The knowledge I hope to accumulate during this trip."

Jack had a long talk with Patrick Wiley early in the trip, over the opportunities of a career in diplomacy: "He is intensely interesting and extremely well-read—just such a man as the country should be proud to have in its service." Wiley gave Jack pointers on preparing for the Foreign Service examinations that were to be offered in January. Jack saw diplomacy as "engrossing with a great range for useful and patriotic service."

Jack and Charley volunteered together to serve on a committee for managing a series of deck sports. A young mustachioed Brazilian engaged Jack in a long game of shuffleboard, with a lively gallery cheering them on. The crew exercised their prerogative of ceremoniously dunking everyone who had not previously crossed the equator, but afterwards "we all got together and threw Neptune and his cohorts, with all their paraphernalia, tridents, wigs, masks, etc. into the tank. I had the pleasure of pouring two buckets of 'lather' over the head of the ship's doctor who had assisted Neptune at the ceremonies. It was fine sport and everyone, especially the neophytes, enjoyed it."

Shipboard contacts brought Jack to the realization that there was a high quality of business acumen among South Americans. He wrote in his journal: "The South American men of affairs, and particularly the Brazilians and Argentinians, are fully capable of meeting the most astute Americans of the 'North' in industrial and commercial fields. It is a shrewd man who can best them in a bargain."

Jack had developed into a good bridge player during his college years. He, Charley and the Wileys played a progressive bridge tournament. Throughout this summer, bridge was a frequent pastime with all sorts of partners.

According to this journal, Jack mostly chose something like orangeade to drink while others might choose beer or spirits.

Jack's journal entry on June 25 is indicative of his broad interest in science and natural phenomena, as well as human affairs. "The equatorial current separates into two divisions at Cape St. Roque," he wrote, "half of its water going northward to warm the Caribbean Sea and half tracing a southerly course along the coast of Brazil. During the past few days we have been breasting the northern current and our speed increased perceptibly as soon as we had rounded the Cape and secured the benefit of the same force we had been combatting."

He was concerned at the lack of United States flag vessels in South American trade. So far, down to Rio, he had seen none.

At Rio de Janeiro Jack and Charley took time to see the city and its spectacular setting. One day they took a taxi up to Tijuca, the highest of the peaks behind the city. They were hailed by a group of Brazilians picnicking by a waterfall. The group urged them to join the party—beer and sandwiches. Portuguese, broken English and Spanish combined to make it a warm and friendly time. "It is such little incidents as these," Jack wrote, "which make traveling so attractive—the unending fascination of meeting new people and making new friends."

Wherever they went on this trip they took in theatre or cabaret or whatever was the specialty of the place, although they stayed away from the more raunchy attractions. Commenting on the Casino Antarctica in São Paulo, Jack wrote that it "was the same if not better than the open air theatres of Paris. The auditorium was far larger than the theatres on the Champs-Elysées, people appeared to spend money just as freely, the demimondane (*sic*) were more repellent but better dressed, and the "cantoras" on the stage sang just as badly but had on a few more clothes than their Parisian prototypes. Altogether it was quite 'Bohemian' and Charley and I left early."

Contacts among their student shipmates on the *Byron* yielded some nice benefits. One of the boys, with his father and five siblings, entertained Charley and Jack at luncheon in their family villa. They took them on a long drive, to a soccer match of "old boys" from the young man's school against a Scottish team, and a gracious dinner at home. They then took them to the theatre.

From São Paolo the next step was the *Alcantara*, a beautiful new steamer of the Royal Mail Steam Packet Company, sailing from Santos, the port of São Paolo, to Montevideo and Buenos Aires—the ship's maiden voyage. As the *Alcantara* steamed away, Jack summarized his impressions of Brazil:

> We have of course been impressed by her unequalled resources. Her cities have delighted and revolted us. Her people have charmed us by their consideration and hospitality but their flagrant disregard of morality and the corrupting influence of a weak church have shown us their deficiencies. Brazil's problems are not commercial; they are not agricultural. Her material welfare is assured. But her greatest need is a national conscience, a religious and moral awakening to which end we in the North can aid her to far better advantage than by promoting her industries. My advice to the prospective investor in Brazil is to keep his capital at home. The competition is tremendous, the government is jealous of foreign enterprise, and the Brazilians themselves are fully alive to their own opportunities.
>
> The future of Brazil, although shaded by the ethical problems she must face, is bright. Her politics are being purified. Fonseca, a thorough incompetent and a grafter, finishes his term this November and gives way to Lao Braz, the leader of the P.C.R. party (Liberals). Her crops, as far as can be predicted, will be excellent for several years to come which should launch her on a new era of prosperity. Financially she is at present in a bad way but by 1916 her paper will all be redeemable. She is struggling under a tremendous import tariff and her excise taxes are extortionly high but there is hope that with a new Congress these taxes will be lowered and the demoralizing Federal lotteries done away with. When these reforms have been made, when foreign capital is welcomed as it should be, and when the people awake to their lamentable degeneracy Brazil will become a power among nations.

After a brief call in Montevideo, Uruguay, they arrived in Buenos Aires. Jack and Charley called at the office of the Munson Steamship Line with a letter of introduction to a Mr. Thomas. He became their guide for much of their stay: to the opera at the Colon theatre, to the cathedral, to the races at Palermo, to the Bolsa (the stock exchange). One of Jack's strong impressions was that the United States was missing a great opportunity by not being well represented in banking. "High time" it was, he wrote.

Further inland, they were received at the large meat-packing plant of Swift & Co., whose major owner was the father of a Yale classmate, Phil

Swift. A couple they had met on the *Byron* took them on the plant tour. This was one of a number of tours they had of shipping, manufacturing, farming and other enterprises.

After an extensive visit in Argentina they boarded the Pacific Mail Steam Navigation ship *Orissa* bound for the Falkland Islands and then the west coast. Their companions aboard were quite varied: a French dramatic troupe, a Chilean businessman, four American salesmen, a courteous English borax prospector, and a sheep rancher who was returning to the Islands. Bridge, deck tennis, and of course reading kept Jack busy.

Port Stanley in the Falklands was cold and dreary, but they met the town baker, an Englishman named Summers. He took them to his shop "and set one of the best lunches before us that I have ever eaten. For over an hour we sat in the comfortable parlor of his establishment while he and his family served us with mutton, mashed potatoes, fine yellow turnips grown in the front yard, and tapioca pudding. The room was heated by a glowing peat fire which he replenished from time to time as he watched us eat. He told us many interesting things about the islands, which he has never left except for one short visit to Punta Arena. . . . Two thousand people, one million sheep!"

Then the *Orissa* took them through the Straits of Magellan and to the southernmost town of the world, Punta Arenas, Chile.

When they landed at Coronel, Chile, five days later, they got their first news that war in Europe was imminent, that Austria had declared war on Serbia, and that matters were coming to a head. This was July 29, 1914. They went to the English Club to get what news was available. Then on, by train, to Santiago.

Jack found the capital of Chile to be a more pleasant city than either Rio de Janeiro or Buenos Aires. Among other things, he noted that there were fewer taxis and more barouches (a type of four-wheeled carriage), or other horse-drawn conveyances. The crowds, he felt, were less cosmopolitan and more Chilean. The impending war however had affected the rate of exchange. Chile depended heavily on her export of nitrates, and this trade was so sharply reduced that the mines were virtually unworked. The value of the peso had slipped from about eighteen English pence to just over seven.

Traveling by train to Valparaiso, they saw nine large German ships tied up in the port, afraid to put out to sea. And there were a number of American lumber schooners in the harbor, "a welcome sight." Jack commented frequently on the squalor that he saw, and the vast difference between South American cities and those of the United States and Europe. In Valparaiso they took in a "moving picture show," an exciting tale in which the hero eloped with the heroine in a Zeppelin.

Back on the *Orissa*, there was discomfort all around because among the passengers were several German reserves. While on board Jack had a sharp attack of appendicitis. The ship's doctor came to his stateroom to see him. "Charley did everything in the world that there was to be done," Jack wrote, "and although I felt rather uncomfortable for a time it soon began to wear off. The last thing I heard before I went to sleep was Charley trying to tell me that we were going at half speed with all our lights out and that a mysterious battleship, perhaps a German cruiser, had been sighted." The mystery ship turned out to be a Chilean cruiser, one of several going into Antofagasta to check on labor unrest among unemployed nitrate workers.

Antofagasta was a desolate port, the chief nitrate port of the country, where rain had never been known to fall. A German cavalry officer was among the guests at their hotel, and when he found out that they were Americans he outlined the German campaign to them: to take France, give Finland to Sweden, make Poland autonomous and take away France's colonial possessions. He could not understand why England had ever entered the war, and admitted that at present the outlook was dark for Germany.

The train trip from Antofagasta to La Paz, Bolivia, was spectacular. Jack recorded details of the narrow gauge rail line, the American-made locomotives and cars, the climb to 13,000 feet in 223 miles, and the descent into La Paz. They found it a very picturesque place, but troops were everywhere to keep peace as the unemployment and unrest caused by conditions in Europe were palpable. They had a talk about the situation with the American minister, the Honorable John D. O'Rear.

"We were awakened this morning," Jack wrote, "by the flare of bugles and the rattle of drums and on looking out of our windows discovered that the Plaza was full of troops escorting a funeral cortege through the streets. Hurriedly dressing, we followed the procession, which was the funeral of the Bishop of La Paz, and went with it to one of the oldest and most imposing churches in the town where the remains were laid in state at the foot of the high altar.

"The interior of the church was ablaze with candles and along each side of the long central aisle were two rows of seats where the President of the Republic, the high dignitaries of the church and state, and the general staff of the army in glittering gold lace and resplendent uniforms were seated. In the transepts were crowds of Aymara women in their most brilliant costumes and in the dark recesses of the chapels and along the sides of the nave under the shadows of the pillars were the poorer Indians reverently kneeling and holding wax tapers. All eyes were focused on the open sarcophagus where the Bishop lay in his white robes, wearing his great hat, and peacefully sleeping. . . .

"We returned to the Plaza for breakfast to an excellent little tea shop where we enjoyed a far better meal than we could have had in the hotel. We tried to bring the Indian guide into the place and give him a good lunch and a plate of ice cream but the proprietor objected and all the Bolivians in the place looked horrified when they saw a bare footed Indian come in. Caste feeling is quite strong in Bolivia and the old Spanish families and wealthy Aymaras draw a sharp line of social distinction between themselves and the poorer Indians. . . .

"Our three days in La Paz were the most interesting we have so far spent."

As the train taking them on from La Paz to Lake Titicaca stopped to fix something, they had the chance to sit and contemplate. "Across the valley with its patchwork fields and floor of roofs rose the steep foothills of the Andes, rugged cliffs colored every conceivable hue, red, blue and brown, and behind a higher range of peaks colored deep copper fusing into brown and capped with snow preparing one for the background of stupendous white mountains dominated by the tremendous height of Illimani. The coloring, the peace, the quiet and the majesty of the scene were incomparable. Only the troops of llamas on the winding road near by, the occasional crowing of a cock, and the cracking of a twig by an old Indian woman gathering brush broke the perfect stillness."

They arrived in Arequipa, Peru, and, lowered by a steam crane in a heavy oaken chair into a little rowboat, were rowed out to the *Chili*, which carried a load of cattle for ports up the coast, and decks loaded with vegetables and other provisions for sale at each stop. On to Lima for two days of sightseeing—including the bones of the conqueror Pizarro. They then boarded the *Palena* for Panama. The boat was overcrowded with Germans returning home for the war, and notices were posted in four languages forbidding discussion of the European situation.

In Panama, the train took them along the banks of the canal to Colón, where they boarded the United Fruit Company's *Abangarez* for New Orleans.

On September [the date left blank] Jack and Charley pulled into Pennsylvania Station in New York, after what Jack called "an ideal summer vacation."

On the campus in the fall of 1914, the war stories in The *Yale Daily News* shared space with events such as the dedication of the Yale Bowl, still the site of Yale football games. This particular story blocked war coverage off the front page for the first time in many editions. The Harvard-Yale game that autumn in the new bowl was front-page news, although the score was Harvard 36, Yale 0.

With Jack as business manager, the *News* ran an extensive campaign to boost circulation, much of it in prominent boxes on Page One. Jack was treasurer of the Yale Red Cross Fund (unspecified dates); in October of 1914 the *News* announced a "mammoth mass meeting in Woolsey Hall" under the auspices of the *News*, in aid of the Red Cross. They raised $1400. The paper carried many articles on the work of the Red Cross, a natural corollary of the paper's war coverage.

This was a vigorous time to be in college. Many students had been abroad. The *Yale Daily News* carried a story in the October 8, 1914 issue headlined "Neutrality at Yale." William Howard Taft, who had been the twenty-seventh president of the United States (1909 to 1913) and was now Professor of Law at Yale, was quoted concerning the important part that American universities would have to play in bringing about a peaceful settlement of the struggle in Europe. He urged Yale men to help keep the "national attitude" in a way that would not mark the United States as being in sympathy with either side more than the other. Taft urged particularly that such an attitude would help his successor, President Woodrow Wilson, in the conduct of the nation's affairs.

The Yale Class of 1915's yearbook was edited by Albert H. Ely Jr., Class Secretary. In his preface, he writes: "Ours has been a unique Class. Bursting upon New Haven in 1911, it has passed as a thunderstorm and in its transit has refreshed and clarified the atmosphere. As we graduate we can review an illustrious record. Our future collectively is bright. Our future individually is assuredly worthy of record—of interest to our classmates and to posterity. Keep your Secretary informed!"

In the yearbook's notes on the Junior year, Jack is mentioned as organizing the Class Party held at the Taft Hotel under the auspices of the *Yale Daily News*. "Due to the careful planning and able organization of Jack Ely," it says, "an elaborate entertainment has been prepared, which provoked enthusiastic applause by its scope and variety." And in comments about their Senior year, it says: "Of necessity must we pass over the Mallory-Ely occupation of South America."

4

Career and Marriage

SOMETIME NEAR HIS GRADUATION, in the spring of 1915, Jack apparently talked with Yale alumnus Henry L. Stimson of the class of 1888, a fellow member of the Psi Upsilon fraternity. Stimson suggested to Jack that he might go to work with him and learn the field of diplomacy. This was a strong pull, coupled with Jack's experiences in his summer of touring South America, for Stimson was one of America's most distinguished citizens and a member of the law firm of Root, Howard, Winthrop & Stimson. In 1911 President William Howard Taft had appointed Stimson Secretary of War, and reforms that he put into effect had a major effect on our Army. Among Yale men he was especially revered.

In the event, Jack spent the summer after graduation with "Doc" Swift,[1] a professor who conducted a preparatory session at the Columbia Summer School, and entered the Columbia Law School in the fall of 1915. According to his daughter Day, Jack originally went to law school as a preparation for the Foreign Service. But he began to realize that the family's lifestyle was eating more than his father's medical practice could produce and that they were in debt; to help out, he would need more income than a beginning Foreign Service salary could provide. He therefore determined to enter the practice of law.

While at law school Jack lived on West 56th Street with his father, mother, and younger brother Francis, and undoubtedly took part in the

New York social scene in which both his parents were so intimately involved. The family's summer home out at Southampton must also have been a great asset to Jack, both for relaxation and for a place to entertain his friends.

Maud had tired of Elyria on Southampton's Ox Pasture Road, and in 1917 she and Al embarked upon an impressive project. Maud had bought twenty-five acres of land adjacent to a golf course in the Shinnecock Hills section, and near to the Shinnecock Indian Reservation. She had begun construction of a great summer house which was to be called "Fort Hill," named for a fort the British had built nearby in 1777. It had a massive entrance hall, spacious library and a dining room measuring thirty by forty feet, a sun parlor opening on a large terrace facing the ocean, with a guestroom and bath on the ground floor.

Fort Hill had a servants' dining room in addition to the kitchen facilities and a butler's bedroom and bath; seven family bedrooms with five baths; six servants' bedrooms, and extra servants' rooms on the third floor—on and on, with generous linen rooms, laundry, storage and supply rooms, a six-car garage, an artesian water supply. Fort Hill was frequently described in the gossip columns as "one of the largest and most pretentious in Southampton," and "beautifully situated on one of the highest points in the Hills with a view of the ocean and of Shinnecock Bay . . . It is scarcely visible from the Montauk Highway, and has extensive grounds reaching to the roadway."[2]

Maud had become a friend of Elizabeth Arden, an energetic and determined woman ten years younger. A biography of Miss Arden states that Maud traveled with her across Europe in 1935. Jack's cousin John Merchant recounts that the ladies visited Germany together to spend some of the Arden profits which could not be taken as cash from the country. They gave lavish parties there, and Maud talked about meeting the "handsome Hermann Goering" and was flattered by his attentions. Maud also took on the job of decorating a new salon that Elizabeth Arden opened in Southampton, and designing the landscaping. She claimed that she had given Arden the thought of naming her famous line "Blue Grass."[3]

Jack received two degrees from Columbia in the spring of 1917, the Bachelor of Laws and Master of Arts, just as the United States was entering the world war. His thesis for his Master's degree was entitled "The Central American Court of Justice" and it must have been of some note, as it was translated into Spanish and published that November in *La Revista del Mundo*, a quarterly publication of Doubleday, Page & Co., the Spanish-language edition of their *World's Work* publication.

Either just after graduation, or prior to it, Jack served for a brief time in the law offices of Kirlin, Woolsey & Hickox, 27 William Street, New York City, specializing in Admiralty Law. In March of 1917 he enlisted in the U.S. Naval Reserve Force, and on April 8 was commissioned an Assistant Paymaster with the rank of Ensign—just two days after the United States declared war on Germany.

Jack served as Commissary Officer at the Naval Reserve Barracks at Newport, Rhode Island. His responsibilities included the submarine bases there. Jack's two daughters remember stories of his being "the only mounted officer in the United States Navy," doing inspections on horseback. In recommending him for promotion in April of 1918, the Commandant wrote, "He has handled his department in an exceptionally skillful manner. Has unusual zeal and initiative, and is especially efficient in successfully carrying out all duties to which he has been assigned."

In May 1918 he was promoted to Lieutenant Junior Grade. That October he made formal application through channels for sea duty, or at least service overseas. This request went up the chain of command, with an endorsement from his superior recommending its favorable consideration, although noting that a qualified replacement would be needed. The letter moved upwards until it reached the Bureau of Supplies and Accounts, where the officials stated that they had no one to replace him and recommended it stop right there. So back down the chain of command came the accumulation, now eight pages thick.

On November 11, 1918, the Armistice was signed in Europe, ending World War I.

In early January of 1919 Jack was assigned to the U.S.S. *Panaman*, as Supply Officer. The *Panaman* was a cargo ship with a displacement of 14,500 tons. She had been taken over by the Navy from her owner, the American Hawaiian Steamship Company, in August of 1918 and had made two crossings to France with food and military supplies. While she was not a dashing warship, she had, nevertheless, had to ply waters hazardous with German submarines. At the time Jack was assigned to her, she was at Newport News being refitted to carry troops. His short month of duty with her was spent on shore. In notes on his career that he sent to Yale, Jack later wrote, "My interest in the sea, aroused by enforced duty at naval shore stations during the war, led me to enter an admiralty law office."

Jack was discharged from active duty on February 10, 1919. A statement from the Office of the Auditor, Department of the Navy, states that

Jack's accounts as supply officer of the *Panaman* were in balance, the gross dollar amount of the provisions, clothing, supplies and stores for which he was responsible being some $81,000. The *Panaman* continued to serve the Navy until September of that year, and brought home more than 10,000 soldiers from the war.

An affidavit dated March 28, 1919 from the District Enrolling Officer of the Second Naval District, Newport, Rhode Island, states that Ely's duties had "required his entire time and prevented him from securing a leave of absence of sufficient length to take the New York Bar examinations in June and October of 1917." It requests "that his application for admission to the New York Bar without examination, under the provisions of the amended rules of the New York Court of Appeals, be favorably considered." Jack was entered into the State Bar of New York on June 17, 1919.

A police report on Jack's fitness to be accepted for the Bar stated that "nothing was found against the character of the applicant," although "he stated that he was summoned once for speeding, and discharged."

An interesting footnote to Jack's attitude to life and to the war is found in a letter apparently addressed to alumni of Yale University on May 1, 1917, signed by William Howard Taft on behalf of the "Committee of Seventy-One" of which Taft was chairman. The Committee was calling strongly for a curtailing of drinking on the campus—and in American life—in consonance with the sentiments of British Prime Minister David Lloyd George, who had said of his own country's wartime fitness, "We are fighting three enemies, Germany, Austria and Drink." Among the Committee are listed Henry L. Stimson, Class of 1888, and Albert H. Ely, Jr., 1915.

After his discharge from the Navy in February 1919, Jack spent several weeks resting and recuperating.

During this time Jack's younger brother Francis was a boarding student at the Ridgefield School in Connecticut, spending weekends and vacations at home in New York. He had been at The Hill School for a year but did not do well there and was regularly taunted by the other boys. His cousin, John Merchant, believes that Francis had a compulsive eating disorder that caused him to be overweight. "I think Francis was babied to the nth degree by his mother," John says, "and in fact that may have been a big part of his problem."

On the strong recommendation of Hill headmaster Dwight Meigs, the Elys took Francis out of the Hill School in favor of a smaller school where his needs could better be met. Francis remained at Ridgefield School until June 1920.

Only a few days after joining the Navy, Jack had received a letter from Charles R. Hickox of Kirlin, Woolsey & Hickox. The letter told him that the law firm would be glad to see him join them after the war was over. After Jack left the Navy, he received a letter from John Woolsey of the same firm inviting him to come in and discuss a position. This letter was written in April and he was almost immediately received into the firm as a law clerk.

Jack's work with this firm is reflected in several bound volumes of legal papers from that period, 1919 to 1923. By this time the firm was Kirlin, Woolsey, Campbell, Hickox & Keating. The cases in Jack's portfolio dealt with damage to ships or their cargoes, damage to bridges or wharves caused by ships, and accidents to crew or stevedores. He handled suits arising out of delays in delivering cargoes, and the intricacies involved in the leasing of ships; cases ranging from claims of three or four hundred dollars to hundreds of thousands of dollars. Cases dealing with charters, insurance claims, cargoes of hides, fuels, sugar, cotton oil, lumber, bales of burlap, cotton, magnesite, disputed charges, demurrage, loss from theft or pilfering. Correspondence with Bermuda, London, Buenos Aires, Philadelphia, New Orleans, Baltimore, Norfolk, Charleston, Newcastle-on-Tyne, Glasgow, Rotterdam, Cleveland, Calcutta, Antwerp, Bordeaux.

Jack loved it. There was the intricacy of getting depositions from crewmen traveling between various ports and arranging with the U.S. consul in these ports to take the depositions under legally admissible conditions. The questions to be answered were complex. Would the ship have carried enough coal for a particular trip? What was the rate of fuel consumption, and what sizes were the hatch grates? Then there was the maintenance of cordial relations in intricate cases and much citing of the law of the U.S. and the laws of other countries. Dealing with disputes over grain loading charges and who had the right to choose the stevedoring company, the ship's owners or the company chartering the vessel from the owners, and so on. Determining what causes certain damage—the sweating of a ship's steel structure in various weather conditions, the effect of a load of damp rain-soaked rags on the rest of the cargo. Ascertaining who is liable for the damage in the collision of a ship with a drawbridge. Handling the case of injury to a man on a gangway. What is the value to be compensated in the case of standing by a distressed vessel at her request, even though in the event no assistance is actually rendered?

In 1920 Jack also found time, at age twenty-six, to serve as a special assistant attorney general of the State of New York, a temporary appointment in connection with enforcement of the election laws.

Those days must have involved some turmoil in the Ely household. In the summer of 1920 Dr. Ely made a 28,000-mile journey to the Far East— Japan, Korea, North China, Manchuria, Southern China, the Philippines, Honolulu. He described this as making a study of the soybean. His passport identified him as "attending physician," but whom he was attending is not specified. Maud did not go with him, and the gossip columnist made much of this fact, taking the occasion to speculate upon the state of the Ely marriage. She commented:

> [Dr. Ely] has come up very rapidly in his profession and has made considerable money; but within the past twenty years he has built two elaborate country houses and reared two sons—one of them a renowned *enfant terrible*—expensively. Anyhow the sons are expensive looking. In this respect they resemble their remarkably handsome brunette mother who has steadily grown less matronly looking with the passing of the decades. She now presents the appearance—if you look at her swiftly—of a sub-deb. So great is the miracle accomplished by a marvelous make-up, the latest in hip-reducers and a wide-brimmed hat!

The columnist went on to comment on various bits of gossip concerning Maud's activities with other men in her husband's absence. This was often the tone taken by this particular columnist about the Elys, and frequently it was much more biting.

Warren G. Harding was elected handily to the presidency of the United States in the fall of 1920. Early in the next year, before his inauguration in March, Harding took a trip to Florida, and spent time on a houseboat owned by Senator Joseph S. Freylinghuysen of New Jersey. The party included Senator A.W. Fall of New Mexico, Henry Fletcher, U.S. Ambassador to Mexico, and Dr. Albert H. Ely, who acted as personal physician to the President-elect. Harding was an Ohio man, and one might speculate that Dr. Ely's connection with him was based on their common tie to Ohio.

The press covered the event, especially the fact that the houseboat was stuck in the mud of the Indian River at one point. Press photos showed assortments of tuna and marlin, which the group apparently had caught, and the party all in coats and neckties. Reporters commented that "the personal physician's agreeableness is standing the tests nobly, and the president-elect is forming a fast friendship for him." For over forty years, the marlin which Al caught on this occasion hung, mounted, first in Fort Hill and then in Jack's study in Washington. Senator Fall, who became Secretary of the Interior in Harding's cabinet, was the key player in the infamous

Teapot Dome oil scandal and served time in prison for it.

Dr. Ely apparently was a guest at Harding's inauguration.

The next summer the press was abuzz with speculation on where the President was going to vacation. He had received dozens of invitations, among them one from Dr. and Mrs. Ely to be their guest at Fort Hill. In fact, Harding did journey in the yacht *Mayflower* to Gardiner's Island, near Southampton, where he invited Ely and his friend Stephen Metcalf to join him for the night. The next day Metcalf's yacht *Sachem* brought Harding and Senator Freylinghuysen to the National Golf Club in the Shinnecock Hills, which abutted on the Fort Hill property. After eighteen holes of golf the party, which also included Mrs. Harding and General Sawyer, the President's personal physician, were the guests of the Elys at lunch.[4] There were twenty-four at the table, including the Secretary of War, the Attorney General, the Under Secretary of State and his wife, the Commander of the *Mayflower* and his wife, and Jack. They visited Fort Hill before returning to Gardiner's Island.

Jack balanced his work life with plenty of recreation—tennis, squash, swimming, sailing, horseback riding. In 1922 he joined Squadron A, of the New York National Guard.

Squadron A was a mounted unit, dating from 1889, that had a certain social aura to it. It was a favorite of the dashing young men of the city, and their lady friends. They wore beautiful nineteenth-century uniforms on ceremonial occasions, and World War I Army cavalry olive drab on regular drills or appearances. In World War I they had served with distinction overseas as a machine-gun company. Jack was commissioned a corporal in May of 1924. This unit had gone to the Mexican border in 1916, in the action against Pancho Villa. Villa had raided at least one town in New Mexico in the course of his battle against the governing party in his own country.[5]

During Jack's three years with Squadron A, the unit had its share of ceremonial duties. The squadron provided an escort for Marshal Joffre, the French military hero of World War I, participated in at least one Memorial Day parade, and was reviewed by the Commanding General of the 51st Cavalry Brigade. They held weekly drills and took field training of two weeks a year, sometimes at New City, up the Hudson River, sometimes at Camp Dix in New Jersey, or at Fort Ethan Allen in Vermont. And they played polo. Jack told his children that on one summer trip, someone had inexpertly loaded their horses into a van in such a way that the horses were head to tail. In the stress of the journey each horse had his tail bitten off by the horse behind him; when they were unloaded they had no tails.

As time went on Jack was doing more and more representation of cases for his law firm, whereas in the beginning he had been doing the donkey work of preparing the cases for one of the partners.

The family delights in a case that Jack solved, in which he was defending a shipping company against a claim of seawater damage to the contents of a woman's steamer trunk—those great old things which carried a lady's belongings abroad in pre-World War II days. The trunk was stood on end in her stateroom and opened out to reveal an elaborate hanging section, and opposite that a stack of drawers. Jack had some laboratory tests done to the damaged contents; it was found that the water stains were of fresh water, not salt. He checked the route the trunk had taken, from a city in the Midwest to the pier in New York and found there had been a rainstorm during the time the trunk was sitting on the railroad platform in the city of origin. Ergo, the damage was not the fault of the steamship company.

In September of 1923 Jack ventured forth with two others to establish the firm of Harris, Dawson & Ely. The venture lasted just over three years. In one case he defended the Colonic Irrigation Institute against the claim of a technician that she had cut her hand on a broken test tube, and that a long, costly healing process had resulted. The claim was for about $400, a more substantial sum in 1923 than today. The case went on for about three years. Miss Frances Perkins of the Industrial Board of the State of New York was the hearing officer. A few months later the claim was bumped up to over a thousand dollars. In early 1926, the Appellate Court of New York reduced the award almost by half. Frances Perkins went on to become the first female member of a U.S. president's cabinet, as Secretary of Labor for Franklin D. Roosevelt.

By November 1926 Jack was working for the larger firm of Kobbe, Thatcher, Frederick & Hoar. In the course of his legal career he was admitted to practice law before the federal courts in New York and before the United States Supreme Court.

Meanwhile, in the fall of 1920, Francis Ely had entered the Riverdale School in the Bronx. One of those who supported Francis' application to the school was Jack's cousin, Frederick E. Williamson. Eighteen years older than Jack, Fred was the son of Dr. Ely's sister Edith. Fred and his wife Hilda had their house in Riverdale and an apartment in Manhattan. Fred was enjoying a career as a prominent railroad executive, and at this time was President of the New York Central Railroad.[6]

Francis's school record at Riverdale was abysmal, with grades in the 50 to 60 percent range and numerous demerits. The demerits were for talking in class and in study hall, lateness, eating in study hall, silliness in class, entering the office at inappropriate times, disorderly and disrespectful conduct.

John Merchant remembers Francis chiefly for the visits the boy paid to the Merchant clan in the summers. He sometimes came for a visit to the Pleasant Point Club on the shore of Lake Ontario near Oswego, New York, where the Merchant family would take a cottage for several weeks. John remembers that Francis had quite a crush on a younger cousin, Elizabeth Smith. Francis was nineteen or twenty years old at this time. He seemed to enjoy these visits very much.

At Southampton, Eugene Edgel took special care of Francis; this must have been a great gift to the young man, who had experienced few friendships, little empathy from schoolmates and in addition had a poor relationship with his father. In a letter to his mother written in April 1923, Francis refers to his father thinking that Francis was always spending money and never earning any—Francis being now twenty-one and still in boarding school. Francis then outlines a plan for earning some money that summer. Maud sent the letter to Jack to read and return.

The end of Francis's story came very suddenly. He died in the New York Hospital on September 3, 1925. The cause of death was acute myocarditis, complicated by bronchial pneumonia—an illness of only three days. Francis was twenty-two years old.

John Merchant, Francis's and Jack's cousin, remembers well the funeral, which took place at the Merchant family plot in the Mt. Hope Cemetery in Rochester. Dr. and Mrs. Ely and Jack, then twenty-nine years of age, accompanied the casket and stayed with Maud's sister, Elinor French, and her husband, Frank. "It was pouring rain," John says, "and Aunt Maud was weeping copiously; she said aloud that the rain was God's tears for Francis."

*   *   *

Jack was a popular young man, and an eligible bachelor. The social columnist who had written so often about Jack's family over the years was not reticent about him. She printed an item about Cornelius Vanderbilt Jr. spending some days with Albert H. Ely Jr. and John W. Brodie, in Miami. She also claimed to be the first to promote the possibility that young Ely was leading the field of contenders for the hand of Grace Vanderbilt, the most famous debutante of her day. However, by 1926 Jack had begun to think seriously about his former neighbor on West 56th Street, Constance Jennings.

By the time Jack was graduated from Yale, their neighbors, the Walter Jennings family, had moved to East 70th Street, while Jack lived with his parents at 829 Park Avenue. Burrwood and Fort Hill, the two families' summer residences, were some sixty miles apart. But social life has a way of catching people up with each other, and the tall young lawyer began to be serious about the tall young woman with the deep-set blue eyes.

Connie was very much an outdoor person. And she was very practical; if her car was balky she would replace a spark plug; if a flat tire developed, she would change it. She had her work at New York Hospital and at Christodora House. She was twenty-six, and she felt romance and marriage had passed her by.

The society columnist wrote, "Connie Jennings is really coming out again now that she is enjoying the company of Hugh D. Auchincloss's very animated young wife, who was Maya de Chrapovitsky before her marriage . . . It was at this dance that I made note of Connie's animation. Just before taking her seat at one of the tables, for instance, Connie said 'I am really thrilled about this party.' And Connie, as was proper . . . had put on a stunning black velvet gown with godets entirely covered with rhinestones. . . . In the past she has been chiefly interested in outdoor events such as the horse shows and 'such like' at Piping Rock."

In December 1925 Connie went to India with her father, mother, and brother Oliver. En route, they celebrated Christmas on the Suez Canal. In India they stayed with Viscount Lytton, the Viceroy, and also with the Maharaja of Jaipur. They camped at the Khyber Pass. They returned home through Europe, stopping in Paris to see Jean Jennings' sister Florence, and her husband Eugene Lentilhon. When they were settled again at home, Connie worked up a formal lecture on India, with movies she had taken, which she presented wearing a sari and bare feet.

By this time Jack had become serious in his courtship, although Connie and her parents were not taking it very seriously. While they were in Paris, Jack cabled to Connie from New York, "Following with Portfolio." The Jennings then moved on to England, where they had rented the gorgeous estate of Lord Lytton and his family at Knebworth, outside London. Meanwhile Jack and a client named Portfolio arrived in France to take depositions in a case Jack was handling. When their legal business was finished, Jack flew to London in a Handley Page twin-engined biplane—his first flight in an aeroplane—to see the Jennings family before they departed for home. At that point Connie's family realized that this young man was serious about their daughter.[7]

Homes of the Ely and Jennings families on Long Island. Above, Burrwood, home of Connie's parents, Walter and Jean Jennings. Left, Elyston, home of Jack and Connie Ely. Below left, Fort Hill, home of Jack's parents, Al and Maud Ely. The Walter Jennings gate at Burrwood, below right, is the only piece of these houses still standing as of 1995.

Dr. and Mrs. Ely in
Palm Beach, circa 1910

Jack in St. Mark's
Square, Venice, 1911

Francis Sherburne Ely
1904-1925

Dr. Thomas S. Southworth

Eugene Edgel, factotum for the Elys
in Southampton for forty years

Issy le Molineux, France: Dr. Ely, Jack, Francis, and Eugene Edgel try to fix a tire

Jack, right, with Cornelius Vanderbilt and J.W. Brodie, on the way to Key West, 1920

Jack in São Paulo, 1914

Jack, a mounted Lieutenant, jg, USN, 1918 in Newport

The Jennings family on tour. The photos on this page were taken by Jean Brown Jennings and mounted on glass slides.

On a tour of the hill towns in Tuscany, 1909

Connie Jennings in Egypt, 1908

The Khyber Pass, 1925: The caravan is approaching the border of Afghanistan

Connie filming in India, 1925

Walter Jennings in his private sitting room in a Rome hotel, 1909

Walter Jennings and friends at the Jekyll Island Club, 1925. J.P. Morgan is bowling

William Avery Rockefeller, left, with his nephew Walter Jennings in Oyster Bay, Long Island, 1895

Jean, Connie, Annie Burr and Walter Jennings at the launching of the Standard Oil tanker S.S. Walter Jennings in 1921

Connie and her father enter St. John's Church, September 24, 1927

Connie on the Burrwood staircase, using hundred-year-old lace from Brussels

Jack and Connie's wedding party, Burrwood, 1927

"Southend," Burrwood, 1929: Connie and baby Day
with Dr. Al and Maud Ely

Connie in a hat on the beach
at St. Jean de Luz, France,
1930

Jack in his Manhattan law offices, 1930

Connie, right,
with her aunt
Florence and
uncle Eugene
Lentilhon,
England, 1930

View from the lawn at Elyston, looking north over Long Island Sound

Connie and her daughters lunching on the terrace at Elyston, 1936

Jack and Dr. H.E. Hale on the Jock Scott, Long Island Sound

Jean Brown Jennings, right, with Isa de Rivas Jennings in Wyoming, 1931

In later years, Connie would sometimes say that she had said "yes" to Jack, who was six years older than she, because she was twenty-seven and nobody had proposed to her and she wasn't sure she would get asked again.

The Long Island gossip columnist had a field day with this engagement. "Widespread in interest is the announcement of the engagement of Constance Jennings and Albert H. Ely Jr. The bride-to-be, who is a tall, broadshouldered girl and has often been seen in and around the ring at the horse shows held at Piping Rock, is a daughter of Mr. and Mrs. Walter Jennings, a niece of Oliver Gould Jennings and also of Mrs. Walter B. James, a cousin of Eunice James who married Henry E. Coe Jr., and of Oliver B. James who married Angeline Krech. Her sister, Jeannette Jennings, was married about nine years ago to Henry C. Taylor, who is a son of the William Ambrose Taylors, a nephew of Mrs. E.S. Harkness and a brother of William A. Taylor Jr., who in May was married to Rebecca Lindon Smith.

"The happy Albert, the future benedick, is a son of Dr. and Mrs. Albert H. Ely who are among the New Yorkers prominent in the summer colony at Southampton. That he is one of the young men who at one time, according to rumor, would win the hand and the heart of Grace Vanderbilt, now the wife of Henry G. Davis 3rd, in no way detracts, of course, from his prestige. At the time, in fact, when such a rumor was rife about him, it was also remarked that he was one of the most interesting of the eligibles in New York and very clever and intellectual—which quite puts him more than a step above that 'also ran' class which is dignified by the name of runner-up."

Miss Charlotte insisted that Connie bring her fiancé down to Foxcroft School. She gave an engagement party for Connie and Jack, a feature of which—Connie remembered fifty years later—was a great big watermelon which had been pumped full of champagne, and tasted delicious.

Jack Ely was well aware that his parents were in tight financial straits with the costs of building and maintaining Fort Hill as well as their residence on Park Avenue, and their lavish lifestyle. But his mother gave him a ring that a grateful patient had given Dr. Ely, a large yellow diamond, as big as a fingernail, set in white gold, surrounded by little diamonds. In the 1950s, Connie told Day that when she saw this ring "it was the first time I flung my arms around him with real enthusiasm." (In the 1980s, Connie vehemently denied ever saying such a thing!) She wore the ring with great joy. She wore it to bed that night; the next morning when she woke up her face was covered in bloody scratches. The sharp points of the setting had cut her in her sleep. So they took the ring to a jeweler and had it remade to

Connie's own design, one less flashy than the original.

The wedding took place on September 24, 1927 at St. John's Church in Cold Spring Harbor, with the reception at Burrwood. The family had never had a big wedding, as Jeannette's had been in wartime, and Ollie was still single. Connie's mother carefully forced many pots of Connie's favorite flower, lily-of-the-valley, a springtime flower, so that they would bloom in late September. Walter Jennings hired buses to pick up his guests at the Plaza Hotel in New York City. Connie had six bridesmaids, with Jeannette as matron of honor. Charlie Ames, one of the six ushers, played an active part in Jack's later life. Jack's best man was his college roommate, Colles Coe. They remained friends for life, and the family kept up the friendship with Coe's widow after both Jack and he were dead.

The wedding was a society columnist's dream. One account described Connie's attendants: "Their frocks repeated the autumn hues of the dahlias, which mixed with grasses made their bouquets. Some of the frocks were yellowish in tone, and others pink, while a deeper, richer shade like flame or tangerine was worn by the matron of honor, the bride's sister."

Connie walked down the aisle on the arm of her father. She was concerned because she was taller than he, so she walked "with my knees bent and my shoulders curved over." Then when Jack joined her at the altar she could straighten up, for he was six feet two to her five foot ten. Connie's gown, from Worth of Paris, was of white velvet, and in the fashion of the time ended above her knees. Her train was of Brussels lace that her great-great uncle Henry Bergh had bought for her grandmother, Agnes Isabella Pollock Brown, in about 1830. She did not carry a bouquet, but had tied lily-of-the-valley in the ribbon markers of her prayer book.

Miss Charlotte attended the wedding ceremony, as did a number of Connie's Foxcroft friends. The Foxcroft crowd freely sounded off with the school's songs and cheers. Connie noted many years later that her more proper New York friends were fascinated with them. The girls raided her closet, and as the bridal couple were driven away, they hurled shoes after them. Connie wore a large bruise on her left shoulder for days afterwards.

Friends of the family captured the festivities on film. There in black & white were Maud, with Al never in the same frame with her; Jean and Walter Jennings; Florence Sullivan, a close family friend; many others of the older generation; and a great flock of young blades and ladies. Connie noted that it was a gorgeous day, and that beyond the estate you could see six-meter sloops racing on the blue Sound. The party seemed to end with all the younger folk going off on Walter Jennings' powerboat, the *Jock Scott*, for a swim, some in bathing suits, some (involuntarily) in their finery.

Jack's parents had thoughtfully provided Fort Hill for their first few nights and days. It was lovely fall weather, and they walked on the beach at Montauk Point. They found two glass balls that Connie always kept in their home after that.

Then they sailed for Europe for a honeymoon of six weeks. Of course they had both been there many times. But being on a trip to Europe with Connie's parents had been very different; the Jennings did not really absorb things. Walter Jennings' idea of "doing" Rome, for instance, had been to take in all 365 churches in the city, so many per day. So on this trip, Jack showed her the things he loved.

In those days, honeymoons and their destinations were a closely kept secret. By chance, Connie's brother Ollie was booked on the same ship. This embarrassed him so much that, to make up for it, he loaned them his touring car and chauffeur for the European part of the honeymoon. In it he put a lap robe, heavy as a buffalo robe, which still serves the family for picnics and traveling today.

Jack felt himself a part of this remarkable family right from the beginning. Mrs. Jennings wrote heartwarming letters to Connie: "Please thank Jack for his lovely letter. Mogens [a Danish architect, friend of Ollie's, who had become close to the family] said the ship was filled with flowers, and Henry Carter told Father he had never seen so many people to see anyone off. Jeannette packed all your silver in the vault. Tell Jack I am playing the part of interfering mother-in-law and am going to keep Uncle Otto's clock. Your father seemed quite hurt to think it should be exchanged and so I shall leave it for your further consideration.

"Ask him to be lenient (Jack I mean!) Well, of course, Thursday morning after you sailed I woke up with a grand attack of bronchitis and have been in bed ever since. So many people have written about the wedding, how lovely it was, what good food. Mary Harkness said she'd thought it the most delightful wedding she had ever seen, the peace and happiness of it all. I feel the bridegroom contributed to that, because your father and I both feel so happy to know you are safe with Jack. Your house is being painted grey with white trimmings. Any amount of love, your loving Mother." She also wrote to let them know that Jack's furniture had come and was safely stored in the Coach House at Burrwood.

"Your house" referred to a house that Walter Jennings had built at the south end of the Burrwood property, called "Southend," which he was lending to the young couple. Walter's mentality was that each of his family should have a country home on the estate. As his children were married each of them would assume ownership of one of the five-acre plots he had designated for them to build on.

Mogens Tvede, the Danish architect, had designed a four-bedroom cottage for Walter and Jean Jennings at Jekyll Island, off the Georgia coast; now that it was completed Jean was very pleased with it: "The house is simply delightful. The sun is always in the sitting room and everyone loves the place—or at least they say so!" Walter Jennings had joined the private Jekyll Island Club, whose original members included John Pierpont Morgan, Pierre Lorillard, William Kissan Vanderbilt, Henry Hyde, Joseph Pulitzer, Marshall Field and the like. The William Rockefellers joined early in its history. The Club had from the beginning a family character, with simplicity of style. Walter and Jean and others of the family regularly spent part of the winter at Jekyll Island. Aunt Annie Burr, the Walter Jameses and others of the family became members of the Club as well.

Ollie had occasional contact with the couple during their honeymoon, arranging rooms for them in favorite places, and Jeannette wrote affectionate letters: "Dearest Bam, Ma has been wretched since you left, but now is picking up. Your house is plastered [she refers to Southend]. . . . Aunt Annie wants us to come in costume Xmas night . . . please bring the children a chicken that walks across the floor and lays eggs. . . . I have returned most of the presents and you have fine credits."

It was a good trip, with Jack taking them "on a Browning pilgrimage in Italy." Jack wrote in notes to his Yale Class of 1915 for their fifteenth anniversary: "To Fano (November 23, 1927) where my wife and I saw Guercino's *Guardian Angel* and thereby became members of Billy Phelps' Fano Club." "Billy Phelps" was the affectionate way the Yalies referred to William Lyon Phelps, the distinguished professor of English at Yale for forty years until his death in 1943.

Later, Jack was telling someone about their honeymoon visit to Delft, in Holland, and the blue-and-white china factory, when Connie cut in: "Jack, we were in Delft on a Sunday, and everything was closed" and Jack grumbled, "Another story spoiled by a damned eye-witness!"

They began a collection of door knockers. And they bought a copy of the brand-new children's book, A.A. Milne's *Winnie the Pooh*. They read it aloud together, and gave each other loving nicknames from it: Jack called Connie "Pooh" because she was "always ready to eat a little something"; Connie called Jack "Tigger," because he "bounced." From then on, Jack signed many of his intimate letters to her "T."

They returned, in December, to another gracious provision. The Jennings planned to spend the winter at Jekyll Island, and they asked Connie and Jack to move into their city house on East 70th Street, with its staff of servants, and look after things for the winter. Jack resumed his legal practice, and they had the winter to get used to married life. This also gave them time to find an apartment they liked nearby, and to prepare it and to move in when Walter and Jean were ready to return to New York.

A few months after their wedding, Jack brought Connie to meet the Merchant side of the family, in Rochester.

At the end of January 1928 Jean Jennings wrote to her daughter, "I can't tell you with what joy your Father and I read of your child to come. . . . You will, of course, suffer discomfort and have to alter your life in many ways, but I can assure you it is worth it. My mother gave up much for me, and I did for you, and now you are passing it on. Be careful not to take too much exercise on the monthly dates. Your loving Mother."

Jack stayed on the job while Connie spent time with her parents and aunts at Jekyll Island. "Dearest," he wrote to her in March, "I hate being a bachelor! I had dinner with Colles. Yesterday I dined with the family and heard from Father that Dr. Hildreth [an obstetrician that Dr. Ely had recommended] liked you so much that he will arrange to be within call at all times—if you should decide you wish to have him. Dr. Hildreth, his nurse and the entire office force thought you the most delightful patient they had ever had. Saturday, I met Reggie, Morris and several other congenial playmates at the Union, and gave them all a lesson in poker. It's heavenly warm here—65 degrees—so I'm going to start walking down town. Do take care of yourself. Are you sure you are all right? Devotedly, Jack."

Brother Ollie had taken an extended cruise during the winter in the waters off Tahiti, with a party including a young woman of Venezuelan nationality, Isabella (Isa) de Rivas. Then in March he announced that he was joining her in Paris where her parents lived, and that they would be married in June. This caused a flurry of activity. The Jennings parents made hurried plans and sailed to attend the wedding, as did Jeannette, and Mogens Tvede also.

Ollie was a little concerned about how his sudden move had hit the family. "Dear Connie," he had written, "glad to get your letter. I wanted to hear how the news struck the family. I am glad that they seem pleased considering the circumstances, and I think everyone should get on all right together. I got a very nice letter from Jack yesterday for which please thank him as I don't know if I shall get time as among other things I am writing the 200 or so invitations. Much love, Ollie."

Walter Jennings wrote to Connie from the Princess Hotel in Paris: "Oliver has given Isa an Algerian rabbit hound; he has bitten a few people. I'm trying to persuade Oliver to leave him here as he probably prefers French blood which has a more alcoholic flavor. Aunt Florence happened to get on the track of Mrs. Ely [Jack's mother] and invited her. She looked well and very pretty. We like Isa but she certainly is most foreign and will create a sensation on Long Island. She is very handsome and dresses beautifully and her face is painted like a Gilbert Stuart. I hope she will leave some of it off when she gets home. If she doesn't I will get Mrs. Chandler to give her a few turns in the washing machine. Lots of love from us all. Affectionately, Father."[8]

On the 20th of September, 1928, Connie gave birth to their daughter Constance Day.

Miss Charlotte signed a typed note, "My dear Mrs. Ely: it gives me great pleasure to enter your daughter, Constance Day, for 1942 when she will be fourteen. . . . I am wondering how you heard of Foxcroft and if you know any girls who have gone here." And the girl who had typed this form letter added "Ha!! Ha!! Captain Jinks!! When are you coming down to see us and bring the baby? Cordially, Moorish."

Jack presented this poem to his wife, written four days later:

Since that joyous day in the fall of last year
When you winked in the aisle dispelling my fears,
I have known you as lover, companion and friend,
And so may it be, ever world without end.
I have known your dear smile, I have felt your dear heart,
Beating close to my heart, 'tis only apart
That I suffer, but then on returning to you
Earth fades from my sight, and heaven I view
And so my madonna, my dearest and best,
May your strength give me strength, may I pass every test,
As down through the years, you order my life
May I prove my self worthy to have such a wife.

. . . .

Notes

1. "Doc" Swift was noted in this way in Jack's personal history in the Yale Class of 1915 yearbooks. The author has found no trace of "Doc" Swift in researching at Yale, or Columbia, or Columbia Law School.

2. The gossip columnist cited by the author in this book is apparently always the same one, from the same publication. Maud Ely's scrapbook contains many clippings, all of which are in the same type, same style of paper and style of writing. However, Maud cut them out of the so-far unidentified periodical, leaving no date or attribution. The columns she clipped apparently run from the early 1900s to about 1928. Much time spent trying to identify the source—at the New York Public Library and through their research service, the New York Historical Society, the Southampton and the Huntington, Long Island, historical societies, has yielded nothing.

3. Apparently Maud led her son to do some of Miss Arden's legal work, for his biography in the *National Cyclopedia of American Biography* says, "For many years Ely represented the numerous interests of the cosmetics enterprise of Elizabeth Arden in this country and in France and England."

4. The account of the lunch is not clear, but it seems to have been held at the National Golf Club at Shinnecock.

5. There was a feeling in Jack's family that he had participated in this action. But there is no record in the annals of this unit in Albany that he was in it or in any other unit engaged on the Border in 1916. He is listed as a member from 1922 to 1925. This is also in conflict with a note someone made on a photo of Jack seated at a machine gun that the date was 1920. Wartime Squadron A had duties as a machine gun company.

6. Fred Williamson was also a director of the First National Bank and of the Federal Reserve Bank of New York. During World War II he was one of a handful of men called by the government to operate the nation's wartime railroad system.

7. The souvenirs of this flight from Paris to London in 1926 were preserved in Maud's scrapbook. "Oldest air service in the world," the brochure announced, offering deluxe accommodations—wicker arm chairs with cushions, Marconi Wireless Telephone, lavatory, newspapers and magazines. "Luncheon with spirits may be ordered."

8. Ollie and Isa were good friends to the end of their lives. However, she moved out of his house a few years after their marriage. She liked Ben, Ollie's true partner—all the family did—but some of the guests at "gay" parties Isa did not find congenial. A good Catholic, Isa never asked for a divorce.

5

Something Brand New

M R. AND MRS. ALBERT H. ELY JR. were living the life of the New
Yorker—he with his daily work at the law office, she with her traditional activities plus a half-hour a day, at tea time, with her small
daughter. They lived in a rented apartment at 125 East 72nd Street. And
they were planning their new home at Cold Spring Harbor on the land that
Walter Jennings had given them in the Burrwood estate.

Like other well-to-do mothers of that era, Connie had spent two weeks
in the hospital after delivery. At the end of the second week she returned
home with a hospital nurse, Miss Dunworth, whom she called "Dunnie."
When this registered nurse was no longer needed, she was replaced by
Miss Mabel Wilks, an English nanny. Miss Wilks took total care of the
baby around the clock, full time, with the assistance of a nursery maid. Miss
Wilks had one day off each week when Connie, with the help of the maid,
looked after her daughter.

Connie's confidence as a mother was undermined in the hospital by
her doctor, who told her that she couldn't nurse the baby because her milk
was giving the baby jaundice. Following this news, Miss Wilks dominated
the nursery and practically everything to do with the daily life of little Day.

Burrwood was in the midst of a flurry of activity, as the two young
married couples—Connie and Jack, Ollie and Isa—prepared to build on
the land that Mr. Jennings had given them. Connie and Jack had engaged

Mogens Tvede to design their home, which would be called "Elyston." It was along to the east of Burrwood at about the same elevation, through the woods. Ollie and Isa had been given a parcel between the two, and had elected to build at the foot of the bluff, almost on the shoreline. They would name their home "Dark Hollow."

In Jack's history, as reported to the Yale Class of 1915, he wrote, "Since 1923, although retaining a professional interest in hulls, cargoes, and their underwriters, my work has been less specialized . . . I have been in Cuba and Mexico and have spent several vacations in Bermuda. . . . Squadron A trooper [National Guard] in camp at Fort Ethan Allen and elsewhere, with Colles in the ranks [his Yale roommate and best man] and Tommy Tompkins as our Top Sergeant."

Jack also cited some of his activities in the city: "Secretary of the class since graduation . . . Member of the Committee on the Law of Aviation of the New York Bar Association . . . Maritime Law Association, the 15th Assembly District Republican Club, the Ex-Members Association of Squadron A, the University, Union, Yale and Lawyers clubs, the Down Town Association, and Holland Lodge No. 8 [Masonic order]." He was also a member of the Knickerbocker Greys Veterans Corps.

The Ely seniors lived at 299 Park Avenue and at Fort Hill. They took pleasure in their granddaughter, and in their in-laws. Mrs. Jennings wrote to Connie from Jekyll Island, "Dr. Ely's coffee is a rare treat and if he knew how welcome it was to a poor family living on an uninhabited island off the coast of Georgia he would not mind the trouble he took to send it. It really is delicious and I shall write him tomorrow."

Day was baptized on December 23, 1928, in her grandparents' drawing room at 9 East 70th Street by the rector of St. James's Church, the church the Jennings family attended when they were in town. The parson told Jack, "I shall always cherish the memory of the lovely little service we had and how beautiful your little girl was—the most beautiful baby, I think, I have ever seen."

"My Mother got Dad's agreement that first babies should be named after a member of the father's family and that girl babies should be given only one christened name to simplify things when they married," Day Ely Ravenscroft reports. "They settled on Day, the maiden name of Dad's grandmother. During the service Dad got to thinking that if he didn't have another daughter, this would be his only chance to name a daughter after his beloved wife. When the priest asked my Godmother, 'What do we name this child?' Dad called out 'Constance Day' and Mother was too shy to shout, 'No we don't!'"

Walter and Jean Jennings were gratified that in March both Jack and Connie were able to pay a visit to Jekyll Island. It was Jack's first time there. The Jennings had declined to have Day included, as the island community was not really geared for infants. The parents stayed about ten days, and in that time Nanny Wilks kept them informed about "The Babs," as they sometimes referred to little Day. She reported that Dr. Ely had telephoned to arrange a visit to see his granddaughter. On the ninth of the month Nanny sent a wire, "I CUT MY FIRST TOOTH TODAY AM FEELING FINE LOVE DAY."

One of Connie's most constant correspondents was Eugene Lentilhon, her Aunt Florence's husband. Born of French parents but raised and educated in America, he had a droll cosmopolitan sense of humor. Sometimes he sent gifts, including a shipment of partridges destined for Walter Jennings. He went to the races, commented on women's fashions, did not like the Germans. And he frequently commented on Aunt Florence's energy, and she on his: "He can only go out four nights a week," she said at one point. "I am having great fun making pumpkin pies," Uncle Eugene confided to Connie, "for my friends who have country places and send me pumpkins every week, but I refuse to divulge my recipe, as I know they would turn it over to their French chefs, who would probably add a smattering of garlic and mushrooms and so spoil the show. I tried my corned beef hash recipe on one outfit with the above result." He often closed the flaps of his envelopes with sealing wax and his signet ring.

Connie had kept in touch with Hermione, the daughter of Lord and Lady Lytton. Hermione wrote in March 1930 from London, "My darling Connie, my life at the moment is exciting and lovely beyond all belief . . . marrying Kim Cobbold—you met each other in India. We will be married at Knebworth and live out in Milan, where he will be General Manager of an insurance company. . . . Please don't ever forget how much I love you."

Despite supportive families, a wealth of friends, interesting activities and ample means, Connie and Jack were apparently finding marriage more difficult and less satisfying than they had hoped. In later years when someone asked them what they would be doing if their lives had not turned around at this time, Jack replied, "Oh, floating around on a yacht." And Connie is reported to have responded, quick as a flash, "Two yachts. Yours and mine." They were drifting apart in their basic interests; furthermore, Connie apparently missed the male-dominant family structure that she had grown up with, and felt that Jack did not assert his place as head of the family. Connie began to think seriously of divorce.

One day early in 1930 Connie was invited to a tea party by her close friend, Florence S. Sullivan, to meet a man "who was doing so much for young people." Miss Sullivan, who had never married, was an old family friend and godmother to baby Day, part of the circle of intimates of Connie's parents and the Arthur Curtiss Jameses, and shared many of their interests such as Christodora House. She was distressed that Connie had no real faith in her life and that in fact she was thinking of a divorce. When she found that she herself could not help Connie find a faith, she was not too proud to look for someone else to try. So she planned the tea party to see if this man she had met could give anything to Connie that would help her to have a more satisfying life.

Connie did not immediately respond to what she heard that day; she knew that Florence Sullivan had planned the tea party because she was concerned about her and her husband. "God," Connie said in telling the story, "was somebody on a throne with sapphires all around him, way off there somewhere. He meant nothing in my life." But the person she met fascinated her. The hostess introduced a man who was much like an ordinary businessman: balding, a rather long nose, spectacles, and a very pleasant expression on his face. Instead of launching in to tell the guests what he was doing, he introduced a woman from South Africa, Jessie Sheffield, who told the guests about some simple experiences that were transforming her life. She then introduced another woman, who spoke and then introduced another. So it went.

And "the businessman"? He simply sat at the side. Connie was watching him, while he was watching the guests and studying their reactions to what the speakers were saying. It struck Connie that this man was responsible for bringing these people, and yet was not controlling them in any sense. He was leaving his friends free to do what they felt they should do.

The man was Frank N.D. Buchman, and what Connie had heard was a simple exposition of what was resulting from his life and work—helping people to find a fresh experience of the Holy Spirit in their lives and building a network of such people across the world. But Connie was "not very religious," her husband was not very religious. They had their life to live, and Sunday mornings often were the best time of the week to play tennis. Connie left the tea party and went about her business.

A couple of weeks later Florence Sullivan asked her to lunch. She went. At the luncheon was one of the people who had spoken at the tea party. She told Connie that she was working with Frank Buchman and had been transformed from "a great big hulking shy person into a great big hulking outgoing person." Her name was Alys St.Onge.

Talk about shyness hit Connie right where it counted, for she was a shy person. Alys had spoken about listening to God, and said that God could give you what you needed. Connie began to try this.

She and Jack were to motor out to the country on the weekend. One of her pet peeves with Jack, one of the things that was driving them apart, was that when Jack drove the car he ground the gears. This was in the days before there was the automatic gearshift, and you had to shift gears by hand. Connie loved cars, and grinding the gears was one of the worst failings she could think of. Much of the time Connie simply got into the driver's seat so she would not have to put up with gear-grinding, although she hated to have her friends and family see "the wife" doing the driving. That morning, she tried listening to God. The thought came clearly to her: "Let Jack drive the car." Her reaction was, this is one of the things that creates tension between us; I love my car; I cannot stand to have the gears ground. The thought persisted, "Let Jack drive the car."

So Connie came down the stairs carrying baby Day and said, "Jack, you drive." He was surprised. He said "Are you sure?" She said, "I'll get the mail. You get the car." They drove out to Cold Spring Harbor. Afterwards, Connie realized that she had not noticed whether Jack ground the gears that day or not. She did not know whether his driving had improved, or whether she simply had not noticed. There was no tension between them. This seemed to her a miracle. They arrived at Burrwood, and went to look at Southend, which her father was lending them for a country place until the house they were planning could be built. They had a really happy weekend. Dr. Buchman liked to say, "When man listens, God speaks. When man obeys, God acts. When men change, nations change." As far as Connie was concerned, she had listened, God had spoken, she had obeyed, God had acted.

Soon after this, she went with Alys to a meeting where people like herself were sharing what these simple things meant in their lives. During the meeting when they all tried listening to God together, she had the thought to tell what had happened with her husband and his driving. She thought, I can't! I am too shy! Her next thought was, "Be not afraid. I will give you the words to say." She did, God did, and she spoke quite peacefully of what was happening when she tried listening and obeying.

After a few experiences like this, of God directing her and her obeying and a simple miracle happening, she said to Jack, "I want you to come with me to a weekend house party at Briarcliffe Manor to meet these people who have meant such a lot to me." Briarcliffe Manor was not far out from New York City, and Dr. Buchman's friends were holding houseparties there. Jack went to his father and asked him what he thought of this thing that Connie had gotten mixed up in. Dr. Ely, the obstetrician and gynecologist, told Jack that you had to be careful, that he knew many women who had gone off the deep end with religious enthusiasm. Nevertheless, Jack decided to go to Briarcliffe with Connie—and was captured by what he saw. He saw the big picture, the third part of Buchman's thought, "When man listens, God speaks. When man obeys, God acts. When men change, nations change." Jack made the connection. He had been experiencing what happened when his wife followed the God-given thoughts. Now he grasped the implication.

That implication needs to be seen in light of where the world was in 1930. It was a time of great dislocation, a time of much economic and social stress and unrest. The Great Depression in the United States followed the crash of the stock market in 1929, and its reverberations were felt throughout the world. The aftermath of World War I, still extremely serious in Europe, saw the coming of Fascism in Italy and the growth of Nazism in Germany. The rise of a dynamic nationalism was beginning in Japan, and the little brown man in India, Mahatma Gandhi, was shaking the foundations of the British Empire. And in the Soviet Union there was the growth of something very little understood in the world, the militant ideology that Karl Marx had articulated and that Lenin had used to take over the nation.

And for Jack and Connie, this was the beginning of an adventure that transformed everything in their lives. It led very quickly to a commitment for each of them; a realization that their own wills divided them from each other and that seeking God's will could bring them together in ways better than either of them could imagine; that in fact their marriage was worth saving. The commitment that each of them made, individually, was to seek God's will for the rest of their lives, and obey it. From that point, Jack lived for thirty-four years, and stuck with that commitment until his death in 1964; Connie lived to be ninety-one, and remained true to her faith until she died.

Some things began to change right away. They began to add new friends to their collection of many old ones, friends who encouraged them and with whom they could share what was happening to them. Alys St. Onge was now a friend to Connie and Jack. She was about to marry one of this group of people who had been influenced by Dr. Buchman, the Rev. J.

Herbert "Jack" Smith.

Jack Smith was assistant to the rector of Calvary Church, an Episcopal parish at Gramercy Park, on 23rd Street in Manhattan. The rector was the Rev. Samuel Moor Shoemaker. Shoemaker, a bit younger than Buchman, had experienced a powerful change in his life through contact with Buchman that had galvanized his ministry. This was the spirit prevailing at Calvary Church, where Connie and Jack began to attend services and meetings.

One of Connie's early experiences in obeying the guidance of God concerned money. She had the thought to give $2.50 to a lady working without salary at Calvary Church. The lady said, "Thanks so much. Now I can get my only other pair of shoes from the cobbler. I was 100 percent broke and it costs exactly $2.50." They each walked on. Suddenly Connie realized that the lady would again be without money after paying for the shoe repair, so she ran after her and gave her some more.

Sam Shoemaker's association with Frank Buchman was such that Calvary Church had become the focal point, the headquarters for what Buchman was doing in America. Buchman had a strategy. He felt that the world needed a great outpouring of the Holy Spirit. Each life that he touched was to him another element in this outpouring, and it was meant to affect the world. His work had almost no shape at all; it was growing in lives made fresh and filled with an infectious spirit. It did not really have a name, although when pressed to identify it, Buchman and his colleagues called it "A First-Century Christian Fellowship"—the Fellowship, for short. And lately, as Buchman and some of his close collaborators had been meeting and working with students at Oxford University in England, people were beginning to know it as the Oxford Group. It was also sometimes just called the Group, or the Groups.

March, 1930—a letter came to Connie at the Arthur Curtiss James address in Florida, from Florence Sullivan. "Connie dearest, what a balm your letter has been to my bruised spirit. I did so need the encouragement of your new 'risen' life to help me today." She recounted a number of accidents and deaths that had recently shaken her. "All this to prove how much I need your prayers. You are wise to let Jack find himself—no two people are led alike, taught alike or develop alike. Your sweetness, your joy, your faithfulness will help him to understand." In a subsequent letter Florence said, "Kiss my baby—whether you shall kiss Jack I leave to you!"

A letter from Connie to Buchman on the first of June of that same year describes Jack recovering from several weeks of what she believed to be rheumatic fever. In the letter Connie outlines their plan to take baby

Day and her nannie to England by steamer and to see Buchman at a houseparty at Oxford University. Apparently, in a very few short months of association, the Elys had become personal friends with Buchman. Connie continues, "Things are going along quite smoothly—we're watched and a few quiet digs are made and mouths opened et cetera but nothing openly unpleasant." And she finishes, "Ever with sincere friendship, Connie Ely."

In July of 1930 Jack and Connie sailed to England on the S.S. *Tuscania* with their two-year old daughter, Day, and her nanny, Miss Wilks. They landed at Plymouth and took rooms in a cottage, "St.Bruno," in the town of Failand, hosted by a Mr. and Mrs. Neil. The Ely entourage traveled with three trunks, seven suitcases, two prams, one folding cot, and assorted smaller items. Day and Miss Wilks spent two months at "St. Bruno" while Jack and Connie traveled extensively.

Jack and Connie rented a Buick and toured cathedrals, ruined abbeys, small towns, backwoods and byways, and delightful small hotels—in Bath, Wells, Tisbury, Salisbury, Stonehenge, the Cotswolds. In Devonshire they picked out two Exmoor ponies, Laura and Topsy, and had them shipped to Burrwood. There was mention of the ponies in the Long Island newspaper, "the first of their kind ever to be exported to this country from England."

They visited Guernsey, Jersey, St. Malo, the Côte d'Azur and Carcassonne. In Paris, they had tea with United States Ambassador and Mrs. Walter E. Edge, and met Mr. and Mrs. de Rivas, the parents of Ollie Jennings' wife, Isa. In London they breakfasted at Brown's Hotel with Buchman and Sam Shoemaker, and participated in a houseparty in Oxford attended by some 400 people.

While they were away, Florence Sullivan took time to chat with Walter and Jean Jennings about "the Buchmanites" as some called the Group. "I did my best," she wrote to Connie, "and I thought Father drank in more responsively than Mother. Of course I said that I had had a hand in your 'conversion,' and they said you certainly showed signs of new life. They said they were very glad to have had the talk."

It was on this trip that Jack and Connie began seriously to improve the quality of their photography. They produced an album of pictures of the trip, and after that Jack became an avid photographer.

In Jack's mind, and perhaps in Connie's too, this was a second honeymoon, celebrating the new life and the new marriage they were finding. They had a happy summer, and returned on the S.S. *Olympic* on the twenty-fourth of September.

Dr. Ely, at age sixty-one, was not well. Dr. George Marshall, who was married to Ely's sister Harriet, arranged for him to consult some of the fine specialists in the Philadelphia area. The diagnosis was throat cancer. Apparently Emdee, as Dr. Ely was often called by the family, was advised to see the specialists at the Mayo Clinic in Rochester, Minnesota.

Dr. Ely wrote that summer to Connie, at the St. Bruno address, the first of what became a series of very affectionate letters. In this one he mentioned that his wife, Maud— "Granny" —had found a new way to go from their apartment on Park Avenue to Fort Hill, by amphibian airplane, in forty minutes. "The young Granny . . . as usual has vamped the company so they almost pay her to fly. If the ship [on which they sailed to England] is a peach so are you. . . . The old grandpa seems to carry on with obstetrics and other professional diversions. Hug Day for me and always remember I love thee trio [*sic*] more than words can tell. Your affectionate Emdee." In August he wrote that he was planning to go to the Mayo Clinic. "Granny is in Maine visiting the Lewises [Elizabeth Arden and her husband Tom]. Shall be mighty glad to see the Jennings for I honestly miss them as I am very strongly attached to the whole bunch."

A few weeks later Dr. Ely cut back severely on his medical work, and announced to Jack and Connie that "having cleared my financial and professional decks I shall let them [the Mayo Clinic] go the limit to effect a radical cure both above and below. Dr. Bohren [a New York colleague] offered to go with me but I am so sure of Dr. [illegible] and trust him to stand by me that I really prefer to take what's coming to me alone. Of course if anything goes wrong Granny will come out immediately. Shall be in Rochester [Minnesota] at least three weeks 'enjoying' vacation. Yet I would prescribe the same treatment for any fellow in like condition, so why not take my own medicine. So here's to all being well when you return and happy summer. Affectionately Dad."

And he outlined his itinerary to Rochester via the Lewises' "wonderful place in Maine" where he would be with Granny, then via Montreal and the Canadian Pacific to St. Paul. In the same correspondence, Emdee mentioned that had the summer developed differently, he wished he and Granny could have gone over to the Dublin Horse Show and then "catch a glimpse of you" in England.

Later Emdee mentioned that "Granny left today to sail on Montgomery's yacht with the Bigelows and I shall join them at Pine Orchard to have a visit with the Heman Elys over Labor Day." John Ely, Jack's cousin and the son of Heman Ely III, recounted later that he understood there had been quite an extended romance between Maud and Monty, as

John called this same Montgomery. John told of having in his own home a cushion on which Maud had embroidered—for Monty—a sailing ship.

Life was exciting for Connie and Jack as they worked with people who were accepting the new element that had so changed their own lives. Many among their families and friends did not respond. Some ridiculed; some were wistful of what they saw, but didn't dare to step out and try it. This cost Jack and Connie a great deal. Their Yale friends by and large did not respond, nor did many of the Cold Spring Harbor and Southampton set. Others did respond, however, and many meetings of the Fellowship took place in Sayville, Setauket, Southampton and other Long Island towns.

As time went on, Jack's mother Maud began going to meetings with them, and was with them when they entertained their new friends; she ultimately took in a great deal of what Jack and Connie were living.

Connie paid a visit to Foxcroft in November, where she stayed in "her" house, "Spur & Spoon," and visited with Miss Charlotte. Jack wrote her a plaintive note from Manhattan, "Miss you. Played squash with Colles (beat him), backgammon at the Union with some of my old playmates. Emdee and I had breakfast together this morning. If you should change your plans and wish me to come down I'll take the first train. Yours, Tigger."

Miss Charlotte wrote to Connie later, "The old days when we sat by the fire dear Con are gone. You know I think of you and hope all goes well. Nobody has or will take your place and your years down here will surely shine in your crown."

Jack kept date books, little three by five inch pocket diaries that allowed about one and a quarter inches for each day. The earliest extant is for 1931. On the first day of January, 1931 (a Thursday, naturally a business holiday), Jack took his baby daughter, Day—The Babs—for a walk from their apartment on East 72nd Street in Manhattan. She was two and a half years old. He and Connie went to Gramercy Park to Calvary Church for a noon New Years Day communion service. In the afternoon they explored the English section of the Metropolitan Museum of Art, and the Altman Collection; then they dined with his father, Dr. Ely, at Park Lane.

There were two prongs to this new life, and both appealed to Jack greatly. The one prong was what had happened to him and to Connie: they had begun to change from selfish, self-centered people to people who wanted God to be in charge of their lives. A personal change, a personal reorienting of life's priorities that was dynamic.

The other prong was that God could use them in his plan to change the world. This was a colossal idea, giving a tremendous perspective to personal change.

As life unfolded, each of them was free to work this new thing out in their own way, not conforming to some theory or formula. Typical is a letter Connie wrote in June 1930 to one of her new friends, Elsa Purdy. Elsa's husband, Ray Foote Purdy, had given up a promising career in business to work with Buchman, and now had no livelihood other than that provided by the God they were serving. They called this "living by faith and prayer." Connie wrote to Elsa: "Come swim? A female jaunt. We collect a few congenial souls and some pagan friends and have ourselves a whirl in the briny deep." And she added, "I marvel continually at the way things are managed when we keep our hands off!" And she mentioned Florence Sullivan: "She has been so much to me this last little time. I mean the last few years that the germ of divine discontent was fermenting in me. She is a wonderful person and full of the most fascinating knowledge of the Bible and things Spiritual, a constant source of inspiration to me."

In this letter Connie also mentions an illness Jack has just had, calling it "a real, genuine attack of rheumatic fever." She attributes this to his doing several things that perhaps he should not have done. But modern medicine would also link this with his childhood illness at the Hill School, and further developments in his health toward the end of his life.

While consciously living a new life based on obedience to the guidance of God, Connie and Jack were also living fully the life into which they had been born. This was the Manhattan city life of an attorney and Yale alumnus, with their apartment on fashionable East 72nd Street, their club affiliations, concerts, plays, museums, many friends; and the gracious estate of Connie's father and mother, Burrwood, at Cold Spring Harbor on Long Island's North Shore. Also in their life was the senior Elys' home at Fort Hill on the South Shore.

Weekends were largely spent at Burrwood. Jack had a favorite horse, Peter; Connie liked to ride Laura, one of the Exmoor mares. There was tennis, sailing, swimming and the beach at the foot of the Burrwood property, occasionally golf, parties, friends. The family belonged to private clubs; Piping Rock, Sewanaka Cove Yacht Club, and Garden City Golf Club. Burrwood kept a permanent staff busy, even when Mr. and Mrs. Jennings were not in residence, and meals at that welcoming country house often included relatives and friends from near and far. Connie's sister Jeannette, and her husband, Henry Taylor, lived on the slope of the hill overlooking Snake Hill Road, which led down toward Cold Spring Harbor. They called their home "Cheridore," after their red-painted front door. Her brother

Ollie and his wife Isa (the Oliver Burr Jennings), were building their country home, Dark Hollow, near the land upon which Jack and Connie had begun building Elyston.

Walter Jennings and other landowners of Lloyd Harbor, the town of which Burrwood was a part, took note of the effects of the Depression on their town and the toll being taken by unemployment. They decided the best solution was local responsibility, and created a fund. In the winter of 1931-32, the Lloyd Harbor street commissioner was instructed to employ four men for four days each week, at a basic wage. The village clerk drew up a list of unemployed in the village, giving preference to heads of families. Men were employed in this way for road repair work and other public-service projects. There are sidewalks in the little town today that were laid by those men in the early '30s. Another lasting result of this project is a charming small brick library in a shore-side park with lawns, flowerbeds, and flowering bushes. Soon the W.P.A., Franklin Roosevelt's Works Progress Administration, took hold and gave employment such as this all across the country. Lloyd Harbor issued bonds in 1936 to continue taking care of "its own."

Jeannette and Henry Taylor lived a full life at Cheridore, and also maintained a house in town, on East 79th Street. They were raising four children. Henry was in the textile business, principally manufacturing cotton goods. In time he became a yachtsman of some standing in the New York Yacht Club. He had a 72-foot sloop built, the *Baruna*, and with it he entered and won several of the prestigious New York to Bermuda races.

Jack's work with Kobbe, Thatcher, Frederick & Hoare was a combination of corporate law, real estate, and personal estate matters, which included a good deal of work on wills. He also served on the board of directors of Christodora House, the charitable establishment in Manhattan that Jean Jennings, Florence Sullivan and others of that circle supported. Connie had been secretary of the organization for two years. Jack also did considerable work as secretary of the Class of 1915 at Yale.

Jack's new interest in photography increased as he watched his wife and her mother taking pictures. Being an intensely competitive person he went into it whole-hog. He bought good equipment and took a lot of pictures, both still shots and moving pictures. As he went along in his life with the Fellowship, he realized photography was important in their work, and he often took shots of what they were doing.

In the city, Jack frequently walked to or from his office. Sometimes he lunched with his mother or with a friend at the Yale Club, the University

Club, the Down Town Association, or Christodora House. With his friends of the Fellowship, sometimes he went down to Calvary House for lunch, or dinner, or a meeting. Or he met one of them in midtown for lunch—William "Bill" Wilkes, a partner in the investment house of Kidder, Peabody & Co., or realtor Hanford "Han" Twitchell. The Rev. Jack Smith, of Calvary Church, who had married Alys St. Onge, was a good friend, as were Sam Shoemaker and others of the group who met at Calvary.

Jack and Connie's families became friends. Connie's mother, Jean Brown Jennings, wrote to Jack's father: "My dear Dr. Ely: Thank you so much for your kind letter telling me the good news of your progress at Rochester. I can't tell you how happy we both are and how sincerely we rejoice with you and Mrs. Ely. You have been so cheerful with it all and shown such marvelous courage, that you deserve to get well and to have all the happiness in life . . . Your description of the wonderful place and . . . the intelligent and sympathetic minds who developed it . . . You were dear to remind me of our conversation about the Mayos and I am proud that I encouraged you . . . and glad to be associated in your mind with so sensible a decision and am quite 'preening' myself on my excellent advice!"

The conclusion of Dr. Ely's various consultations was that he needed an operation. He apparently elected to have a colleague in the New York area do the surgery, for Jack took his father to Columbia Presbyterian Medical Center for the preliminaries. Emdee was installed in the Harkness Pavilion, the fine facility of Columbia Presbyterian devoted to private patients. Jack and his mother were there when Emdee emerged from the anesthetic. During the days of recovery, Jack noted in his diary that he visited Emdee every day, and sometimes they had good "talks" together. Emdee could not speak and had to write his side of the conversation on a pad. From this point on, Emdee had to take his food through a tube in his side.

By the beginning of 1931 the house at Elyston was being finished. Weekends at Burrwood included inspecting the new building, conferring with decorators on materials, and laying out the landscaping. There was the driveway to plan; paddocks for their horses; plantings to select and stake out. Jack did a lot of cutting of brush and trees, for the site was still very wooded. This went on for months, almost any time he could spend on it, and he loved doing it himself.

Jack had told Connie about his heart condition, which apparently dated from the episode at Hill School when his track coach got him out of the infirmary to run in a meet. His doctors had said that he would be bedridden by the time he was forty. In their new home, the Elys built a ground-floor bedroom with a complete bath, and with a nurse's room next to it. (As it turned out, Jack had his first heart attack at age fifty-nine.) Connie used that bedroom for her den, and Jack used the nurse's room for his photo storage.

Two things were a constant in Jack's daily notes: observations on the weather, usually very appreciative, and on food. "Black bean soup—good!" He enjoyed food, and loved its wide variety. And Jack always noted who won at squash or tennis. He was the winner at least half the time!

With equal faithfulness he noted, in these days of a new and experimenting life, what the Sunday sermon was about and whether it was a good one. This went hand in hand with a new interest in the Bible. This winter of 1930-31 Jack and Connie were studying at Calvary in a confirmation class, once a week in the evening. The Jack Smiths came out to Burrwood to spend the night from time to time, and there would be long walks and long talks. Sometimes Jack Smith would get into a good conversation with Maud. Sam Shoemaker had recently married, and he and his bride, Helen, would come out on occasion also, as would other friends from Calvary, including Jack's realtor friend Han Twitchell and his brother H. Kenaston "Ken" Twitchell, and their wives. Ken was one of Buchman's close associates.

Connie had Miss Wilks to look after the intimate details of her baby's existence, so that—like hundreds of married women in the affluent world—she was free to come and go as she saw fit. But by and large she was at home and around New York City and Burrwood. Jack was freer, provided he made arrangements in his law practice, to move afield with the Oxford Group. Early in the spring of 1931 he took an overnight train to Boston, on a Saturday, and participated with others from Calvary in a church service in the suburb of Milton. He was back at home in New York by Sunday evening.

They planned a week of meetings in Louisville, Kentucky, for April. Jack was one of a dozen of the Group who traveled there. They were guests in homes of those interested in what God was doing, and they held a well-planned series of sessions. There were large public meetings and individual encounters where various ones of them talked with people who asked for personal interviews, about the realities in their own lives and how to begin. This was the heart of the matter. For Buchman had a favorite saying: You can't dispense eye medicine out of a second-story window; you need an eyedropper up close.

Jack sent a letter home to Connie from Louisville, noting "personal work with Bill Hoge, president of a lumber company, and I thought of the way you shut your eyes and ask for help. Thrillingly exciting it is . . . perfectly amazing to see this situation unfold. The first meeting we had perhaps a hundred people. Last night the great ballroom of this hotel was jammed to capacity, 500-600 hungry people who took in every word. Enthusiastic reception we have had from all the ministers, without regard to creed or color, and from the press. I'm going out on the war path now with George Smith to try to win Hugh Caperton, my Hill School friend. . . . With all my love, Tigger."

In the course of this week in Louisville Jack took on the task of setting up a large-scale meeting at Louisville University. He presided at the meeting at the end of the week, with 1,600 people in the audience.

In another letter home he wrote, "Darling, I am desperately lonely without you and want to come home but feel impelled to stay here by my guidance until Saturday. . . . Today for instance I have had two interviews which have resulted in decisions [people giving their lives to God], but I must stay until the decisions are registered. . . . Mr. Anderson got into a long theological discussion, and when he was out of breath he paused for me to say something. I closed my eyes as you taught me and thought to ask him if he was happy. It drew the cork and we shared deeply. I tell you, dear, it certainly makes one feel eternally grateful and very humble to be used and see changes come before your eyes. . . . From your bouncing but lonely Tigger."

At Burrwood, Bishop Julius Walter Atwood was a frequent guest of the senior Jennings. Bishop Atwood had retired as Bishop of Arizona, and now lived in the New York area. Jack took a long walk with him after a luncheon that spring, and they had a good talk about the Fellowship. Jack's interest in the Episcopal Church was growing all the time, he having been baptized into it at St. Thomas's on Fifth Avenue shortly after his birth. As these years developed he took an increasingly important part with the Church in his work with the Fellowship. Connie got a transfer from her family's city church, St. James's, to Calvary Church, as Jack was being confirmed there.

For Jack's thirty-seventh birthday, he got a telephone call from his almost-three-year-old daughter Day, saying "Happy Birthday Daddy—bring me some birthday cake, please."

On May 1, 1931, Connie and Jack celebrated their first night in their new home at Elyston. There was still a lot of work to get it into the condition they wanted it to be, and every weekend they hung pictures, sorted and shelved books, and made further choices of furnishings from the Jennings house at 9 East 70th Street, which was being closed. Elyston was to become a lovely country home.

The meetings at Calvary and other locations around the area must have evoked substantial interest, for a dinner meeting they organized for Tuesday, May 26, drew a thousand people to the Plaza Hotel. Jack changed into his evening clothes at the senior Elys' apartment on Park Avenue, and met with the speakers before dinner for prayer and a time of seeking inspiration. Jack presided, and felt the evening to be a whole-hearted success.

Han Twitchell wrote a note to Connie, who had stayed at Elyston because of her condition—she was in the ninth month of pregnancy with her second child: "Wish you might have heard Jack: dignity, poise, compactness yet completeness of what he said. A great boost to watch him carry his share of the load that has been heavy for you both. God bless you."

Jack's diary note for June 3, 1931 reads: "About 3 A.M. Florence commenced to make further sleep impossible & at 6 she came into the world—a beautiful 9 lb. baby. C. was a real soldier & was sustained mightily by her faith. What a glorious, happy end of our 2nd honeymoon." Florence was born in their new home. Dunnie, the registered nurse who had come home with Day when she was born in the hospital, spent the next few weeks with them looking after Florence and Connie.

After this there is a lift to Jack's diary notes. This summer was a full and happy one, what with the social season, tennis, the beach, sailing, and solid work to do at the office. The house at Elyston was shaping up and guests were being entertained; his work with the Fellowship was interwoven with it all and he found it very satisfying.

His father, Dr. Ely, had gone up to the Berkshire mountains in western Massachusetts to recuperate from his throat surgery, bringing with him Miss Katheryn Flynn as a nurse. He wired upon his arrival, "EVERYTHING POSSIBLE BEING DONE FOR ME BY THE MOST EFFICIENT NURSE TEN YEARS UNDER DOCTOR ST JOHN THEY ALL SAY FOOD WONDERFUL I HAVE TO TAKE THEIR WORD FOR IT LOVE EMDEE"

Practically all of the notes and telegrams from Emdee that survive are directed to Connie, not to Connie and Jack.

Jack's mother was dividing her time between her apartment on Park Avenue and visits to Southampton, Elyston and Burrwood. Jack drove up to see his father frequently, often with Connie and sometimes taking Maud, or "Granny," with him. They would take the ferry from Long Island, avoiding the drive through New York City. Granny Maud said in a note to Connie,

"According to Miss Sullivan, Florence Ely is the most remarkable baby in the world. I will telephone on Saturday to find out the best hour to visit you and your new treasure." And she added, "I am very happy about Dr. Ely—he certainly is stronger. Affectionately, M.L.E."

After his time in the Berkshires, evidently Emdee and Miss Flynn moved back to Fort Hill. Jack, Connie and Day visited him there, and Maud dropped them a note about their visit: "It was a joy to see you three looking so well and happy yesterday. And didn't you think my invalid had a new lease of life? We are going to keep Fort Hill open until late, as Emdee says he can get better food there."

In November Connie made one of her trips to Foxcroft. Jack hosted his parents at Elyston without her. Maud sent them, in thanks, some monogrammed linens, saying "Thank you from the bottom of my heart."

Jack wrote to Connie from his law office, "Dearest Pooh, I will go up to Fairfield for the game. A beautiful cake for Emdee at tea. Father was greatly touched, and Day came down, with Nannie, to help, and ate an 'normous piece. We dined at Burrwood and again Emdee was the center of attraction as he sat next to your mother. Your father made a graceful little speech congratulating Emdee on his becoming of age. The George Brewsters, Larry Noyes, Taylors, OBJs, Memey and Granny were all there. Granny and I had a long talk which was not as satisfactory as I had hoped and prayed it would be, although we did pray together. She persists in living in memory of the past and will not forgive Father for 'the way he has treated her.' The tragic part of it is that Emdee feels so sorry for Granny that it affects his condition.

"Now Granny says she thinks she will go to Paris and work over there with Mrs. Graham this winter as she is 'not needed here.' Yesterday she stayed in the country all day repacking the trunks from Southampton which I took out of the vault for her, and then insisted on taking the 7:11 train back to town so that she could be ready to motor down to Fort Hill with Mrs. Lewis in case the man who wishes to look at the house could make the trip.[1] I feel that the friendships Mother is making with our friends will result in her complete cure. She likes Irene [Dr. Irene Gates, one of the Fellowship] immensely and had a nice talk with her."

The Elys would occasionally take a favorite jaunt up to Newport and Hammersmith Farm to visit Aunt Emma and her husband Hugh D. Auchincloss. Or they would take the boat to Nantucket and sail with Ollie and Isa. Tea at the Yacht Club. Crabbing and scallops. Tennis. Golf. And calling on their friends who put in at Newport in their large yachts. They would stop on the way for tea at Watch Hill with "Aunt Lillie," one of Connie's godmothers.

The truth of the family situation was that Jack and Connie were paying most of the bills for Maud and Al, or Granny and Emdee as their children and grandchildren now called them. By 1931 Emdee had ceased to practice medicine. Whatever the value of his medical practice had been, the cost of their life-style—Fort Hill, 299 Park Avenue, trips to Europe, fine clothes, gracious dining, and now medical bills—meant that little was left. Jack, with Connie's support, took care of their bills, made arrangements to lease Fort Hill from time to time, and conducted negotiations to borrow money on the value of what property his parents owned.

For Day's third birthday party, in September 1931, Granny came all the way from Maine. Jack and Connie worked on the party together. Jack noted, "Heaps and heaps of fun. Day loved it." That night Fred drove them in to Penn Station to take the train with a group of the Fellowship, to the General Convention of the Episcopal Church in Denver, Colorado.

This was a major event for the Fellowship. The Presiding Bishop of the Church, Bishop James DeWolf Perry, was much impressed with the work they were doing and had urged them to be in Denver for the convention. He wanted his bishops to experience what was being done, for it was far beyond what was happening in most churches.[2]

The group planned carefully what they would do at Denver. The train trip to the West in those days was hot and dirty, with a change in Chicago. Canon B.H. Streeter of Oxford University, one of the English churchmen on whom Dr. Buchman's work had had a profound effect, was with them. James D. Newton, one of the most able and attractive of the younger businessmen who were active in the Oxford Group, came to Denver with his friend Russell ("Bud") Firestone. Bud was the second son of Harvey Firestone, America's number one automobile tire manufacturer at Akron, Ohio. Jim Newton was Mr. Firestone's personal assistant. Bud, with Jim's help, was in the process of emerging from a serious alcohol problem. Through some of those in the Group, a vital solution to alcoholism was being found, and within a year or two of this time, particularly with the help of the Rev. Sam Shoemaker, several of their friends were to found Alcoholics Anonymous.

Jack and the Group rallied around Bud and Jimmy; between sessions and meetings they managed automobile trips to see Lookout Mountain and other scenic points. Dr. Irene Gates, a physician with a profound belief in the power of prayer and the effectiveness of listening to God, was paying close attention to Bud Firestone's condition; the withdrawal process from a life saturated with alcohol was not easy. Irene was becoming a real and valued friend to Jack and Connie as well.

After the convention Bud Firestone and Jim Newton joined the party traveling by private railway car back to New York. During the train journey Bud and Sam Shoemaker got into a serious discussion and went into one of the compartments. An hour or two later they emerged, Jim Newton said later, "and I could see the difference in Bud's face. He had made a decision to turn his life over to Christ, and to let go the things that had been holding him." Jack and Connie invited Bud to spend the next few days at Elyston.

"I went back to Akron," Jim Newton continued, "and told Bud's father what had happened. Next day the Old Man and I got on a train and went to New York and out to Cold Spring Harbor. When we went up the hill to the house they were sitting on the lawn, Bud and some others. Mr. Firestone got about ten or twenty feet from Bud and just stopped, stock still. I could see the sense of awe on his face when he saw the change—not felt but saw—the change in his son. Quite miraculous. That convinced him—here his son was given back to him."

Bud stuck with his decision, and although he had a lapse or two along the way, he remained essentially a sober man for the rest of his life.

Jim Newton later recounted something that had impressed him about Jack Ely during that time at Elyston. Jack was keen to see the right atmosphere sustained so that the several guests would find something of the Holy Spirit. Jack said to Jim, "You carry your weight, don't you." Jack had been watching each person there, and had noticed that Jim did his best to help create the right atmosphere.

Connie's uncle, Eugene Lentilhon, expressed what was typical of many of his class in his reaction to what Connie and Jack were experiencing: "Religion is a funny thing. I have found that there are many hypocrites in and out of the church, but I always felt and was brought up to believe in the divinity, and many times it has been a great comfort to me. However as my Daddy often told me, there are two things, Eugene my boy, that you should never discuss with your friends. They are politics and religion. So I feel, Connie dear, that if you and Jack have found something beautiful in life, why should you not enjoy it to the full. Let the others go hang."

One of the characteristics of Connie and Jack's relationship that began to be an important force in their lives was the way their lives worked together. On a day in early 1931 there is this note in Jack's diary: "Felt spiritually low but C fixed that quickly." Connie did not waste words. Her daughter often speaks of the quiet way Connie would put her finger on the point, with a minimum of words. No lecture, no philosophy, just highlighting a simple point. "Is that what you really want to do?" "Could you be jealous?" Simple, effective, leaving the conclusion up to you.

Jack took time, when he felt it was appropriate, to let people around him know what he was finding in his life. He commented in his diary one day, when he had been working around Fort Hill, that he had shared with Eugene Edgel what was on his mind, and the inner battle to live what he had decided to live. He did the same on at least one occasion with Fred, a Jennings man-of-all-work around Burrwood and Elyston. Jack was normally reticent about personal matters, and it cost him a good bit to confide in people in this way. But he knew the value of trusting a person like Eugene or Fred, who was physically close to him, with the issues which he wrestled with and which might help the other man personally.

This was one of the elements in Frank Buchman's work which his associates were learning—the art of real friendship—how you could use the things in your own life that you had to overcome to help someone else. Someone described the Group as "a bunch of sinners who have quit bluffing." Some called it life-changing. Whatever you called it, it was at the heart of the vibrant Christian fellowship that was the Oxford Group.

Jack had gotten to know Philip Marshall Brown, a professor of international law and diplomacy at Princeton. Dr. Brown had served in the diplomatic corps early in the century. His career had included postings to Constantinople and Guatemala, and he was American minister to Honduras from 1908 to 1910. He had become a convinced Christian, and was a lively part of the work of the Oxford Group. In February 1932 he and Jack drove from Princeton toward the South, arriving at Gainesville, Florida, for a houseparty at the University of Florida. One of the people who attended some of their meetings was Charles Bennett, who later represented northern Florida in the U.S. Congress for forty years, and remains today a staunch supporter of their work.

Jack reported to Connie, "The houseparty was a huge success. All of the meetings were well attended and many decisions were made. . . . Your own humble little Tigger has talked a great deal but I fear has not been a real life changer. One boy who works in the local newspaper office I think I have helped. Another man I am conscious of having helped is Karl Puison, one of Mr. Firestone's secretaries, holding a position like Jim Newton, who was sent up here from Miami by Bud and Dot. On Sunday I conducted a men's Bible class of 200 at the Baptist Church and preached late at the

Episcopal Church from the chancel rail. Mostly personal witness, with an attempt to stir peoples' imaginations to the implications of this movement. My text— 'Whosoever commiteth sin is the servant of sin'—a subject on which I easily qualified as an expert.

"Today Phil Brown and I were asked to lunch with the Lions, a men's club, and later rode horseback through the pines and palmettos. An invitation has come from Mr. Firestone Sr. for Phil and me to visit them for a few days in Miami. I have been asked to 'address' the Asheville Bar Association! By the time I come home, Pooh dearest, I will be a very tired, love-hungry Tigger. There is a real joy being a 'lion'-hunting evangelist. Tomorrow Phil and I 'have a go' at the Rotarians—they are another kind of men's club. Love and Hugs for Day, Florence and Granny and extra bestest love to Mummie from T."

Afterwards they drove over to Florida's Gulf Coast. They visited Emdee, who wrote to Connie about their visit: "Enjoyed Professor Brown's and Jack's short visit immensely. Washed much soiled linen and ironed out of my thoughts many worries. Professor Brown was one of those, who from like personal experience, did much to straighten out my various antagonisms. He told me Jack was a grand man and doing wonderful work for the welfare of all types of human beings. Have made a new deal so I can now honestly subscribe to what you are doing. Love to Day and a hug for Florence, Affectionately, Emdee." Jack's report about this visit was that "Father was better physically but in a depressed way spiritually, feeling that I was wasting my life in the fellowship work."

Jack and Brown went fishing with Dr. Southworth, who had retired to Venice, Florida.[3] Their trip also included Miami, to take up the invitation to stay with the Harvey Firestones. They were able to have time with Bud. Jack said of the Firestone home, "This place is really lovely. Right on the water at the extreme end of Miami Beach far from the madding crowd and set apart in its palms and beautiful flowers. Regards from Dot, Bud, Ma and Pa Firestone, and most of all your Tigger."

Then, Jack notes, they flew in a Curtis Condor to Newark, with stops at Savannah, Charleston, Florence, Raleigh, Richmond, Washington, Baltimore and Camden. That was commercial flying in 1932!

In 1937 Philip Marshall Brown had a small book published, *The Venture of Belief*, which became a source of inspiration for Jack.[4] He studied and meditated on the book often in his life, quoting from it to reinforce his own conduct.

When he got back, Jack did something he had contemplated for almost a year: he registered at the General Theological Seminary in Manhattan, and embarked on a schedule that involved him one way or another six days a week for at least a couple of hours each day. His courses included a study of the Old Testament, the New Testament, Church History, Pastoral Theology and Dogmatic Theology, as well as two weekly lectures on selected subjects. Jack's diary for 1932 makes clear how serious a matter it was for him. He worked at it. He must have played a greatly diminished role in his law firm, for often he not only attended classes but spent hours before or afterward at the Yale Club or at the Seminary, studying. His evenings and weekends at home bore the same marks of concentration.

In the twenties and early thirties many of Dr. Buchman's circle pursued theological studies. Having made a commitment to give their lives to God, it was a natural next step to see what that had meant for people down the ages in the Christian faith, and to see what more it might mean for them. A few went on to be ordained in the denomination of their choice. Jack did not, because his bishop told him he would be more use if the world were his parish rather than just one church.

During this time Jack and Connie often saw the new rector at St. John's Church in Cold Spring Harbor, The Rev. Mr. Lyman Bleecker. Mr. Bleecker and his wife were frequently among the guests at Burrwood, and occasionally at Elyston. Jack often spent time walking and talking with him. Connie's parents were staunch members of St. John's.

Nurse Katheryn Flynn wrote to Connie fairly regularly of Dr. Ely's progress. There was a prolonged stint in Philadelphia, staying with Emdee's sister Harriet and her husband Dr. Marshall. A renowned surgeon named Chevalier Jackson did some work to improve Emdee's condition. Miss Flynn described it in detail. "It is uncomprehensible [*sic*] the torture he went thru—and this treatment lasted one hour. I must say he showed wonderful sportsmanship thru it all. The expense of it all as well as Mrs. Ely's attitude is giving him quite a little worry. Mrs. Marshall [Harriet Putnam Ely Marshall, Emdee's sister] is without doubt one of the loveliest women I have ever met. She has been a great comfort to Dr. Ely and is anxious to have him with her. I realize that you both are terribly busy, but it would be a great help if one of you could either drop him a line or telephone some evening, for he has been down in the depths all this week with good reasons—although I am not admitting that to him. It has been a great pleasure to see Dr. Ely through this awful ordeal, and I trust it will not be long now before you will all be repaid for your faith, patience and courage."

Then Mrs. Marshall wrote to Connie: "It would seem to me that there must have been some malicious tale bearing. From our careful observation we feel that Miss Flynn takes faithful care of her patient and helps his morale. Poor man, he needs an understanding friend. When he first came to Philadelphia, and later in the discouragement of the bronchitis, suicide seemed an escape. Why not? So little incentive to live unless he could again be useful. Why do you not write to Dr. Jackson about his opinion of Miss Flynn and her ability? Jack told me his mother would feel the same about anyone who came into such close relation and gave to her husband what she cannot give. Katheryn Flynn seems to me quite above any unwholesome or unrighteous affection but of course she is fond of my brother and in the long time of close companionship he has depended upon her and she is, sometimes, more familiar in manner than I like—still I have faith in her and believe that her influence is good and founded in deep religious convictions."

In June of 1932 a number of the Oxford Group people from around the country took up an invitation from Henry Ford to spend some days in and around Dearborn, Michigan. At the time of Thomas Edison's death in 1931, the Ford family and the Firestone family (with Jim Newton, Harvey Firestone's personal assistant) had attended the funeral in New Jersey and then had gone to the Firestone apartment in Manhattan at the Ritz Carleton Hotel.[5] There Bud Firestone had told them all the story of what had happened to him. The Ford and Firestone families had often shared family gatherings, and Ford had known the Firestone boys over the years. Henry Ford had been much impressed by Bud's story. There were some key members of his industrial empire who had problems with alcohol.

The group that assembled in Dearborn included Connie and Jack Ely and Bud and Dorothy Firestone. There were meetings in nearby Bloomfield Hills, and at the lovely Dearborn Inn which Mr. Ford had created as a guest and meeting facility. One of those who joined in sharing their experience with Ford's people was Bill Pickle, a former bootlegger whose life had been changed through Frank Buchman's work at Pennsylvania State College. Bill had become a charming and powerful force for good on the campus. His story played a key part in the ten days in Dearborn and in what Henry Ford wanted his people to hear.[6]

On the train returning home from Dearborn, Connie and Jack had the company of Bill Pickle as far as State College, and Pickle and Jack had a good conversation during the journey.

Just before New Year's Day, 1933, Mr. and Mrs. Jennings went as usual to Jekyll Island by private railway car. The Jekyll Island Club had had a policy forbidding automobiles on their private roads, but that winter Club members were allowed to drive their cars on the private roads for the first time. Walter was driving on the island by himself, when another member ran a stop sign and hit him. Walter sustained a severe blow to the chest, followed by a heart attack. They called a close friend of the family in Baltimore, Dr. Fyror, who came immediately to the island to attend to him. Walter died in his sleep on January 9. Jean Jennings was very careful to help the other driver feel that it was not his fault, that her husband's heart attack was inevitable.

Connie and her sister and Henry Taylor took the night train to Richmond to meet Mrs. Jennings, who came north accompanying her husband's casket. Jack spent the day at St. John's Church and at Burrwood taking messages and making preparations. He and Lyman Bleecker met the train in Manhattan.

Jack sat next to his mother-in-law at luncheon upon her arrival. They had what he describes as a victorious service at the church, with favorite hymns like "Ten thousand times ten thousand in sparkling raiment bright."

The next day they visited the grave together, Jean Jennings, Connie, Jeannette and Jack, admiring the flowers, and then lunched with the children. The children were a great comfort for them all, Jack noted in his diary. They spent much time walking and talking and visiting. On Ascension Day the little church dedicated a memorial tablet to Walter Jennings.

Emdee wrote to Connie, "Dearest Connie, what a wonderful letter you wrote me, such a graphic description of the services held for your dear father—a Christian Gentleman who was to me one of the most human and understanding men I have ever known. His sudden calling was a great shock to me. Faithfully, Emdee."

Oliver and Isa Jennings had been in Europe, and now they hastened back on the S.S. *Paris*. Jack and Connie met them. With the family all together, Mr. Jennings' will was read, his legal affairs being handled by Henry Stimson's law firm. Among Walter Jennings' bequests was his Gilbert Stuart portrait of George Washington, which he left to the National Gallery in Washington, and his famous painting of the U.S.S. *Constitution* battling the British warship *Guerriere*, which he gave to the U.S. Naval Academy at Annapolis.

Jack pursued the theological studies he had begun at General Theological Seminary in New York for a full year. In April 1933 he attended the graduation exercises; the record shows that he did not attain a degree, but was given a certificate of completion of the courses he had studied. The exams were fair, Jack noted, and Connie had helped him prepare for them. His final marks were A in Church History and Pastoral Theology, C in Old Testament, B in New Testament and a C in Dogmatics. It had been an intensive year of study, and he was both sorry and glad when it was over.

There followed another trip for Jack to England, on the S.S. *Europa*. The houseparties at Oxford were growing in popularity, with over 2,500 registered in advance for this one. Jack saw a good bit of Frank Buchman, and took a full part in the meetings. He jotted on a postcard to his mother, "In a few short weeks I have met more world leaders than most people meet in a lifetime." He enjoyed liberal doses of tennis, with such partners as Loudon Hamilton, the first man Buchman had brought to a new experience at Oxford, and Eric Bentley, a debonair Canadian. He noted that in tennis he was about even with Bentley.

The work at Oxford spilled over across the British Isles, with teams going to Chester, Carlisle, Sheffield, Derbyshire, and south to Bath and Bristol. From Sheffield Jack wrote, "Last Sunday I preached from three pulpits." Jack and others sailed home on the S.S. *Bremen*, where there was excitement when a seaplane was catapulted from the ship to hasten mail to the shore.

Among the friends whom the Elys got to know in these days were Takasumi Mitsui and his wife Hideko. Sumi, as his friends called him, was a member of the great Mitsui banking and industrial family of Japan and founder of Keimei School. He had gotten to know the Group while spending a year studying at Oxford. At one time, en route from his home in Japan to be with Buchman and his colleagues, Sumi spent a night unexpectedly at Elyston. Jack lent him a pair of pajamas. Sumi said afterward that in Jack's pajamas he would take three steps before the pajamas started to move. Jack and Connie became fast friends with the Mitsui couple.

Back home again, there was time for activities with the children. Jack took both Day and Florence to their first experience of a movie, *The Three Little Pigs*. They did some reading together, and walked in the woods and fields—a trip with Florence to see newborn lambs, games of great imagination with Day. Occasionally Jack had lunch with Day, just the two of them, and he was always impressed with the way her mind worked.

Day recalls that one dark, rainy day at Elyston her mother introduced her to knitting. They went to the basement and there made giant, easy-to-use knitting needles out of kindling. Connie sanded the pieces smooth, cut points on one end and covered the blunt ends with red sealing wax. "Voila, knitting needles for a clumsy child whose motor coordination was nonexistent," Day says. "With some rope-like bright wool she taught me to knit. We could both then knit regular stitches in the dark without looking at our work."

. . . .

NOTES

1. In this letter Jack uses two of Elizabeth Arden's name names. She was born Florence Nightingale Graham in Canada in 1878. In about 1910 she went into business as "Elizabeth Arden." She married her banker, Tom Lewis, who had a hand in managing her business. They later divorced. She used the names Graham and Lewis at various times, including in her career as an owner of race horses.

2. The author's father, the Reverend Charles Jarvis Harriman, a priest of the Episcopal Church, had met Buchman and his associates at about this time. Mr. Harriman felt he was seeing and experiencing what God meant the church to be. What he found greatly influenced his ministry.

3. Dr. Thomas Southworth died in 1940. His son, Dr. Hamilton Southworth, also a Yale graduate, treated Jack in 1952 in New York, when Jack needed medical attention. Dr. Thomas Southworth's grandson, Hamilton Southworth Jr., sent the author a photograph of his grandfather—Jack Ely's godfather—which appears in this volume.

4. Philip Marshall Brown, *The Venture of Belief* (New York: Fleming H. Revell Co., 1937).

5. For the full story of Newton's friendship with Edison, Ford, and Firestone, see James Newton, *Uncommon Friends* (New York: Harcourt Brace Jovanovich, 1987).

6. The story of Bill Pickle is one of the key episodes in Frank Buchman's life and work. See Garth Lean's book *On the Tail of a Comet* and *Pickle Hill*, a video produced by Moral Re-Armament.

6

A Growing Family

A S THE OXFORD GROUP PEOPLE MOVED back and forth across the Atlantic, the Elys were getting to know a host of international people committed to this work. This fascinated Jack Ely in particular. As was shown in the journal Jack wrote about South America during his years at Yale, concern for the world was a compelling interest for him. To fulfill whatever role God had for him in the gathering storm of world affairs would be his top priority.

The tempo of life for those involved with the Oxford Group began to pick up in the mid-1930s. The pace of world affairs was accelerating, with the German occupation of the Rhineland, the Italian invasion of Ethiopia, the Japanese assault on Manchuria. These were moves by totalitarian regimes to assert themselves in what was effectively a vacuum of international law, and at the same time there were tremendous upheavals in that mostly unknown world of the Soviet Union.

In Buchman's mind, he and his team were engaged in "a race with time to remake men and nations." That conviction was more and more at the heart of the life of Jack and Connie Ely, who were often in the midst of what Buchman was doing.[1] The houseparties at Oxford became truly large, attracting thousands. There were similar gatherings in Denmark, Sweden, Norway; Holland, and Switzerland. Ten thousand people gathered in some of these events; 25,000 in the British Industries Fair building in Birmingham for one meeting in 1936.

After the death of Connie's father, Walter Jennings, Jack and Connie moved further and further into working fully with the Group. They were also using Connie's now considerable fortune, as they felt God was leading them, to help advance this work which they saw as the work of the Holy Spirit. They crossed the ocean many times to participate at gatherings in Britain and Europe. By 1935 Jack was doing very little legal work, as world-remaking became an ever more urgent priority.

Jack and Connie were each quite clear that God had saved and rebuilt their marriage; and they had come to believe, individually and as a couple, that God was rebuilding society through his actions in peoples' lives. The Elys and others of the Oxford Group team in the New York area developed a conviction that they should cover the Long Island communities. Jack's diary notes meetings in many towns on the Island—at Southampton including Fort Hill, at Oyster Bay, Islip, Sayville, at the Ely home in Cold Spring Harbor, Smithtown. This strategy was thorough, well-planned, and constant. This involved development of new leadership in all these towns. The team also did a round of meetings in Syracuse, Rochester, Akron, Columbus and Cincinnati.

Connie often joined Jack in these excursions. The change in Connie's life style did not go unnoticed by her family. Her mother, Mrs. Jennings, wrote Connie:

> Thank you for your lovely letter. Please do not reproach yourself for anything. I have never complained of your not being a good daughter nor do I think that you have been delinquent. I often regret that you have given up your old friends, on account of your future life and on account of your children's future, but as far as your affection for me goes, I have never doubted it. You have arrived at a time of life when you must make your own decisions, and I have arrived at a time of life when my decisions are made. My life is nearly over, so it is the difference between living in the present and living as an onlooker with only the great hope for the future. I feel you have found happiness and comfort in a way that does not touch me, but that it is a good way, I am sure, and I wish you joy and success in your achievement, so do not, my dear child, feel that anything can come between us. Day and Florence came over this p.m., & they look & seem very well. . . . Any amount of love to you both, your loving Mother.

It was during this time, in Ohio, that Bill Wilson and Dr. Bob began to form Alcoholics Anonymous (AA), based largely on what they had learned through Sam Shoemaker and others who were involved in the work of the Oxford Group. Henrietta Seiberling of the Akron rubber family was often the hostess for the embryonic AA, and Jack stayed in her home several times. "An enormous Teutonic-Tudor pile of stone," Jack called it, but added, "the grounds are lovely."[2]

While working with individuals and giving them the best he had to offer, Jack was always feeling for the broader outreach and the larger implications. He kept up his father's relationship with the Roosevelt family, who had moved into the White House in March of 1933. He also developed a contact with the Honorable Marvin H. McIntyre, President Roosevelt's appointments secretary, who handled many confidential matters for the President.

In Washington, the distinguished German-American poet Hermann Hagedorn, a close friend and biographer of President Theodore Roosevelt, had been profoundly affected by the Oxford Group. Hagedorn was in contact with Franklin Roosevelt's Secretary of Agriculture, Henry A. Wallace. Jack journeyed to Washington in the spring of 1934, stayed with the Hagedorns, and he and Hermann visited Wallace in his office. They called also on McIntyre at the White House.

Later in the spring, Jack took the train to Washington again. This time it was in conjunction with a series of meetings that Buchman and the others were conducting, in particular a large public meeting at the Shoreham Hotel. Buchman had brought several people over from Britain who could speak with authority about the changes taking place as a result of the work of the Oxford Group, men such as George Light, a leader of the unemployed from Warwickshire.

In connection with this meeting Jack and Hagedorn called at the White House, then visited with Frances Perkins, now Roosevelt's Secretary of Labor and the first woman in U.S. history to hold a cabinet position. (A dozen years before, Jack had presented a case of labor law before Perkins when she was a referee for the state of New York.) They also met with Daniel Roper, Secretary of Commerce.

This time they also called on men at the *Washington Star* and the *Post*. Their chief contact at the *Post* was publisher Eugene Meyer, a man of wide experience in finance and government. And they saw the Washington correspondents for the *New York Times* and the *New York Herald*. They also talked to Jack's Yale classmate Dean Acheson, who was then Under Secretary of the Treasury.

Meanwhile Jack had increasing family responsibilities as his father, Emdee, went through many ups and downs in his battle with cancer. Miss Flynn was Emdee's constant support. Early in 1933 he was moved into a cottage on the Burrwood estate, where he could be set up and cared for thoroughly. Jack and Frank, one of the Burrwood workers, strung telephone wire from the Elyston house to the cottage so they could keep better in touch and respond to needs and emergencies. Sometimes Maud was there, sometimes only Miss Flynn. Miss Flynn regularly sent to Jack and Connie accounts of moneys spent, or of anticipated needs like train tickets.

The family was able to take Emdee to the Pocono Mountains of Pennsylvania occasionally for a change. Day remembers her grandfather clearly. Even though he spent most of his days in a bathrobe and pajamas, could not speak and could never eat at the table, she remembers that there was a sense of dignity about him.

After one occasion when Connie and Jack had visited Emdee and Maud, Maud wrote to Connie: "Yesterday when you kissed my hand I was quite touched by it. Was it because I was Jack's Mother? Or because I was Day's Grandmother? or simply because you are discouraged; do not I beg of you tell me it is because the case is hopeless. My love to you and Jack and the two adorables. Devotedly, Granny. P.S. I do not object to signing it as long as I can keep from looking the part."

In the midst of his busy schedule with Buchman's team, Jack twice took the train to visit his father in Macon, Georgia. Emdee and Miss Flynn were staying there for some weeks, at the home of a Mrs. Walker. Jack spent hours with his father. It was clear on the first visit that his father's health was deteriorating. A few days later Jack went again to Macon, this time to bring Emdee back by train to the Huntington Hospital, the closest hospital to Cold Spring Harbor. Emdee was settled into a comfortable room on April 12. Jack kept track of his father, seeing him most days.

On April 25, 1934, Jack and his mother went to call on Emdee, finding him very weak and in considerable discomfort. Jack was called that night to the hospital again, and at 1:40 a.m. his father "was released from pain."

Jack had taken his father along with him to several Group meetings, introduced him to his new friends, and included his father at dinners with many of these interesting people in his own home and at Burrwood. By the time Jack and Connie had really gotten into the work, Emdee had his throat cancer to wrestle with. Jack had found something new, a pearl of great price, and all he could do was to place it before his father for his father to make of it what he would.

Emdee had written to Connie from Sarasota the previous winter, while she was in the Harkness Pavilion with her appendectomy: "Dr. J. H. Jarrett's daily reading in *Yet Another Day* could but register with me this morning.

'My father teach me how to be grateful. May I see thy mercies everywhere.'"

Jack's diary speaks of a victorious service for Emdee at St. John's Church in Cold Spring Harbor. The Rev. Mr. Lyman Bleecker conducted the service, with the Rev. Mr. Samuel Shoemaker assisting. Sam had met Emdee on various occasions. Mrs. Jennings had some of them to lunch afterwards: Aunt Harriet Putnam Marshall from Philadelphia (Emdee's sister); his nephew Heman Ely and Heman's son John; Fred and Hilda Williamson, and representatives of the Elyria family, along with Emdee's widow and Connie and Jack. They drove into town and took the train for Rochester, where Maud's family met them that evening. A memorial service was held at St. Paul's Church, and Maud's sister, Elinor, and her husband, Frank French, had them all to lunch, along with the Frenchs' children and their spouses. The following day Emdee was laid to rest in the Merchant family plot at Mt. Hope Cemetery, near two of his sons, the little boy Gerald and twenty-two-year-old Francis.

Connie and Jack received a telegram of condolence from Allentown, Pennsylvania, the hometown of Frank Buchman:

> Now the laborer's task is o'er,
> Now the battle day is past,
> Now upon the farther shore
> Lands the voyager at last.
> Father in thy gracious keeping
> Leave we now thy servant sleeping.
> May your witness to Jesus and the resurrection glorify God
> who giveth us the victory through our Lord Jesus Christ.

The telegram was signed by Frank Buchman and a host of people whom Connie and Jack knew well.[3] Buchman followed this with a letter saying, "I have just been at my parents' grave, and I shall never forget the sense of radiant happiness that came when I knew my loved ones were safe."

Emdee's career had been a fruitful one. He had reported to his class at Yale that he had delivered 1,637 babies. His work on behalf of the Southampton Hospital had paid off well for that community, as had his work in the Village Improvement Association. His obituary also cited his practice in New York City from 1891 to his retirement in 1931; Fellow of the New York Academy of Medicine; membership on the medical board of the Doctor's Hospital, in the American Medical Association and that of New York State, County and City; and membership in St. Bartholomew's Church in the City and St. Andrew's Dune Church at Southampton.

Maud and Jack were overwhelmed with messages about Emdee over the next weeks:

"He was our truest and best friend; he helped us over many a stile and was always so kind and full of wisdom and understanding."

"He was for so many years, since 1889 I think, the friend and counselor of us all—my grandmother, my father, and ourselves, and so constantly sympathetic and devoted that we looked on him as a member of the family."

"We have lost a lifelong and invaluable friend."

"You know how very fond I was of him, how grateful I have been practically all my life for his sympathetic and skillful care."

"Your father was a most gallant fighter and the courage he showed in his great affliction won all our hearts."

A doctor who knew Emdee in Macon wrote, "He was doubly a hero because he knew he was fighting a fight that he had to lose and one that would give him relief when it was over, and yet he did not end it himself."

Emdee's Yale classmate Frank R. Shipman sent Maud a copy of a dignified memorial booklet the class had printed and sent to all the members:

> He had fought a good fight, he kept his faith. Those of us who remember only the somewhat languid Ely of college days may have wondered at his endurance in the grim battle. During that youthful time he did not let himself be known. His after life proved that whether in health or in illness the real Ely lived with extraordinary energy and fullness. As Cutler suggests on the next page, he was an arduous toiler in his profession, physically and emotionally. Towards the end, though bowed in his bed, speechless, panting, he would snatch the pencil and write on his pads the words that he was so eager to speak. To see him so was to win a new admiration for humanity. F.R.S.

The booklet included this from C.W.C.:

> Al was a dear friend in a group of Yale classmates who had lived and worked together for forty years. . . . His whole work, which was of extreme delicacy and entailed skill of a high order as well as the tact and personality which he had to a large degree, made him of the greatest value to many people who could not be reached by those of us who worked in hospitals and offices. In other words, there are a great many who require not only the skill of a surgeon, but the human interest and sympathy of a friend. What I want especially to mention, however, is the personal friendship which we valued who knew him best, and his fortitude during his long illness. His wife was with him and was a constant support and source of courage to him.

The Ohio Society of New York sent a message of condolence for Emdee, "whose name we were proud to add to our membership in 1921." The New York Obstetrical Society did also.

Jack wrote from Elyston to the rector of St. Paul's Church in Rochester thanking him "for the beautiful service at Father's grave. You gave us renewed assurance of the victory which he has won. The enclosed check goes to you with our love."

Shortly after the service, Jack made a train trip out to Portland, Oregon, to join some of his Oxford Group colleagues. En route he wrote Connie about making friends with "a Hollander, on his way out to California to find a good American brandy to mix with the Dutch. He shared with me that he dislikes this business, knowing the misery it causes. His daughter is interested in the Oxford Group. . . . Kiss the children for me—big bear hugs—ever your T."

From the Arlington Club, Portland, Jack wrote of a "disastrous longshore strike here. The Secretary of the Chamber of Commerce who will welcome us in a meeting tonight is the acting mediator. Until he was challenged yesterday [by Jack and his friends] he had made no attempt to personalize, to know, the leaders of labor or management. . . . My how I wish you were here. Don't let anything interfere with you and Mother coming to Banff."

The days in Portland, and then Seattle, were busy ones for Jack, with large meetings in both cities and a strong team of Buchman's best-trained people. Then on to beautiful Banff, for several days of a houseparty, which included golf and tennis. Jack noted in his diary that Alan Limburg, a fellow New Yorker with whom the family was to have a strong relationship, gave his life to God with Jack and a teammate.

Connie and Maud joined Jack in Banff. After a few more days in this glorious setting they took the Canadian Pacific to Calgary and on to Winnipeg for a meeting of 5,000 people. Jack noted the next day in his diary that the train was skirting Lake Superior all morning, and that their special CPR train had five sleeping cars and an observation car, seventeen cars in all with 311 people. They held more meetings in Toronto, then on to New York.

On almost all of his trips, Jack had gotten into the habit of carrying a small portable typewriter with him on which to make notes and write letters and reports. He typed out poems expressing things that touched him as humorous or moving. Jack also made notes on jokes that he could use—he had a wry and impish sense of humor when he was relaxed. Typical was this joke he recorded in mid-1933: "Seven-year-old in a thunderstorm: 'Poor God.' 'Why is that?' 'Because he's nearer than anyone else.'"

In the summer of 1934, Jack and Connie were once more at the Oxford Group house party in Oxford. This time, their friends Eugene, Janet and baby Schuyler Bedford were back at Elyston looking after Day and Florence, with a French mademoiselle acting as governess. Nanny Wilks had moved on to other employment by this time. Mrs. Jennings, who kept an eye on things when Connie and Jack were away, wrote to them most approvingly of "Mademoiselle" and said that the children were happy with her. When Connie and Jack returned, however, they found their lively little daughter Florence sitting cowed and fearful on a chair with her feet tucked up under her. She had been told there were demons lurking under the furniture who would drag her down into their underworld if they could grab her feet. They dismissed "Mademoiselle," and in cleaning out her room found stacks of empty whiskey bottles hidden away.

After that, Jack and Connie began to study seriously how to find the right people for the care of their children. Connie and her sister and brother had grown up with a staff to look after them, and both Jeannette and Mrs. Jennings expressed strong feelings that professionally trained women should be looking after the Ely children. Connie made a try or two with what might be called traditional governess types, one of whom would dress up the little girls and take them in a chauffeur-driven car around the Burrwood estate where they were supposed to wave to the workers.

Several of the Oxford Group people were focusing their attention on the upbringing of children. Among them was Nell Cochrane, who spent some time with Day and Florence when Connie had her appendix out. Nell introduced Connie and Jack to a young woman named Gladys E. Van Cize, of Scarsdale, New York. Gladys was interested in the Oxford Group, and came to care for Day and Florence. When Connie and Jack were away, Gladys would write often to let them know how the children were faring. The winter 1933-34 was spent largely at Elyston, and Gladys told of "Gar" —the children's nickname for Connie's mother—bursting in on them to tell them to look out the window at a pack of foxhounds and a mounted hunting party streaming by.

Gladys Van Cize did not remain with the children for very long. Mrs. Jennings mentioned in a note from Jekyll Island that "Jack writes you have to get a new governess as Miss Van Size [*sic*] is worn out. A good deal of responsibility for her. She is not the type for a nurse, too highly strung I thought."

Connie consulted with Nell Cochrane about what they should do next. Nell wrote her:

> In larger homes where the nursery is the hub of the child's universe and
> where the nurse, not the parents, is with the child when most of the prob-

lems arise, and when most of the opportunities arise for talking about God and for turning naturally to Jesus in times of decision—then I do feel strongly that that nurse should be a converted person and that you should be willing to move heaven and earth to find one and willing to go through several painful experiences such as Gladys to get one.

I don't blame you for feeling that you'd rather have peace and efficiency with an unconverted one Connie, but I do feel that you are taking the easiest course and that you shouldn't rest until you've found God's choice for your youngsters. I really am concerned. You know how much I love the youngsters (and Poppa and Mommer) and I know that it's through the natural events of the day that a vital relationship with Christ is slowly built with the children. I've been praying for you Connie and this letter is the result.

Connie next hired Lucille Kendrick, a trained children's specialist from Macon, Georgia. Kendie, or Ken as she was known, may or may not have been a "converted" person, but she was highly able and the children found her to be a fascinating storyteller. She took charge of the Ely children's upbringing, beginning in the fall of 1934.

Early in January 1935, Connie showed signs of extreme fatigue. Dr. Irene Gates came out to Elyston by a late train on Sunday night and took charge of the situation. A few weeks later it was found that Connie was pregnant, and due to have her baby in October. Dr. Gates took special care to be sure the pregnancy would go well.

In February, Jack and Connie took their family to Jekyll Island for three weeks. They played tennis and golf, did some reading, visited Savannah, drove around the islands, and visited with some of the Club members. Mrs. Jennings and Aunt Florence joined them; Aunt Annie Burr Jennings was already in residence. Jack read aloud to Connie and Kendie. Picnics, the beach, backgammon. Jack took the children to see a raccoon caught by one of the maintenance men, and they took pictures of young alligators. The Episcopal bishop of Savannah came and dedicated a plaque at the little chapel in honor of Walter Jennings. Day was chosen to unveil the plaque, and Florence wore her little sailor suit.

The Elys left Jekyll and spent ten days in Macon, renewing friendships and continuing the work among people that the Group had met several years before. Kendie, whose health was never robust, became ill, and was operated on. Connie and Jack visited her in the hospital several times before they left for Long Island. Kendie rejoined the family some weeks later.

The Elys bought a new 1935 Ford touring sedan: they had moved from an assorted taste in automobiles to having three Fords in the household. One of the innovations was that these vehicles could have radios! The cars all had names— "Alexander Beetle," "Josephine" and "Jennie."

At the beginning of 1935, Jack laid out a schedule for his days at home— 7:00 a.m., rising time. Breakfast at 8:00. From 9:00 a.m. to 10:00 a.m. work at his desk. From 10:00 to 10:30, planning time. Exercise from then until lunch at 12:30. Rest and reading from lunch until 3:00 p.m. 3:00 to 5:00— open. 5:00 p.m. to 7:00 p.m., tea, and time for the children. Dinner at 7:30.

The Elys frequently attended the theater and the movies, often with Mrs. Jennings and sometimes the Taylors or Florence Sullivan, shows such as *The Scarlet Pimpernel*. In the mid-1930s, the child star Shirley Temple was the rage. Jack and Connie took Day and Florence to all her films— *Curley Top, The Little Colonel*, and the others. And the family was delighted when Connie's brother Ollie discovered an amusing ventriloquist named Edgar Bergen and hired him to entertain at Aunt Annie Burr's Christmas party with his "associate," the sassy dummy Charlie McCarthy. Thereafter Bergen's radio show became a hit with the family.

Radio had become a keen interest to Jack. He had a new set with capability of reaching the world, and he logged the countries and stations he received.

Jack and Connie became aware that Jack's mother, Maud, had gotten into gambling. Gambling had, since Victorian times, been something gentlemen did and some of their less conventional ladyfolk discreetly did as well. Florence tells of playing backgammon with Granny Maud in her apartment in New York, starting when she was four years old. She vividly remembers her Granny's fingernails; it was not proper for a widow to have colored nails, so Granny wore silver ones. The apartment was furnished with lovely things, but Florence, as she grew older, found that her grandmother was holding pawn tickets for some of her finer furnishings. Florence would play her Granny for the pawn tickets, and when she won them she would take them to her father, who would redeem them and retrieve the furniture and precious things for his mother.

Unobtrusively, Connie and Jack were buying Fort Hill from Maud and making regular payments on the purchase. This was a subtle way, accepted by all sides, of keeping the senior Mrs. Ely solvent without too much loss of face. Florence believes that in the same way, Elizabeth Arden engaged Maud, who had fashionable taste, to redecorate some of her salons, knowing that Maud needed money.

Among the Elys' many Oxford Group colleagues, several became close friends socially as well. Alan Limburg, whom Jack had gotten to know at

Banff in 1934, and his wife, Kay, were such friends. Alan had a seat on the New York Stock Exchange, and the Limburgs had homes in Manhattan and in Westchester County. They enjoyed Yale football games together; Alan liked to wear the traditional Ivy League raccoon coat and arrive in an open convertible even in the coldest weather.

The Charles Ameses were occasional social companions of the Elys. Charlie, a stock broker, had been a groomsman at Jack's wedding and Jack was regularly in touch with him about investment matters. Connie had placed her fortune completely in Jack's hands. Jack paid close attention to the financial situation, and bought and sold equities with Charlie's advice. Often the two men had lunch together. As the years went on, Jack's management of Connie's affairs proved wise, prudent, and quite productive.

Some years before, Walter Jennings had set up an instrument, the Burrwood Corporation, to hold and manage his considerable assets, separate from what he had willed to Connie, Jeannette and Ollie. At his death in 1933 the Corporation became operative. Connie asked that Jack take her seat on the board of directors, and he and sometimes both of them attended the regular monthly meetings in New York. Later, after Jack's death, his daughter Day represented her mother's interest on the Burrwood Corporation board. These meetings were sources of excellent information on investments and the state of the national economy, as the corporate holdings were large enough to attract some of the best advisors in the nation.

Jack was asked to become president of the Huntington Hospital. He had done well as chairman of their capital campaign a few years before, and now he agreed to head the hospital board of directors.

One friend of the Elys, and one of the great supporters of the Oxford Group in New York, was Emily Vanderbilt Hammond (Mrs. John Henry Hammond), a granddaughter of Cornelius Vanderbilt. She had a favorite charity, the Berry School in Rome, Georgia, which served disadvantaged children from the Appalachian area. Jack and Connie accompanied Emily Hammond and several others on a visit to Berry. They were met with a torchlight reception and taken over the extensive grounds to see everything—the industrial training facility, home economics department, and the junior school. Jack spoke in the chapel to a student body of some 1,500; Connie and Jack together talked with Berry's 300 high school boys. When he got home, Jack wrote an article about their visit for Mrs. Hammond, and made a film for her to help publicize the school.

With Connie's pregnancy a concern for Dr. Irene Gates, Connie stayed at Elyston instead of accompanying Jack on some of his travels. In giving

Connie a pair of gloves, Jack enclosed this little poem:

These handsome rivals I release
Although I recognize
They'll never give me any peace,
They'll hold her hands, I'll never cease
To envy them their prize!

That summer of 1935, Kendie brought to Elyston a young woman whom she had met in the Girl Scout movement in Georgia. Dona Nicholas turned out to be a wholesome, wholehearted girl who cared for the little girls thoughtfully and well. Dona (pronounced with a long "o," like Mona) lived day and night with the girls, created camp environments on the estate for them and their friends, took them swimming, boating, bicycling, horseback riding, on excursions through the woods and across the fields of the estate and down to the shore. Dona had that delicious sense of the wonder and mystery of life, of hidden spots that fairies might frequent, a world where a child's imagination could flourish. "Miss Con," as Dona called her, told Dona that she had tried several governesses who had attempted to mold the two girls into little aristocrats. She said to Dona, "You are the oldest of seven and you come from a middle-class family. I want you to teach my children the things that your mother taught you." So Dona set to work, under Kendie's direction.

Living at Elyston was quite a change for Dona: her father's business had been wiped out by the depression, and he was unemployed; they had lost their home and were living in two rooms of a friend's house. Twenty-year-old Dona was trying to work her way through college. Being with the Elys "was a wonderful experience for me," Dona said. "I was not reared among such wealth, such culture, among people who had that background. It freed me of a lot of artificiality. It helped me to see that all people are basically alike, same needs, and there is life wherever you go. Rich and 'uppity'? Not so."

Dona described the relationships in the family as she saw them: Connie was shy about showing affection, "not the kind of mother that you would crawl into her lap and cuddle up to." Jack had the softer qualities that would draw anybody. Dona felt that, for the period they lived in and the responsibilities they had, they spent considerable time with the children. "The quality was there," she said, "the depth. They enjoyed their children. The children were fortunate to have two parents who were compatible but not so much alike that life would become dull. Connie would always dress for dinner, and she was a handsome lady. Not beautiful, but she loved to dress in exotic costumes from India and China and she had a jewelry cabinet that just dazzled my eyes. When she came down for dinner, bejeweled and majestic, Jack adored her that way. He needed that kind of a woman."

Dona told of the effect when Jack's mother would visit: "Miss Con dreaded Mrs. Ely's visits. She was petite, the most beautiful eyes I've ever seen. She wore her silver hair high on her head—just a gorgeous creature. Her dress was conservative, which was opposite her deep nature which was provocative, flirtatious, very 'Frenchy.' She exuded this. All the servants loved her. She was diametrically opposed to what was trying to be lived there at Elyston. She didn't laugh much except with her eyes. She just spoke with them. When Mrs. Ely would come I was happy, the servants were happy, Miss Con was miserable, the children were joyous and I think poor Jack just stood in the middle of all of this commotion and femininity that descended on us all at once."

Dona's remarks give a rare indication that Connie did not enjoy her mother-in-law's visits. Over the years, Connie had come to know that Jack had had a horrible childhood, whereas her own upbringing had been filled with the warmth and love of her mother, Jean Brown Jennings. Connie blamed Maud much more than Emdee: Maud had wanted Jack sent off to boarding schools when he was very young, had spoiled Francis and often excluded Jack, and then had demanded financial support from him.

Dona also described their visits to Maud's home, Fort Hill: "Gorgeous—on the tallest point at Southampton. From it you got a view of the bay, and the Sound, and the ocean, on three sides. It was the style of an old English Tudor wood house, and as we drove up there were petunia boxes at all the windows and the petunias were in bloom. Always a breeze, and all the petunias were waving hello."

The Elys made good use of Fort Hill from time to time. They would move the whole family there for a week or two, and invite guests to join them. Usually Granny would be with them. Lyman Bleecker and his family, "Aunt Put" (Harriet Putnam Marshall) from Philadelphia, Mrs. Jennings and Aunt Florence. Eugene Edgel would be there, and the children got to know him. He had white hair, by now, and whiskers, and he was always kind with them.

They would sign on to a charter fishing boat and go out deep-sea fishing. Mrs. Florence Dickerson nearby had good swimming off her place. Crabbing was great fun. They would drive out to Montauk for dinner once in a while.

Granny Maud did needlepoint sometimes. The children remember various of her works around the house and each of them inherited some of it—although they admit it was not really very fine work, especially compared to the beautiful needlepoint that Mrs. Jennings did.

Maud loved the party life. She managed to remain involved with the collegiate football scene. Young John Ely, grandson of Dr. Ely's brother, George Henry Ely, was at Yale with the class of 1935. John recalls that Maud would come up to New Haven by train and that his father Heman would meet her and bring her to the post-game cocktail party in his son's rooms. Maud was quite welcome at these parties. The young men found her fascinating—she loved to flirt with them, and she wore distinctive clothing—veils, chiffon creations, definitely modish. She was witty and got along amazingly well with the college crowd.

That June of 1935, Jack took the ferry to Stamford and proceeded to New Haven to attend his twentieth reunion at Yale. It was a four-day affair, with old friends, picnics, golf, tennis. He wrote, "Four superlatively joyous days with as fine a crowd of men as ever got together. As a class we have found ourselves, and never again will we have any difficulty either with finances or attendance at class affairs. I succeeded in having a committee to help me and share details." At the class dinner he was elected to the executive committee which managed class affairs. Dean Acheson was their speaker, addressing current affairs with pessimism.

. . . .

NOTES

1. The growth of Frank Buchman's work during the mid-1930s and later is well covered in a biography of Buchman by Garth Lean, *Frank Buchman: A Life* (London: Constable, 1985). The American edition, titled *On the Tail of a Comet*, was published by Helmers & Howard, Colorado Springs, in 1988. This book is highly recommended for an understanding of Jack and Connie Ely's work during this period and later.

2. For detailed information on the links between the Oxford Group and Alcoholics Anonymous, see Dick B., *Design for Living: the Oxford Group's Contribution to Early A.A.* (San Rafael, California: Paradise Research Publications, 1995).

3. Among the signatories was the author's father, the Reverend Charles Jarvis Harriman.

7

Growth in Every Way

O N AUGUST 28, 1935, JACK SAILED for Europe on the S.S. *Majestic* as part of a strong American Oxford Group contingent. The group was bound for Geneva to join Frank Buchman at the League of Nations. En route, they met every day to study the situation into which they were heading. Sam Shoemaker suggested that Jack lecture to the group on "Historical Background—Europe since 1815," and lead a discussion on the League of Nations and on the causes of the present world crisis.

Jack's notes for these sessions include: "U.S., England and France are satisfied with the status quo because they have about all the land and materials they need. Italy, Germany and Japan have neither enough land [n]or material . . . expand or explode . . . unless some of us nations go Christian and begin sharing with them and practicing Christian stewardship on a supernational scale. Just as we find life-changing more satisfactory than business competition we can develop what corresponds to life-changing on a national scale—one nation going out to help the others and to make the sacrifices demanded not only for the destruction of war but to lower tariff barriers, give up land, forego the collection of war debts and make other national sacrifices that will help in the reconstruction of peace.

"We as a nation will have to make restitution for our national sins just as we do as individuals before we assume our place of leadership. . . . restore some of the land we grabbed ourselves before we can check Japan or Italy for their land grabbing. The Mexican War resulted in the biggest land grab in history—we also grabbed the Philippines to keep Japan from getting them. . . . We have let freedom to worship God degenerate into freedom to do whatever we please and we have lost our life to the hordes who wanted freedom at no price at all. We have the greatest freedom in the world but no vision, and are perishing from lack of vision despite the fact that our administration is now putting through the greatest project in history, mobilizing more resources and wealth than were ever before known and calling on the best brains in a brilliant country. We will have to take up this mission to lead the world before we find a soul."

Jack worked on this concept throughout the voyage. He wrote Connie, who had remained at home in the late stages of pregnancy: "It has been fun and I have clarified, for myself at least, many questions. I happened to read the life of Dwight Morrow [former U.S. Ambassador to Mexico, noted financier, and the father of Anne Morrow Lindbergh] and was glad to find he had reached many of the same conclusions."

The group disembarked at Cherbourg and took the train for Paris. Jack took several of them out in a hired open touring car to show them "his" Paris—Notre Dame, the tomb of Napoleon, the Eiffel Tower. Arriving in Geneva, they settled into the Carlton Parc Hotel opposite the League of Nations building. Buchman had called together a team of nearly 500 from Britain, America, Scandinavia, Holland, France, South Africa. Some thirty nationalities were represented, as well as several hundred Swiss. The group had the use of the hotel's meeting hall, and decorated it for a series of open meetings. They also held a few larger gatherings in a large downtown public hall, the Salle de la Reformation.

Rudolf Minger, President of the Swiss Confederation, officially welcomed the Oxford Group to Switzerland. The President of the Assembly of the League, Dr. Edouard Benes of Czechoslovakia, gave a luncheon for the delegates to meet Buchman and his team.

Buchman was to say later that the League of Nations failed because nobody was doing the spadework with individuals that could make it function. Otherwise all you had by and large were nations stating their gripes at one another and very little changing. Buchman wanted to see men and women learn the art of effecting change in situations because their own motives changed and caused a chain reaction in others. A reporter for the *Christian Science Monitor* wrote of the deputation from the Oxford Group, "These people are doing what the fine ladies and gentlemen of the League are talking about."

Jack called on Senator James Pope of Idaho, who was in Geneva as an observer. It was always a sore point that the United States Congress had never voted to join the League even though Woodrow Wilson as President had been a strong element in its founding. Pope had introduced a resolution into the United States Senate supporting the League of Nations and felt the United States should be more encouraging to this world-initiative for peace. A few days later Jack gave a tea party for the senator and his wife to meet several of Buchman's team.

Geneva in the summer of 1935 was a magnet for all sorts of people. There was a full slate of counts and countesses, lords and ladies of various nationalities, and people from labor and management. Jack and his friends called on the representatives of the International Business Machines Corporation and of International Harvester, and on representatives at the International Labor Organization. They were guests in the gallery of the Assembly of the League itself. Jack, with Hallen Viney of England, called on League President Benes at his hotel.

Jack and his colleagues found time to play some tennis with delegates from South Africa. They found time also to drive into Italy for lunch, over the Grand St. Bernard Pass. And Sam Shoemaker arranged to take the whole American group—thirty-eight of them—on the steamer that circles Lake Geneva, stopping to see the Chateau de Chillon, "from dungeon to ramparts!" Jack recorded. "A great day for us all!"

Philippe Mottu of Geneva drove with Jack to Bern, where they arranged meetings and receptions for social, governmental, press and diplomatic folk. Philippe was one of the first of the Swiss to become a full-time worker with Buchman, and had known Buchman about as long as Jack and Connie had. From this time on, Jack and Philippe became good friends.

Jack wrote to Connie his impressions of all of the events in Geneva, and of what he saw among the Europeans in the Group: "There is an earnestness about the work here which is lacking at home; a softness in the American work, an almost apologetic way of presenting the message. Already sixteen members of Mogens' family [Mogens Tvede, the Ely's Danish architect] have been changed and his brothers have assumed national leadership."

About the French he wrote: "They are disciplined, courageous, intelligent soldiers fighting in an international army side by side with Germans. We have no idea at home of the momentum and tremendous appeal to intelligent people of the movement over here. Each day I realize more clearly that the appeal is to the will, not the emotions, for the men now being reached are among the leaders in world thought, and unless we wake up—unless the Church at home gets on a life-changing basis—Europe may be preferable to America as a place to live."

With Sam Shoemaker and others, Jack took the train to Zurich and then to Frankfurt, Germany, where they called on Princess Carl Friedrich, the sister of the late Kaiser. They visited with various Germans who were acquainted with their work in Frankfurt, Darmstadt and Saarbrucken, and then on to Paris and Cherbourg. They returned to the United States on the S.S. *Europa* and docked in New York on October 14. Jack's mother and Lucille Kendrick met him at the pier.

At home, Connie was being as restful as she could. She was admitted to Doctors Hospital in New York, and four days after Jack had landed, Mary was born, ahead of schedule. "Very small and precious," Jack recorded. Afterwards, he wrote, "Prayers with Ken." Apparently Mary's chances in the first few moments of birth were so uncertain that she was baptized in the delivery room. Connie and the baby received a spate of cards and gifts, including one from Elizabeth Arden to "great little Honey-Bunch."

According to a note Connie wrote in searching for a nurse for her new baby, Mary was born prematurely, "with a medium inversion of both feet which are now in casts" [at two weeks]. From that precarious beginning there was always concern about Mary. She had spina bifida, a damaged heart, and club feet. Most obviously, she needed corrective orthopedic care for her feet and legs. Jack and Connie consulted with the experts in New York.

The neonatal nurse, Dunnie, who had helped Connie with both Day and Florence, again came home with Mary. Dunnie was a Bellevue nursing school graduate and wore a Bellevue cap, pleated and gathered with a little black ribbon. Kendie hired another Girl Scout from Macon, Edna Reeves, who came within a month of Mary's birth and, under Kendie's direction, took complete care of the baby as if she were her own.

Mary's coming into the family upset four-year-old Florence. Feelings of displacement by "the baby," as one perceived so super special, festered inside. The next summer Florence, aged five, was looking out of an upstairs window and saw Mary in her big black English pram on the slate terrace below. Imagining Mary squashed like strawberry jam if the pram were turned upside down, she proceeded to take that action. As the pram tipped, the mattress came out with Baby Mary surfing on top of it. The grownups gathered around at the screams and praised Florence for her concern over the baby.

That day Florence lost respect for those adults and became skeptical about all others. The very next day her new belief was reinforced when the adults put red pepper on her tongue for apparently lying and denying that she had put her dachshund Muffin into the play pen with Mary. But she hadn't. Apologies followed when the grownups later saw Muffin wriggle in all by herself, unaided. Too late—Florence's respect for adults was forfeited. Florence comments today that she and Mary later became close friends, and laughed about the incident.

Dona Nicholas and Edna Reeves worked together closely in their care of the Ely children. Dona tells of the Burrwood experimental farm, and the four or five brick cottages that housed the key staff people. There was the shepherd and his family—from Germany, Dona thought—plus the cattle herder, and the head gardener, a Cornell graduate. Each one had the opportunity to send their children to college, if they were willing to work hard.

"Mrs. Jennings loved to knit," Dona recalled. "She had the wool processed from their own sheep. She knitted Edna and me each a sweater for Christmas, a great gift from a lady who was very busy. And she was very down to earth. One day, Day and Fluff and I were standing on our heads—I was teaching them balance—and I saw this tweed skirt and work boots and there was Mrs. Jennings. 'That's good,' she said. 'I do that every day in my bedroom.'"

After the eventful time at Geneva and in Switzerland, the Americans of the Oxford Group planned a campaign they called "America Awake!" It employed the figure of Paul Revere on horseback dashing through the night. There would be a large houseparty in the Berkshires in the summer of 1936. Jack was among the team who spent many days in Stockbridge and the surrounding Berkshire towns preparing for a large crowd.

While rooming in the Red Lion Inn in Stockbridge with one of the South Africans who had joined the team there, Jack wrote, "Dearest: working hard preparing for the great numbers expected. My work is chiefly with plans for transportation by bus between sites. Sometime I hope my roommate takes a trip with all his clothes in a very small boat so that he will have to put his things away or find himself hoisting his flannel trousers as the main sheet. . . . The local people are slow-to-move but cooperative. Many, many happy returns of May 16th. Hugs and kisses, yours ever, T."

Dona Nicholas was again at Elyston for that summer and stayed until after Christmas, when she returned home to resume her studies. At about the same time Kendie left the Elys' employ. Connie had another conference about bringing up the children, this time with Olive Jones, a children's specialist who was closely associated with Calvary Church and the Oxford Group. Olive and Connie discussed how to raise children in an atmosphere where God was a normal part of life—praying to him and listening to him, loving him and his son Jesus Christ. And about how a child could find Jesus as her dear and personal friend. Connie decided that from then on she would seek to have people around the children who had that attitude to life.

Shortly after Christmas in 1936 little Mary developed a severe case of pneumonia. When she became stable enough to travel, the whole family departed for Fort Myers Beach, Florida, to stay in the hotel owned by Jim Newton's parents, where Mary could recuperate in the warm weather. Connie took Mary and Florence by train, and because of Mary's continuing problems she also took along Dunnie, the neonatal professional.

Jack and eight-year-old Day made the trip by car, a journey Day recalls with great relish. Jack stopped in Annapolis to show his daughter the Naval Academy. Then on south. Day remembers especially the drive to the Gulf Coast on the Tamiami Trail through the Everglades. It was a two-lane road, and her father took great care in passing a fleet of eleven buses. Shortly after Jack passed them all, Day told her father she had to go to the bathroom. They made a stop. When Day rejoined her father he remarked that all eleven busses had just finished passing them again. "He was sweet about it," Day remembers.

It was a happy winter in Florida. Day had attended the Lloyd Harbor School in 1935, and was enrolled there again. While in Florida, Jack was supposed to tutor Day in her fourth-grade subjects, but she remembers that neither of them was able to make the tutoring work very well.

"Gar [the children's name for Mrs. Jennings] came down to visit us," Day recollects, "and we were so happy that finally after three years of mourning she wore a lovely turquoise blue-green velveteen housecoat for family breakfast. Mother used to get so annoyed because Dad and I had to read every word on the cereal boxes before serving ourselves and passing them on. We loved the movies Dad took when he and Mum went deep sea fishing, of Mum's mobile face making all kinds of imitations of fish and rabbits and jack o'lanterns." By April Jack had returned to New York, while Connie and the children remained at Fort Myers Beach until well into May. Connie's mother wrote from Burrwood, "Dearest Connie, I had such a nice time with Jack and we discussed everything, the Relation of the Oxford Group to Society and everything else!"

Back in New York, Jack noted the anniversary of his father's death,

". . . and I am having dinner with Grannie at her apartment. Two classmates at the Yale Club were really interested to hear about the Oxford Group. Frank [one of the Burrwood staff] met me at the train in Huntington, and drove me to Elyston. Elsie had the house looking good. Dinner at Burrwood. Ollie was there. Gar looked well. A walk around the farm after church with Gar and Ollie." At Calvary House, the Group's headquarters, he worked on photo equipment used in producing the Group's illustrated printed material. Jack was learning to develop black & white photographs. He had a darkroom in the Elyston cellar.

Jack wrote often to Connie in Fort Myers Beach. In May he shared with her his thoughts about "quiet times," the practice of listening to God for direction. "For long stretches quiet times were unreal to me and, as you know, I never had any real guidance. But for the past week there has come back a sense of God's presence and of His companionship which has made my heart almost sing in the mornings. Gradually I have become really dependent on them.

"Went down to Burrwood, lunch with your Mother and Mrs. Atterbury—I felt a tremendous sense of love for your Mother with a realization of how greatly I have failed her in the past. My dearest love, Pooh, and I promise to love you for your own self."

Connie and the girls returned home from Florida in the station wagon that Jack and Day had driven down. Connie's mother had written, "Would you like a private [railway] car for the trip home? I can arrange it. We could put your car on board." But they drove. Day recalls stopping in St. Augustine on the way north and exploring the old Spanish fort, and the discomfort of having to wear shoes again after five months of running barefoot on the beach.

In that year, 1937, Jack formally left the practice of law and became in his own mind a full-time worker for God. Their base was at Elyston, in Cold Spring Harbor—they had closed the apartment in the city when Elyston was ready to live in.

8

Prelude to Major Change

I N 1937 A YOUNG WOMAN NAMED ANNA HALE appeared in the Ely household. Anna was a devoted Christian for whom the Oxford Group's ideas
had unleashed great creativity. Like the Elys and the Jennings, she was
of a pioneering family who had come to the New World as Puritans in
1633; perhaps the most famous of her family was the Revolutionary patriot
Nathan Hale. Anna had studied theology in college in hopes of being a
missionary in Asia, as so many of her family had been, but the depression
had prevented her church from financing her in the mission field. She found
that she had great skill with children and could use her talents to free parents like Connie and Jack for "missionary work."

Anna had lived for several years with Alan and Kay Limburg, taking
care of Myles and Phyllis, the Limburg children. Connie had let it be known
that she would very much like to have Anna work with the Ely children, as
her effect on the Limburgs had been so noticeable. Anna remained involved
with the Ely family for life. When the children were young they called her
by her college nickname of Bobby. She was a resourceful person with a very
real faith.

At Cold Spring Harbor Anna Hale initiated, with Connie's enthusiastic participation, a camping program for Day and Florence and a dozen
children of the Elys' friends. Day remembers nature studies, raising the
flag and saying the Pledge of Allegiance, and learning to cook around a

campfire. There were lessons in boating, swimming, diving (Anna had spent many summers on Lake George in the Adirondacks and was an expert diver). Everyone had the chance to pass Red Cross safety and rescue tests. At the end of each camp there was a water show for parents and friends. The children would demonstrate such skills as righting a canoe and climbing in again after being tipped out in the water while wearing heavy clothes over bathing suits.

Anna's contribution to the well-being and effective functioning of the Ely family was multifaceted. Although there were several servants to do the housework, Anna went to Connie one day and suggested that it would be healthy for Day and Florence to learn to make their own beds and take care of their own rooms.

"All went well at first," Anna said. "Novelty made the chore exciting, but trouble came. One morning I found Day on the floor of her room sitting in a swirl of sheets and blankets, so angry she was crying. I sat down in the nest of bedclothes beside her. When she was quiet I explained to her why her mother and I wanted her to make her bed every day, as part of her education and growing-up process. Day had her father's keen brain and she took this in. After a bit she accepted this new lesson, not with pleasure but with understanding. In the same way later she and Florence learned skills like cooking and childcare.

"Florence did not enjoy the routine of bed-making any more than Day, but typically her approach to the subject was different. One day, having decided she would not make her bed, she found the chambermaid and turned upon that young woman all the charm of her dark brown eyes and warm smile. 'Rowena,' she wheedled, 'You'll make my bed for me today—won't you? Please?' Rowena grinned at the six-year-old. 'Why yes, Miss Florence—I'll be glad to if Miss Hale says I can.'"

Florence wrote this recollection some fifty years later. "When Anna came to be part of our family, I had become a child terrified, paralyzed, by fear of the dark. Previously I'd loved the night, especially outside in the woods of Long Island. Anna didn't scoff at my fears nor did she give in, or not care. She explained instead that I should put my fear into an imaginary box; we could tie it with strong rope, kneel down and give the box to Jesus. Jesus is polite, she explained, too polite to grab my fear if I was choosing to hang onto it; Jesus respects our possessions and would keep the box so should I ever want my fear back, I could choose to have it. We did this together, identifying the specific fears, putting them into the box, closing it—it was very real to me. Then we knelt down and I gave my box to Jesus.

He took it and the fears are still in his keeping.

"I have been sorely tempted several times to grab my box back," Florence continued, "especially during Mau Mau in Kenya, during bad storms, in front of cold audiences. It is my choice. To experience this relationship with Jesus has made faith real to me, beyond any reasonable doubt. I *know*."

As the summer of 1937 wore on with the children growing older, it seemed to Connie and Jack that the Lloyd Harbor School was no longer what they wanted for them. In a schoolhouse with three grades in each room, Day had entered the second grade and was quickly moved into the room with the third, fourth and fifth graders, where she had an excellent time. Soon she could recite all the lessons anyone in her room was learning. Then had come the winter in Fort Myers Beach; both Day and Florence had had some tutoring by their father. Now they were getting ready to begin another school year.

So the question was, where should they live? Connie and Jack talked a lot about it and raised various possibilities. Connie loved the atmosphere of San Francisco, although she didn't know many people there. Jack's mind and his recent work tended to suggest Washington, D.C., as the place where his commitment and world vision would be very useful.

Frank Buchman and a number of his people made one of their many trips to America that autumn. The pace at which they were working throughout Europe and Britain was repeatedly matched by campaigns in the United States, although the response in Europe was deeper and more substantial, probably because the danger was more palpable. On this occasion, Connie went down to meet their ship alone, because Jack was ill. Buchman came off the ship and he and Connie talked beside the pile of luggage that was accumulating as the party disembarked.

Connie recalled the conversation: "I told him we had a decision to make, and he said 'Well, let's make it.' We sat on trunks and bags and boxes and things that were piled up there, and I told him the advantages of San Francisco in my mind and of Washington in Jack's mind, and he said 'I think God knows, and let's just be quiet.' There in all the hustle and bustle of people getting off, Frank just looked down at the floor, and I kind of looked down at the floor too—I didn't know what to do, I wasn't very accustomed to listening to God in strange places. Frank looked up all of a sudden and said, 'Well, you're married to the man, why don't you go where he wants?' and I replied, 'Well, that's fine, it suits me.'"

So they moved to Washington. It is a commentary on Connie and Jack's stature in the social world that their names are immediately listed in the 1937 edition of the prestigious *Social List of Washington and Social Precedence in Washington*, and in every edition thereafter until Connie moved away more than thirty years later. *The Social List* was a privately compiled directory, founded by Helen Ray Hagner and continued by her daughter Carolyn Hagner Shaw, as a guide to protocol for Washington entertaining and diplomatic functions.

When Jack came to Washington, he was among the most formal of men. He wore double-breasted three-piece suits; he wore starched collars, even when they were attached-collar shirts. A pearl stickpin in his tie. A handkerchief in his breast pocket and another in his trousers for use— "a hankie for show and another for blow." And spats. And his accessories matched. He always wore a homburg, usually gray. He bought his suits ready-made by Brooks Brothers, probably because their styles fitted him well. He wore Brooks shirts, embroidered on the pocket with his initials, until he learned from his brother-in-law, Henry Taylor, that J.C. Penney's shirts were of finer cotton than Brooks's. (Taylor's company wove cotton for large users, and the thread count that Penney specified was finer than the thread count Brooks ordered.)

The Elys scouted for a house to rent, to enable them to get the feel of the city and of where they ought to settle. They chose a house on Kalorama Road, near a great many of the embassies. They moved in September 1937. Day was nine, Florence six, Mary two. Day and Florence were enrolled in the Potomac School, which was near their new home. Later Mary went there too. Eventually Day went to the National Cathedral School and Florence and Mary to Madeira School.

It must have been satisfying for Connie to be near her old school, Foxcroft, for Middleburg, Virginia, was a scant hour out of Washington. They kept their home at Cold Spring Harbor, primarily for summer use, but their life very substantially centered in Washington. In the next three years they rented three other houses on Kalorama Road, searching for the perfect one.

Connie was asked, years later, about the move, why she was so willing to make that decision on the strength of what Dr. Buchman said. "I felt he had such good judgment," she replied, "and he had so much vision, and I knew he wanted to have my husband where he could see more of him because I felt his confidence in Jack. I felt Frank's interest in the development of my husband."

The year 1938 was an important one in the work of the Oxford Group. Buchman was searching for what might turn this movement of the Spirit into a force that could affect the tide of history. He felt that it did not require a whole nation of individuals to turn history around but a few key people in a few strategic places. Buchman took up a phrase that a Swedish trade union leader had written to him: "We must rearm morally." The phrase "moral re-armament" quickly became Buchman's program, the program of the Oxford Group.

Through much of this time, Jack and Connie knew that she was pregnant. Mary got pneumonia again that winter, and in March Mrs. Jennings invited the family to join her in Aiken, South Carolina. She installed them all in Willcox's, an old-fashioned hotel that had very few guests at that time. There was a dry river of sand and it was a wonderful place to play and picnic. Day and Anna Hale did some horseback riding—the stable groom decided Day could handle a former race horse, and she loved the pounding runs along the bridle paths with Anna close behind her. And Connie loved the carriage driving that was available.

Jack spent much of the time in Washington. "Mother has just been too dear for words," Connie wrote to him, "flowers in all our rooms—lilies of the valley for me! Little animals and books and toys for the kids—she insists we are her guests!" She wrote her observations on how the stable boy handled the horses. They had her open convertible with them. "Good night, Jake," she concluded a letter, "consider yourself kissed!"

Connie wrote that her mother was beginning to understand the Oxford Group better. "Oh darling," she wrote, "My guidance yesterday was that I was afraid of having my feelings hurt by the family and so I shut up. Now I don't have to, with JJ [short for Jeannette Jennings] and Ma both having been to meetings the ice is broken. My beloved, this comes with all my love."

As Connie's day drew near and they returned to Washington, Day contracted the measles. By the time Connie checked into Doctors Hospital in New York for her delivery, she had caught the measles too. On May 6, 1939, Connie gave birth to a son, Nathaniel Jennings Ely. Connie was not allowed to touch the baby until she had recovered. "Call in the cleaners," Day wrote to her mother in the hospital, "to remove the spots."

"Dearest Bam," Jeannette wrote to her from her home on East 79th Street, "we are too thrilled! How grand to have a son! I'm sorry I can't come to see you but I know you probably are not allowed visitors and I've never had the measles either!" And Maud wrote, "Dearest Connie, My love to you and your son. If he had waited until May 7 he would have been born on his great-grandmother's birthday [Mary Day Ely, Emdee's mother]. But you couldn't really blame him for wanting to get away from a case of measles. I suppose Jack's chest line has grown some since 1:30 this morning. Much love to you six, Granny."

Niel, everyone called him. What a heritage his name celebrated—all that Nathaniel Ely, "the emigrant" and his descendants had gone through and accomplished. A son to join three daughters. It was a proud and grateful father who welcomed his son into the world. But Niel had some of the problems that Mary had. His legs and feet were misformed, and almost immediately he had plaster casts on his legs, as Mary had had.

This of course was difficult for Jack and Connie. Two healthy, vigorous children, and two happy but frail and heavily disabled ones. One thing people quickly noticed was that the family did not cater to the children's problems. With both Mary and Niel, there was no false sentiment. Anna Hale recalls bringing Mary, then a crawling infant, in to meet some of Connie's friends at tea one day. Anna put the child down on the rug, and Mary began immediately to crawl around on the plaster knees of her casts. One of the ladies started to voice something on the order of, "Oh the poor little thing." Connie, quick as a flash, said, "Mary wears casts, and takes them for granted. She does not have to feel sorry for herself now or ever." The same was true for Niel.

Anna Hale was Niel's godmother and looked upon him as virtually her own son. Peggy Bond, daughter of one of the Elys' friends in Sayville, Long Island, had come to work at Elyston for two summers; when Niel was born she spent a year taking care of him, to earn her way through college. Later Peggy recalled, "Connie kept Niel in touch with his memories of me, such a gracious lovely thing to do. Every time I saw him in the succeeding years it was as though we had just parted."

Shortly before Niel was born, another person had joined the Ely household—Brooks McKinley Onley. Brooks was an expert driver, and was recommended to them by Philip Marshall Brown. Brooks became chauffeur and man-of-all-work with the family, both in Washington and at Elyston, until he retired some thirty years later.

Brooks had learned to drive a car very, very smoothly, when he worked for Professor Brown. They would drive from the Brown home in Princeton, for instance, to Georgia; that meant going through a good many places where Dr. Brown had friends; if he were awake in the car, he would want to stop and visit here and there. If Brooks drove carefully and the professor slept they would cover much more ground. The issue for Brooks, an African American, was where, if they stopped, he could find a place to eat or to stay. That was the reality of life in America before the Civil Rights movement. So a shrewd man like Brooks would take measures whenever he could to avoid stopping where he was not welcome.

Jack and Connie Ely moved into action with the others to help make Buchman's concept of Moral Re-Armament a national affair. There was a series of events to publicize it in 1939: a large meeting at Madison Square Garden; a meeting in Constitution Hall in Washington, where they now lived; and a gathering of 30,000 people at the Hollywood Bowl, with many hundreds turned away.

A special railway train was organized to bring people from the East to the Hollywood Bowl. By the time the train left, with Jack on board, they had required twenty-two sleeping cars, which was some kind of a railroading record. At one stop, Jack realized there was a perfect opportunity to get a photograph of the whole train if he could go ahead up the track and climb a bridge with his camera. Jack Ravenscroft, who eventually married Jack's daughter Day, saw Jack huffing and puffing with his equipment, and figured the older man was going to have heart trouble. So Ravenscroft helped Ely with his equipment, and they got the picture.

After the Hollywood Bowl meeting and another event in San Francisco, Buchman, Jack Ely, and several others visited Mexico City, where they had been invited to the inauguration of President Manuel Avila Camacho. The manager of the Hotel Reforma, in which they stayed, gave a party for them on his roof-garden. Jack took many photos of the occasion, which made a hit with the manager and his staff. The trip itself gave the party a bit of a respite from their work. Jack brought back three *china-poblana* national costumes for his three daughters—red skirts with broad green bands at the bottom and sequined embroidery.

September 1, 1939: in spite of all the efforts to prevent it, Europe went to war.

As Washingtonians, the Elys got to know many of the diplomatic corps stationed in the capital. The Japanese embassy was near the Ely home and the Elys became friends of Japanese ambassador Kensuke Horinouchi and his wife, Toshiko, who had had some touch with the Oxford Group in Japan. The Horinouchis had endeavored to practice what they understood of the Group's message. Partly as a result of this commitment, Ambassador Horinouchi found himself in the minority opinion against the militarist faction of the country, who were determined to pursue what became known as the Greater East Asia Co-Prosperity Sphere.

Horinouchi did his best to represent Japan's foreign policy vis-à-vis the United States, but by 1940 he felt that he could not dissemble to the American government as his country's plans for war were maturing. He resigned his post that summer, and as he was leaving the country he came to Elyston, where the Elys were spending their summer, to pay his respects and to say goodbye to the family.

Later in the summer of 1940, Jack joined Buchman and a number of his people out in the San Francisco Bay area. He stayed for some days at the Pine Inn, Carmel. "California is quite different from anything that I had expected," he wrote to Connie. "Firstly, it is actually cold!" He went on to describe some of the scenery. "Arroyos," he said, "Fluffy will like that word." He wrote of "MRA [Moral Re-Armament] Day" at the San Francisco Exposition on Treasure Island. He was working with his colleague Sciff Wishard on a 16mm film of the Hollywood Bowl meeting.

During that summer, Jack and some of his friends were also in Chicago for the 1940 national convention of the Democratic Party. Jack wrote to Connie from his room at the Chicago Athletic Club: "Mr. Bankhead's secretary [William B. Bankhead was Speaker of the House of Representatives] came to us yesterday with a draft of the keynote speech and said, 'We hope you will like the last paragraphs. We tried to make it MRA and we took out some things which were not in the spirit of MRA.' As I went over this draft of the speech—delivered last night—I saw phrases, little sarcastic digs, innuendoes etc. which had been pencilled out because they were on a personal level and would have tended to create unnecessary bitterness. . . . [so and so] introduced us to Mr. Avery, head of Montgomery Ward. I'm dining there tonight. Today I'm moving up to stay with Lauren Drake, President of Union Tank Car Co., on Lake Shore Drive. Devotedly, T."

From July to September of 1940, the core of men and women giving their full time to work with Buchman held a kind of retreat in a chalet lent to them on the shore of Lake Tahoe in Nevada. It was a soul-searching time, a period of examining where they were and what their commitment was individually in this "race with time to remake men and nations." Jack flew there from Washington to be part of it. They emerged from several weeks together with a simple conviction for the ordinary American, and a vehicle to use in promoting that conviction: a musical revue called *You Can Defend America*, and a booklet by the same title which set forth their ideas in a clear and simple form.

The booklet *You Can Defend America* was published in late 1940 with a foreword by America's one genuine military statesman of that period, General of the Armies John J. "Black Jack" Pershing, whose concluding words were, "I commend its message to every American." Well over four million copies were in use world wide, distributed by the civil defense people, war production industries, labor unions and others. It was impressive to see how ordinary Americans responded to this statement of what their nation stood for.

By the summer of 1941, both the booklet and the musical review *You Can Defend America* had begun to make their mark across the country. That summer, at the suggestion of the governor of Maine, a number of people convinced of the need for MRA at this critical time gathered for training sessions in morale-building at an old hotel on Lake Maranacook, just west of the city of Augusta. They handled housekeeping and cooking and other chores themselves, like an extended family.

The Elys took a cottage at the resort and pitched in with the practical work of the gathering. The family, including Anna Hale, loved the simple environment, despite the fact that the roof over Mary's bed leaked and Connie had to set out buckets and umbrellas to keep her daughter dry. All but Jack got into the informality of the scene—as usual, he dressed in a coat and tie.

The children at Maranacook had their own program. They organized as "Minute Men" and "Minute Maids." Day and Florence were Minute Maids, and enthusiastically took part in songs and skits. Day recalls helping lead the children in singing "We're the Minute Men of Maranacook. We always have our guidance book. We always have our pencil too. We hope the same applies to you. . . ."

"Simple as it was," Day says, "the climate of concern for the war against Hitler was such that people got the point of cooperation and seeking God's inspiration for solving problems and for changing our ways of living." When the time came for the children to return to Washington and school, they gathered for a farewell breakfast, with all the grown-ups attending, and told the assembled crowd what they had learned during the summer. Expecting some simple but profound truth from ten-year-old Florence, they put her on a chair so everyone could see her. "I learned to wiggle my ears, like my big sister Day," she reported, and demonstrated.

Meanwhile, Britain and all of Europe were at war. The celebrated British author Daphne Du Maurier, author of *Rebecca*, had written a book of true accounts of how ordinary people in Britain were coping with the war, using stories gathered by her friends in MRA. The resulting book, *Come Wind, Come Weather*, was published in England and proved to be a great morale booster. Miss Du Maurier arranged for it to be published in the United States also, with the royalties paid to Moral Re-Armament.

Jack wrote to Buchman suggesting that as "the royalties from the book [the British edition] were given by her to the Soldiers', Sailors' and Airmen's Families Association, would it not be appropriate in this country to donate the royalties to the American Red Cross?" Jack suggested that such a move would help a universally accepted organization and probably would secure their help in getting wide distribution of the book.

Buchman wrote back, tactfully disagreeing: "Daphne Du Maurier wisely saw that she could not constantly draw upon the source who fed her with her inspiration and life without in some way giving some return. MRA gave the work of all our people free to help her. . . . Daphne has asked MRA to have the royalties on the American edition. She is the first to realize, as you always have been, that to carry forward such a needed work at such sacrifice needs constant undergirding. I am sure a reasonable reduction could be given to the Red Cross if they were interested in large numbers. You might yourself find out just what the possibilities might be."

This exchange may have focused something for Jack, and perhaps also for Connie. Buchman wrestled with the constant need to pay the expenses of this ever-widening work. And also, he sought to focus the thinking, energies and means of his friends on the essential battle to bring a deep and drastic change in the motives of key people. Day Ely Ravenscroft has this perspective: "Father really felt that there were other important ways of working for God beside MRA. He would try to understand other people's concerns and be their friend and support them in finding God's plan, not just try to get them into our program." While Jack and Connie saw MRA as a major priority for their time and money, their primary commitment was to God rather than to any movement.

The musical revue *You Can Defend America* was invited to play in communities coast to coast. Setting up a schedule for responding to the flood of invitations involved Jack and Connie and many of their friends, and Connie in particular became a vital part of the cast. Basically a shy person, she played the role of "Mrs. Citizen" in the revue with vigor. The show toured the land—Detroit, Indianapolis, Columbus, Boston, Philadelphia, Washington, Richmond, Atlanta, Raleigh, Miami and other Florida cities, San Francisco, Seattle, and across the states of Maine, Connecticut, and Massachusetts. The beat of the music was infectious and sent audiences out of the theaters with heads up and feet marching.

One notable American who responded was Mary McLeod Bethune, an African American born of slave parents who had founded her own

Sketch of "2419" by Reginald Hale of England, a frequent visitor

Jack hosts Buddhist abbot at lunch in the garden, 1957

Connie on the cover of Town & Country, February 1952, in connection with an exhibition at the Corcoran Gallery of notable paintings from private collections

Frank Buchman and Brooks Onley in living room at "2419"

Ely Christmas card, 1944

Tea with Earl and Patty McQueen; "Rumpus" begs for treats

Eric Parfit's sketch of himself arriving for dinner at "2419"

The Elys host a dinner at home for Sibnath Banerjee, leader of the Calcutta dock workers. At the right is Irene Laure, head of the Socialist women of France.

Day and Harriet Jackson Addison in the "2419" kitchen

Jack in uniform of the U.S. Coast Guard Auxiliary, 1942

Jean Jennings' boat the Jock Scott II, used by the Coast Guard on wartime patrols

Senator Harry Truman of Missouri and Representative James Wadsworth of New York, co-sponsors of premiere of The Forgotten Factor

Frank Buchman and Jack in Tallwood, Maine, 1941

Florence and Day at President Franklin Roosevelt's inaugural parade, 1941

Connie with Niel, 1941

Connie as "Mrs. Citizen" in the wartime revue You Can Defend America

Midnight work in the Mackinac kitchen: from left, Grete Morrison Hale, Maisry MacCracken, Day, Connie, Eleanor Forde Newton

Pumping water at the MRA conference in Tallwood, 1941

Jack the photographer, typically loaded down with equipment

Connie in Virginia, 1948

A selection of Jack's photos from the 35th reunion of the Class of 1915 at Yale. From left, Jack with George Stewart; Archibald MacLeish; and Colonel Truman Smith.

Tea at Elyston, 1941; from left, Florence Lentilhon, Maud Ely, and Jean Jennings

New York, 1948; Connie, Mary and Niel en route to Wyoming after one of Niel's foot operations

Jack and Day showing Mt. Vernon to overseas guests, 1959

Connie (left) with Dr. Mary McLeod Bethune (right), founder of Bethune-Cookman College and advisor to President Roosevelt

*Saturday walk: Jack and his son
Niel, 1942 or 1943*

*Mary Ely's funeral, January
1958. Above left, St. John's
Church, Washington; above right,
Dr. S. Douglas Cornell, executive
director of the National Academy
of Sciences, pays tribute to Mary's
life; left, U.S. Navy Honor
Guard carrying Mary to her final
resting place at Arlington
National Cemetery*

college and done her utmost to give black people an opportunity to move ahead in life. She was an advisor to President Roosevelt on race matters, and Jack and Connie had gotten to know her in about 1939. She would come to the house for tea, and the children called her "Aunt Mary." She took lemon in her tea, and Florence remembers hopping on her bicycle to scour the neighborhood for lemon in the days of wartime shortages.

Mrs. Bethune said of *You Can Defend America*, "it breathes the spirit of the Emancipation Proclamation." Jack got to know others of the African-American leaders in Washington. He went to a church meeting with Ken Twitchell, who reported that the minister had introduced Jack saying, "This man looks like a white man but he has a real black heart." Mrs. Bethune asked Jack to serve on the board of trustees of her Bethune-Cookman College, which he did from 1939 to 1949.

Another person with whom Jack Ely worked closely in Washington was Arthur Meigs, a graduate of Princeton and of the University of Pennsylvania Law School. Arthur had become part of the Moral Re-Armament team. He made his home in Washington, where throughout his life he was involved in community issues and had many friends among the city's diverse populations.

Arthur and Jack were similar in their quiet, somewhat reserved and patrician approach to life, and they understood each other. Day says of Arthur, "He was very brainy but not at all snobbish about it." Arthur Meigs was perhaps one of the few persons who knew Jack well; the only one interviewed for this book who said about Jack, "He was my friend."

During this period, the Elys found themselves looking for a house in Washington that they would eventually buy. Some thirty years later, Connie described how she and Jack came to own the house at 2419 Massachusetts Avenue, the house that played such a large part in the rest of this story. The time was early in 1941: "Anna Hale would take our son out in his baby carriage, around the neighborhood, and on down to Sheridan Circle, and one day she overheard a bunch of nannies with their charges, talking about 'that big house of Mary Roberts Rinehart's.' Mrs. Rinehart was a well-known writer of mystery stories. The Swiss ministry, which had been renting Mrs. Rinehart's house, was being moved.

"Anna pricked up her ears. She walked the baby carriage over to Massachusetts Avenue to stroll by the house, and then up the alley so that she could see it from the other side. She saw how much room there was, and told me that this would solve our problem. I thought it was a terrible old house, but she insisted I call up the real estate people."

Connie had also made up her mind, in the four years of experimenting with houses on Kalorama Road and thinking of what they wanted, that
Massachusetts Avenue was one place she did *not* intend to live; with four
children and pets there was too much traffic and too much commotion.

The decision about where to live permanently was made in consulta-
tion with Frank Buchman. Years later, Connie reminisced about this. Their
last move on Kalorama Road had been to a smaller house because, she said,
"My husband had suggested that we not have so many guests all of the
time. He found them irksome and tiring, and they interrupted his already
established friendships." Day recalls, "Mother got what she called 'sheetitis,'
an inflammation of the emotions due to having too many sheets in the wash
from too many guests, and she rented a house where there were no guest
bedrooms."

So it was all the more remarkable that Connie and Jack held the decision about using Mrs. Rinehart's house up to the light of their commitment
to God, and shared the facts with Dr. Buchman and their close colleagues.
They negotiated with Mrs. Rinehart and rented the house. They had moved
in by the middle of September 1941.

They did a prodigious job of renovation and adaptation on the building. Mrs. Rinehart apparently became quite intrigued with their life and
how they used the house. That summer while the Elys were in Maine they
visited Mrs. Rinehart at her summer place on Mt. Desert Island. "She is
charming," Jack said afterwards. "She asked the right questions about MRA.
She was a special investigator for the FBI into subversive activities on the
West Coast. She also asked, 'How can I find the guidance of God?'"

Two years later Mrs. Rinehart let the Elys know that she was receiving
offers to buy the house, and that neither she nor her sons expected to live in
Washington again. By 1944, the Elys had purchased the house from her.

Before Jack and Connie moved from Kalorama Road, Buchman had
raised the possibility that the Rinehart house might be both a family home
and an embassy. That was certainly one of the ways in which Buchman saw
Jack and Connie—as ambassadors of his work at the highest levels of diplomacy, government and society. A handwritten letter to Buchman in Jack's
beautiful script, in May of 1941, states, "I am again grateful to you for
writing me so fully your convictions about the house in Washington for
next year. We share fully your thought that it should be not only a home
but an embassy. And we hope you will spend many days 'in residence' as
Ambassador. But like most embassies I believe that it should have a chancery, apart from the house, where business may be done. The present Swiss

Legation (2419 Massachusetts Avenue) might serve as a combined Embassy-Chancery but not, I am afraid, for a family like ours with small children. . . . I can see that it might have great possibilities. But I do not think that our family could run it, because of the children. . . . Conceivably the time may come when because of the bombing or other reasons it is necessary to have a greater measure of communal living; but at present, I believe, a 'sound home' can best be built on the basis of one family under a roof with lots of guided guests sharing the home, especially where the family have small children."

Perhaps Jack and Connie decided together to accept Buchman's conviction about the house in spite of the things Jack had put into that letter, and in spite of what Connie had thought about the idea of a smaller house. And in spite of her determination not to live on Massachusetts Avenue. Whatever changed their thinking, from then on they juggled the needs of their growing children and the work they felt called to do.

Whether or not Jack was fully happy about the way his home was used is a point of speculation. Some persons interviewed for this book felt he was not, some that he was. In all probability, his feelings were mixed. Certainly for the next twenty-three years, until his death, Jack's home on Massachusetts Avenue was an embassy in the heart of Moral Re-Armament's worldwide work. He and Connie did take the family away during school vacations, usually to Elyston, Mackinac, Wyoming, or Cape Cod. This gave a natural change of pace and some of the family would be together in a more peaceful outdoor setting. Letters and diary entries indicate that Jack, and probably Connie, saw the family home, their growing children, and their involvement in a global effort as pretty much one seamless creation, all part of obedience to God's calling.

Jack's letter to Buchman breezes over an important note, "because of the bombing." It is sobering to think, in the 1990s, that Jack, with his broad view of national and world affairs, even considered that Washington might be bombed in World War II. The reality was that houses in all of the eastern states had blackout curtains at all the windows against the possibility of air raids. For a time, all outdoor lighting was also blacked out. Air raid sirens were mounted on poles in every urban neighborhood.

9

Crisis for America

A CONSIDERABLE AMOUNT OF WORK was done on the house at 2419 Massachusetts Avenue before the Ely family moved in. Thereafter they continued with adjustments and renovations to make the place more efficient for its growing uses. They bought the lot beside the house (to the left, as you looked at it from the street) to expand the garden and make it useful for receptions and garden parties.

Beryl Evans, who lived there and worked closely with Jack as his secretary from 1947 to 1955, described the house: "There were six bedrooms on the second floor, with three bathrooms. Then on the third floor there were four bedrooms and two baths, plus two servants' bedrooms with a half bathroom. The first floor included a large living room, smaller sitting room, dining room, library, Jack's study, sun porch, office space added at the rear, kitchen, serving pantry, and an added staff dining room, called 'the palace.' A patio and lovely walled garden with a pond (goldfish and water lilies), which one entered from the living room, were developed by Connie with Horace Peasley, a fine landscape architect, using many large plants brought from Burrwood after her mother's death. And there was a double garage at the back.

"Always, afternoon tea was served for whomever was in the house at the time, often in the garden when the weather was pleasant. Earl Grey tea was a favorite of Connie's."

"We had a staff of seven people," Connie reminisced, "chauffeur, cook, waitress, downstairs cleaner, upstairs cleaner, laundress, gardener." At first, in wartime, she could not find good cooks. Then Anita Ritter, one of Connie's new friends in Washington, told her that her waitress recommended an aunt, Mamie Shellington. Connie hired her on a live-in basis. The day Aunt Mamie arrived and unpacked, Connie told her there would be five for dinner. Then Jack called and said there were three senators he wanted to talk with, and their wives were free and they would all come. Eleven! Aunt Mamie loved it, loved having people to cook for. This cemented her relationship with Connie immediately.

Day recalls, "We called her 'Aunt Mamie' because she was near retirement age when she came to us and 'Aunt' was the respectful way to address an older woman in her position. . . . Her very personal version of 'crêpes suzette' was our all-time favorite dessert: a high stack of thick, light pancakes as big as an iron skillet in diameter and stuck with butter, strawberry jam, brown sugar and cinnamon."

Mealtimes were important in the Ely household. Day recalls that all meals were eaten together as a family: "No matter what time the first child had to leave the house, breakfast was a sit-down meal with all the house guests in time for that child to take a peaceful part. Mother liked a wide— and wild—variety for breakfast: sometimes oatmeal or eggs and bacon, or scrambled eggs and creamed brains, or sweetbreads on toast or sausage and grits. One of those hot dishes plus fruit and toast, not a huge buffet every day. Sunday was always half grapefruits and waffles with bacon and syrup. Mother had two old and trusty irons at her place and made waffles as fast as possible for all ten to fourteen people at the table. Then we all went to church at St. John's Lafayette Square."

Late in 1941 something happened that shook the growing work of Moral Re-Armament and the Oxford Group. It may have been inevitable, and in some ways it brought a renewed and confirmed sense of conviction to the work. Calvary House, the parish building of Calvary Church, 61 Gramercy Park, New York, had been for several years very much the administrative center of the Group's work in America. The rector, Sam Shoemaker, decided with Jack Smith, his associate, and the vestry of the parish, that Moral Re-Armament's use of the buildings as a center for its national and world work had become overwhelming and incompatible with the building's use for parish work. Shoemaker therefore informed Buchman that the MRA-Oxford Group functions would have to move.

It is understandable that the two functions were competing for space and attention in a parish building. What was added to this, however, was Shoemaker's feeling that he must part ways with Buchman. His rationale was that MRA was concentrating on ideology while his church needed to concentrate on salvation of souls. Shoemaker focused the feeling of numerous people in the Oxford Group that MRA was something different and was on a runaway course that was not what they wanted. For Buchman, it seemed natural that a personal experience of God and Jesus Christ would lead one into thinking beyond oneself and working to see change come in the world.

However it was, at this point various people followed Shoemaker, Smith and others in declining to be drawn along with the work of MRA. Buchman found it excruciating to lose the close teamwork and fellowship with Shoemaker and the others, but he was clear in what he felt led to do; Shoemaker in effect parted company, and had little or nothing to do with MRA thereafter or with Buchman.

Jack and Connie found this very difficult to accept, because their experience of faith was so tied up with both Shoemaker and Buchman. Jack and Buchman exchanged several letters on the subject. Jack was serving on the vestry of Calvary Church at the time, as he had for several years.

From their new home on Massachusetts Avenue Jack wrote to Buchman on October 4, 1941, about driving south from Maine, stopping to see the headmaster at Groton School (which Franklin D. Roosevelt, Averell Harriman and others had attended). The letter continued: "Then we went on and spent the night at Calvary where the next morning I had breakfast with Sam and Jack Smith. My first intimation of the impending tragedy! I told them that I believed you were facing your greatest battle and that there could not be any defection. The Devil's greatest triumph in this generation would be to drive a wedge between you and Sam. It just can't happen. Someone must go to Canossa and there can't be any standing on ceremony.[1]

"Maybe you could both go together. I have now heard both sides, I love you both, and I am bold to say that neither of you are entitled to more than a Scotch verdict.[2] I told Sam that 'no one ever leaves this fellowship for the sake of the Kingdom of God' and I believe it is guided to remind you of what Christ had to say about forgiveness. For myself it has been coming strongly these days that we—and I especially—must deny ourselves the luxury of self-expression, that each one's talents must be used to drive home God's philosophy of change." Then Jack drew on the key scene from the revue *You Can Defend America* where each side realized there was blame on both sides and you had to start with yourself. And added that he would be in New York for a vestry meeting at Calvary and ready to do all he could to prevent a real rift. "Connie and I are both sick at heart over the prospects. . . . It just can't happen. And that's all there is to it."

Jack concluded this letter by reporting that John Roots, Arthur Meigs and he were finding a rich sense of fellowship together as they went about seeing key people in Washington "and are beginning to get together and to find under guidance the plan for each day." And he sent from the whole family "renewed assurances of our affection and gratitude."

Many people who had experienced Buchman's work over the years made the transition in their thinking and moved on with the concept of Moral Re-Armament. Quite a few did not. Eventually Jack and Connie came to understand that there were clear differences in what Buchman and Shoemaker felt commissioned by God to do. The Elys decided that their primary convictions lay with Buchman and Moral Re-Armament, and they reaffirmed in a letter to Frank that they shared his conviction and were with him for life.

On December 7, 1941, Japan attacked American bases at Pearl Harbor, the Philippines, and Wake Island. That afternoon the Ely family, who now lived across Massachusetts Avenue from the Japanese embassy, could see the embassy staff burning records in their garden. America was finally and fully into the war.

Much more could be said of this period, the war years. To many people today it comes as a surprise to learn that gasoline was rationed in the United States during World War II; that sugar was rationed, that meat was rationed. Automobile production for civilian purposes ceased in this country; you had to have a priority rating to buy tires. People today, after the utterly different experience of the Vietnam conflict—which itself is fading from memory—have no concept of a *total* war such as World War II. The Elys along with millions of patriotic countrymen practiced the stewardship of scarce commodities—gasoline, rubber, certain foods, even paper was in short supply. Day recalls that Connie would contrive to feed the many people staying at the home with ration books for just one household.

Florence, who was ten years old at the time of Pearl Harbor, remembers the war years as an exciting time: "What I loved was the sense that we were all needed, and that it counted, and we mattered. For instance, we all collected silver paper off sticks of gum. I think that was used to drop behind airplanes and confuse radar. Every Saturday my Girl Scout troop went to make beds in a gym that was used for soldiers who were in Washington for the weekend. We knit scarves for the soldiers out of khaki wool."

Then there was the draft. Brooks Onley had no birth certificate, and the date of his birth was in question. Jack went with him to the local draft board. "Brooks was born in 1901," Jack told them, "and that is attested to by the middle name his parents gave him—McKinley; McKinley took office as President in 1901; that's his birth date." The draft board accepted Jack's argument; Brooks was too old to be drafted.

There was the battle over whether to have the men who were working full-time with Moral Re-Armament exempted from the draft. Jack, John Roots, Ken Twitchell, Ray Purdy and others fought this issue for two years, with draft boards and the Selective Service administration and the War Manpower Commission. There were endless leads to follow, people to meet and cultivate. Their point was that these MRA men were doing service essential to the war effort and should be free to continue doing it, just as key industrial manpower were doing essential wartime service and were given exemption.

Jack's Yale classmate Truman Smith was intimately involved in the war manpower situation, and he and Jack saw a good bit of each other.[3] It was men like Smith, who began to have a thorough appreciation of what Moral Re-Armament was doing, who were often at the family home on Massachusetts Avenue for a talk or a meal. Others who shared this appreciation included John R. Steelman, director of the U. S. Conciliation Service, Senator Alexander Wiley of Wisconsin, Senator Francis Case of South Dakota, Senator Harry Truman of Missouri, Congressman James Wadsworth of New York. And most of these men came at times to the house with their wives. It was a confirming and vastly creative thing to have these couples spend an evening with Jack and Connie and the children. The Elys were a family whose solidarity was an inspiration to other people.

In mid-1942 the major part of the physically fit manpower of the Group—American, British, and from other European countries—was called up for the American draft. This made it impossible to continue to produce *You Can Defend America*, and the sixteen or seventeen states that were still clamoring for it had to be passed up. Many MRA men who were drafted served with distinction, and returned early after the cessation of war to continue their work with Buchman.

Jack, with his background of service in the Navy in World War I, looked for and found a way to serve in uniform in this conflict also. He became a member of the United States Coast Guard Auxiliary, which had a base at Eaton's Neck near Cold Spring Harbor. Mrs. Jennings had replaced the aging and old-fashioned yacht *Jock Scott*; Jack registered this new powerboat, *Jock Scott II*, as an auxiliary craft. The boat served continuously and Jack spent several days a month on duty on Long Island and patrolling Long Island Sound.

To render these coastal waters more dangerous for enemy operations, all buoys, lights and other aids to navigation had been removed, and often this auxiliary duty was to escort U.S. and allied ships safely through unmarked waters. There would usually be two or three men on each shift—Jack joked that he only had to be the cook once. Florence recalls, "One time Father didn't come home from his Coast Guard drill until thirty-six hours later. They had been patrolling where an aircraft had been shot down into the ocean—they knew a German U-boat would come and try to take the instrumentation off of it. Another time the boat Father was on found a German U-boat in Long Island waters."

Jack had to learn to use semaphore signals in order to get a promotion, and his daughters had to teach him. Florence says, "Day and I would be out there signaling back and forth to each other and trying to get Dad to learn. We learned semaphore, we learned Morse code. Day and I could do Morse code with our ears!"

Sometimes the convoy that Jack's boat helped escort was led by Admiral Sir Edward Cochrane of the Royal Navy, whom Jack had met through their mutual work in MRA. Jack would arrange to be the one to go out to the Admiral's ship. Cochrane, who led many convoys across the Atlantic during these years, would stay at the Ely home when he was in Washington between journeys. He provided an invaluable link with friends in Europe, many of them now in the "underground" on the Continent, and others in Britain. Florence remembers, "We would go scrounging and standing in endless lines to obtain stuff to send to England and France and Holland, to the underground. It was a thrilling time!" By 1943, however, after MRA's draft-age men had been inducted into the armed forces, Jack ceased his Coast Guard activities to give priority to the work of Moral Re-Armament.

Day remembers that after the fall of France in 1940 the Elys heard from the family of Claire Weiss, a French girl her age, and from the Baroness de Watteville. The Baroness told how if they had a lump of sugar they saved it for bedtime because it was so cold and it was easier to fall asleep if they had energy from sugar. She wrote too how difficult it was to get along without soap. "These stories really stuck in our heads and hearts," Day recalls.

The family moved to Elyston for the summer all through the war; sometimes they went to Burrwood for Christmas, but they would stay with

Mrs. Jennings rather than open up Elyston for that short time; they kept the house on Massachusetts Avenue open as well. It had become very much the nerve-center for the MRA work, with three telephone lines. The Elys built a large room behind the library to use for office work—to be the "chancery" of which Jack had written to Buchman. It had six or seven desks for typists and the preparation of letters, news releases, reports and so on. Three telephone lines do not sound like much for a busy place today, but the style of working in the 1940s was much more related to letters and memos than to the telephone.

Despite the demands of their increasingly busy lives, Connie saw to it that Day and Florence had the chance to enjoy what had always been one of her greatest pleasures—horseback riding. The ponies purchased in 1930 from Exmoor, Laura and Topsy, were brought to Washington and stabled in Rock Creek Park, near the Ely home. Sometimes the girls took school friends riding with them. Many weekends, until automobile travel was curtailed by gasoline rationing, they drove to Middleburg, Virginia, and rode horses that they boarded with the Sands, a family Connie had known since her days at Foxcroft. The Elys had purchased three horses: Hydrada, a big gray gelding for Jack; Melody, a chestnut mare for Connie, and Sheriff Downs, a small bay gelding for Day.

Driving back to Washington from Middleburg on Saturday afternoons, the family would tune the car radio to the New York Metropolitan Opera. "We heard and learned the music to dozens of operas over the four or five years that we went regularly to Middleburg," Day says. Music became an important part of the family's life: Florence played the cello and all the three girls played the recorder flute, inspired by the Trapp Family singers. Mary, who had perfect pitch, sang and played the violin. Often on Sunday evening the family and their guests would gather around the big piano in the living room and sing hymns and Scottish ballads.

The Ely children's reports from school in May of 1942 give some insight into what was the fruit of their life at home. Niel's report from nursery school is revealing about the little boy. "Determined to succeed at running and although somewhat awkward, enjoys and frequently indulges in it. Not interested in mechanical toys except the fire engine. Almost too independent. Does not call for aid even though occasionally mauled by other children. Will not cry unless really hurt. Very good expression. Clear, good vocabulary and construction of sentences, reasonable, logical. Attention span superior, is not easily diverted from chosen activity. Cooperative, self-reliant for so young a child, nice sense of humor!"

Mary's report from The Potomac School was equally positive. "Mary is her consistently thoughtful and considerate self. Whatever work she is doing, she maintains dignity and poise, and a thoroughly constructive attitude. She quietly plans what she will do and does it, only asking for help when she absolutely needs it. She is openly affectionate and lovable, gay, playful, with an active sense of humor. She is responsible not only for herself, but helps in the general cleaning up. Her relationship with other children is a natural and pleasant one. Mary deserves the greatest admiration for her thorough good sportsmanship, for her running, jumping, roller-skating and all the other activities that she has made her own through her splendid adjustment."

Florence was doing well at Potomac. Her report read, "Florence has been all year one of the most cooperative, dependable and responsible members of the class. I hope she realizes how much we depend upon her and that she will live up, as she has almost completely, to this trust."

Day's report said, "She seems to be withdrawing into her own world of ideas more rather than less. It is almost inevitable that a girl of her gifts should be individualist at heart, but she must live as a member of a group. She has so much to give her contemporaries, that for their sake as much as for her own she should make an effort to overcome her aloofness." A year later the school noted that "Day has taken a more active part in the class, both socially and in contributing to class discussions and problems. She takes suggestions well and carries them out."

Florence wrote to her mother, who was playing the part of "Mrs. Citizen" in *You Can Defend America* in Detroit that spring, "I am sending fifty cents to Uncle Frank [Buchman] for a birthday present. I biked five miles. Lots of love to 'Mrs. Citizen' from Florence Ely."

. . . .

NOTES

1. This is a reference to King Henry IV of Germany, who in 1077 ended a power struggle with Pope Gregory by standing in the snow, barefoot, before the Canossa castle in which the pope was staying. In 1871 German Chancellor Otto von Bismarck, in a struggle with the Catholic Church, defied the pope by saying, "Have no fear—to Canossa we shall not go…"

2. Jack draws upon the legal reference to Scotland's code of laws, in which in some cases a verdict of "not proven" can be handed down, hence an inconclusive or ambiguous pronouncement.

3. Truman Smith is one of those men, little known outside their own working circles, who poured out their lives for their country. A graduate of Yale, Class of 1915, and of a New England preparatory school before that, Truman Smith was very like Jack and the "wise

men" in his background and education. Smith's career was defined largely by the Army. He saw service on the Mexican border in 1916 and in World War I as an infantry officer, where his division took part in some of the war's severest battles. He then served with the 1918 army of occupation in Germany and was an author of the 1920 history of the military government in Germany. In the 1930s, Smith was assistant military attaché at the U.S. embassy in Berlin, where he was particularly concerned with intelligence. He returned to pursue further career steps in the Army.

10

To Win a War

MRS. HENRY FORD SUGGESTED, in early 1942, that MRA should have a place for unity-building conferences and suggested Mackinac Island, in northern Michigan, where three of the Great Lakes come together. The thought rapidly developed into action, and a vacant hotel on the island, the Island House, was made available. The first such conference at Mackinac took place in the summer of 1942.

In August 1942, Jack, Connie, Day and Florence took the train to Buffalo and boarded a lake steamer overnight to Detroit. Then an overnight boat for the 300-mile voyage north to Mackinac Island. Anna Hale and Peggy Bond were at Elyston with Mary and Niel, and Mrs. Jennings (Gar) looked in on them almost every day.

Anna kept Jack and Connie well informed with news from Cold Spring Harbor. She wrote of a study she and the children made of the Ten Commandments: "I asked Mary if she thought we ever had false gods. She said yes, and when I asked what they were, she thought a second and said 'ourselves.'"

This was the first of many summers the Elys spent on Mackinac Island. For the whole Ely family these were lively times. They took part in the detailed running of the conferences, the physical work as well as the planning and conducting of plenary meetings, small group meetings, training sessions, production of plays and films, and in the personal work that was the hallmark of MRA and the Oxford Group.

Day recalls, "When Mary and Niel were old enough to come to Mackinac, Mother sent up the little pony, Rainbow, given to her by Miss Charlotte Noland of Foxcroft when Niel was born. Brooks Onley came too and drove the pony cart. Brooks and Rainbow were available so that in spite of Mary and Niel's bad feet they could keep up with the other little children on that island, which had no motorized vehicles."

In a handwritten letter from Connie at her Washington home to Buchman, she comments on the wife of one of their close colleagues, who was reluctant to join her husband on a trip to the conference at Mackinac Island. Connie writes. "She does not see the adventure of life once one joins the firm 'giving unlimited.' Seeking the guided things among many, I had to give over many feelings about keeping Mary and Niel in the city, not getting to Mackinac at the time I thought the Lord wanted me to be there. But we are seeing lives changed and jobs done and God is very good in the lavish way he gives new feelings and desires."

Jack's mother, Maud, developed some serious gastrointestinal problems in the fall of 1942. Jack left Connie at Island House and went east to see her. Elinor came from Rochester to support her sister. Dr. Irene Gates had sent Maud to the hospital; leaving her in good hands, Irene went to serve as a doctor at Mackinac. Jack wrote from the Yale Club to Connie at Mackinac, "Tell Irene that there is no doubt of Mother's loyalty and her great confidence. I told her about the new book Irene is writing[1] and Mother is really interested to have it read to her. . . . Your mother sent some lovely flowers to the hospital."

In November 1942, the world force of Moral Re-Armament was deeply shaken by the news that Frank Buchman had suffered a severe stroke. He had gone with a few associates to Saratoga Springs, in upstate New York, to rest and to rethink the strategy of the work, when he collapsed. It was touch and go for several days, while people around the world prayed for him. At the Ely home all the family and the others there prayed together for him. Day recalls that prayers continued, twenty-four hours a day, in the small drawing room.

Buchman had a long, slow convalescence, with little energy. He dictated a letter to Jack and Connie in January, which expressed the hope that Jack would come see him in Saratoga when next he visited his mother in New York. "My visitors are rare," he wrote. "I have followed all your doings. . . . I hear the children had their friends in about the school play [which the MRA children had created] and it was a great success. This is one of my early letters, but you must know what a wealth of joy rests in my heart for you all. Believe me, Your loyal friend, Frank."

Jack replied, "It was a great family event to receive your letter, to know you are better, that our prayers for you have been answered, and that 'the truth goes marching on.' . . . Grateful for your guidance for this as an MRA embassy." He then named nine of Buchman's team who were currently staying in his home along with the family of six, Anna Hale, and several of the Elys' paid staff.

The exchange of letters was frequent, even though Buchman was so weak. A few weeks later Jack gave him an account of a trip to Richmond, during which he and Connie stayed with Mr. and Mrs. Blair Buck. Thirty years earlier, Blair Buck as a young man had been at the center of Buchman's "laboratory" work in changing lives at Pennsylvania State University,[2] and was still faithful to what he had experienced in those days.

Jack wrote a poem, "Thanksgiving—1942":

For homes where love abounds
And people learn "to neighbor" once again.
Where from the children's room there float down sounds
Of friendly voices, sharing joy and pain.
For such faith citadels,
Safe from man's sword,
We thank Thee, Lord!

For teamwork in the nation's industry
And a new caring, conquering hate and greed,
As boss and worker learn how to agree
And work as one to meet the nation's need.
For such a business world,
Forging war's sword,
We thank Thee, Lord!

For a united nation, free and strong,
Turning again to God for her true course;
Seeking how best to banish every wrong;
Filled with repentance, not passing remorse.
For what our country may be,
Saved by Thy sword,
We thank Thee, Lord!

In the spring of 1943, Jack and Connie visited Buchman in North Carolina where he was recuperating. Afterwards Connie thanked him for this visit with a note giving him news of some of his friends in the Washington area. She continued, "You will doubtless be remembered as the man who amongst other things brought to this country the civilizing influence of Afternoon Tea, and so we have sent you a little something to keep it going." Perhaps she sent some choice tea leaves, or it may have been a check to help with expenses.

This sentiment stretched the truth a bit, as Connie knew full well that her own family had been not only Anglophiles but also regular afternoon tea drinkers long before Frank Buchman ever set foot in England!

An especially happy event took place at the Ely home early in 1943. Their friend Jim Newton, now a captain in the Army, had asked Eleanor "Ellie" Forde to marry him. Ellie had been, since 1926, one of Buchman's most trusted workers, and Jim had known her almost since that time. The Elys offered to have the wedding and the reception in their home. It was not that they wouldn't have had the wedding in a church, but Jim wanted to have his close friend, Charles Lindbergh, as his best man, and he knew that Charles would be shy of the press if the wedding were held in such a public place. (The Lindberghs had been wary of publicity ever since their little boy had been kidnapped and murdered before the war, and because of Charles's treatment by the press over his statements about the German war potential.)

Jim went to Detroit, where Lindbergh was working as a consultant to Henry Ford on the production of the B-24 bomber, and talked over the wedding plans. Charles learned that the reception would be catered, which to him meant more employees around and the probability that the word would get out that he was involved. So Jim went back to Washington and arranged that the ceremony itself would take place in private at the home of Van and Migs Rickert, another family close to MRA. Willard Hunter stood by with Jack Ely's Buick convertible, and when the ceremony was over he whisked Charles away and the main party went on for the reception to the Ely residence on Massachusetts Avenue.[3]

The extended family at "2419," as the Elys' home was often called, was fully involved in the campaign to focus America's thinking on how to build unity in the effort to win the war and create a lasting peace. A play by Alan Thornhill, *The Forgotten Factor*, dramatized the industrial struggle and its solution in the story of a management family and a labor leader's family, where the two men were locked in a labor dispute.[4] The "forgotten factor" entered the picture when one of the men listened to the voice of his conscience that told him he needed to change—for his family and for his work. The play's simple message was, "It's not who is right, but what is right."

The Forgotten Factor moved people very deeply. It was to have its formal premiere at the National Theatre in Washington in November 1943, with Senator Harry Truman (Democrat) and Congressman James Wadsworth (Republican) as its sponsors. Truman and Wadsworth were so keen on the play and its message reaching the leadership in Washington that they wrote a thousand individual letters to the people they had in mind.

The Ely home was a nerve center for this campaign. Night after night, volunteer secretaries worked until two or three o'clock in the morning typing these individual letters, on manual typewriters. In that era before computers or even electric machines, a mistake meant starting afresh on a clean sheet of paper. The letters would be rushed each morning to Truman's and Wadsworth's offices for signing and delivering, and more letters would come back to the home to be typed. Because of this concern and effort, at least 300 members of Congress were in the audience for the premiere. Subsequently, *The Forgotten Factor* was presented in many of the cities where *You Can Defend America* had played as well as in others the revue had not had time to reach.

Jack Ely was one of a growing number of men who were working with management in America to inject the "what's right" philosophy into human affairs. Jack was not "management" per se; he represented capital. He found great teammates in the men of industry who were rallying to this concept. One of Buchman's longtime associates, Charles Huston Haines, had done his stint at his family's steel mill, Lukens Steel in Pennsylvania. His father had invented the Haines gauge for measuring the thickness of steel plate while the rolling mill was operating. Charles and Jim Newton, who had worked for eight years as Harvey Firestone's right-hand man, decided that they needed to take the message of MRA and the Oxford Group to top management. The group also included, among others, Parks Shipley, a partner in the international banking house of Brown Brothers Harriman; George Eastman of Los Angeles, a building materials executive; and Bernard Hallward of Canada, a paper-products manufacturer.

Jack's main work, however, was in maintaining and developing contacts and friendships in Washington. Truman Smith came repeatedly to consult with Jack and the others at the Ely home, and Smith and his wife Kay and Jack and Connie frequently had meals together. John R. Steelman and his wife Emma spent time with them, as did members of Congress, and military men.

Willard Hunter, who had driven Lindbergh away after the Newton wedding, worked closely with Jack at this time. Willard recalled that Smith would say to Jack, "How's everything going in Hotel Ely?" Willard saw that Smith had a high regard for Jack. "He seriously wanted Jack to go to North Africa in intelligence," Willard recounted, "because Jack could speak and understand French, and Smith was concerned about America's checkbook diplomacy—not very much understanding but we felt we could buy our way. He thought Jack could get him better information."

Among the wartime residents at the Ely home was A.R.K. "Archie" Mackenzie, a Scotsman in the British Diplomatic Service who had met Buchman and his people at Oxford and had made a decision to let his life be used by God. During the war he was doing political intelligence work for his government, and in that capacity spent the years 1943 to 1945 in Washington.

In 1996, Archie Mackenzie, now retired on the shore of Loch Lomond in Scotland, shared these thoughts on the Ely family: "My first impression was of their courage, vis-à-vis their own 'class,' standing for this thing they'd found that wasn't universally popular with the establishment. They brought all of us into their home—Duncan Corcoran, a Clydeside shipyard worker, Adam McLean, an auto mechanic, Sam Reid, myself—Jack and Connie were absolutely straight with their own class.

"They could have enjoyed their delightful family home just for themselves, but it was used all the time and for a purpose. We must have been a potentially disrupting force, yet I can never remember feeling that from them. They were really remarkable in their generosity.

"Jack and Connie were dedicated to the thing they had found in their own lives and making it available to America and to the world. I have the sense that they didn't spend much money on themselves in separate or private ways. They accepted sacrifice and discipline for what they believed in.

"They were obviously a happy family. There were many problems to face because of the younger children's health, but they were all wonderfully buoyant. It never seemed to make them turn inwards, they were always on the give. Connie did so many things in that high society set of Washington, which we would never have reached otherwise."

In May 1944, Granny Ely—Maud Merchant Ely—died of cancer in New York. In her final years Maud had had a lovely apartment at 220 Madison Avenue, paid for by Jack and Connie.

During those years Maud had gone through a transformation. In her earlier illness, in 1942, she had been the bane of the hospital staff, so demanding and complaining that they tried to avoid going in to answer her often-ringing bell. When Maud was recovering from that hospitalization, she had stayed with the Elys in Washington. Connie sensed that Maud was afraid, and took pains to be so open and empathetic with her that she would talk about her fears. What came out was that Maud was afraid to die because in the next life, in front of God, her husband would see all her sins and she would feel naked. She didn't want all her sins known, especially her infidelities. Connie said, "But God loves you and he'll forgive you and those things won't even be with you when you get to Heaven."

Maud arrived at a complete sense of forgiveness. When she went into the hospital for the last time, she was such a pleasure to serve that the nurses were competing to work with her.

Few people ever realized that for all those earlier years Maud had been nasty to Connie. The gossip columnist had often alluded to the fact that she could be terribly catty with the social set on Long Island; she would cut someone to shreds with cruel and witty remarks, when the object of her scorn was not present. But in her last years Maud had become sympathetic about the work Jack and Connie were doing. A few months before her death, when she was facing an operation, Jack had written to Buchman, "She prayed beforehand for your complete healing and the work."

Elizabeth Arden's biographer says that when Maud was in her final illness, Elizabeth "had overcome her dislike of hospitals to visit her every day, bringing along a flask of scotch. Maudie had smiled, 'No ice.'"

After the funeral service for Maud, the family took the train for Rochester with her casket. They held a memorial service in St. Paul's Church where she had been married, and she was buried beside her husband and two of her sons, near her parents and others of her family in Mt. Hope Cemetery.

Jack and Connie maintained Maud's New York apartment until 1955; it was most useful for the family and for people of MRA during those years. Connie kept a supply of postage stamps on the desk in the apartment labeled "For general use. Note: we are all generals."

Maud had kept in her apartment a cherished collection of things Napoleonic, including prints, paintings, busts and figurines of Napoleon Bonaparte, medallions, commemorative plates, mugs and other memorabilia. When it no longer seemed economical to maintain the apartment, Jack and Connie sent the Napoleon collection to the Louisiana State Museum in New Orleans—the one part of the United States that Napoleon had ever owned. The collection of fifty-five items is housed with other important Napoleonic materials in The Cabildo, on Jackson Square.

The Ely family home in these war years had become a world center for the work of Moral Re-Armament. This meant that certain bedrooms were for the family, on the second floor, with a special one there for Frank Buchman when he should visit. The third floor had several bedrooms that were used much of the time for people associated with the work of MRA.

The house was full. Some lived in the house, like Mary Lou Merrill, a young Vassar graduate who kept the letters and reports and other work flowing. Others might spend a day or two there while some important activity was going on in town; and the men who went into military service might have a few days off to come and visit. A stream of people! Sometimes Jack or Connie would say, "I never know when I go down to breakfast how many people will be there."

Jack Ely took a particular interest in all those service men he had gotten to know as they had worked with MRA. He put together a regular newsletter to all of them, to tell them how the moral and spiritual battle was going and to keep the sense of fellowship and support alive for them. There would be news from across America and from men like Admiral Sir Edward Cochrane, of the British Navy, who would bring reports of what was going on in Britain, and sometimes news smuggled to Britain from occupied France and Norway, Denmark, Holland and Belgium.

The four children took special notice of the service men. Niel would straighten his little body as best he could and ask his father or mother if he were walking like a soldier. The warm-hearted quality of the boy went straight to the hearts of these men who had a few moments or a day or two off from the grim business of preparing and conducting the war effort.

Connie, who had learned from her mother the skills of maintaining a gracious home, maintained her house in that manner. In the spring the curtains were changed, slipcovers went on the upholstered furniture, and all the rugs were changed. The solid doors of the bedrooms were changed for louvered three-quarter-length doors to give air circulation in the hot summer.[5] In the fall the process was reversed. Maintenance was done regularly, by their staff, and by outside contractors as needed.

The Ely children took part in the practical running of the house, along with Connie and the servants. "We learned how to do the laundry with Bertha Carter," Florence recounts. "And we learned how to repair the fine linens from Annie Stewart, an Irish woman who would spend the winter with us. She would teach us how to repair the lace on the place mats and the tablecloths. We learnt what was appropriate to use when—the difference between damask, cotton, and so forth. We used cloth place mats at dinner, and there was no 'drip dry' in those days. Everything had to be washed, starched, and ironed.

"Everybody's beds got a clean top sheet on Saturday, and a clean pillow-case. The used top sheet became the bottom sheet—fitted bottom sheets had not yet been invented. Father taught us how to make a bed military style. If a sheet got frayed in the middle—this was before polyester—we split it down the old fragile middle and brought the sturdy side selvages together to the middle and sewed one flat long seam from top to bottom. The worst parts were cut off. The sheet was narrower and lost its monogram, but could be used for another five or ten years. The same with the bath towels. Nothing was wasted.

"Each room in the house, even a closet, had a number by the hinge at the door. The blankets that were meant to be in that bedroom also had a number on them. You never wasted anything: that was drummed into us from early days. We were stewards of what we had. Though we may have been entrusted with a great deal, we didn't own it, we were stewards of it."

There were changes in the kitchen. Mamie Shellington, the treasured family cook, developed severe diabetes and had to retire. Her niece, Harriet Jackson Addison, who had come to the Elys as chambermaid, took over the cooking. Day remembers: "Mother and Harriet became close friends and Mother discovered that Harriet had been trained as a cook, but that her last employer had been so critical and difficult that Harriet nearly had a nervous breakdown and decided never to cook professionally again. Mother was always appreciative of all good work and it was not long before Harriet began to feel safe again."

Harriet's reign in the kitchen "was a triumph for all concerned," according to Day: "Harriet trained me in running a household. She was very strict on protocol. She felt it made people feel safe to know that things would go in an orderly way. She taught me how to plan menus that would stretch, how to provide food that everyone in the house would enjoy." Ultimately, three of Harriet's sisters also worked at the home. Day and Florence considered the Jackson sisters an integral part of the family.

There was no attempt to shield the children from all the activity at the house at 2419. Living at the center of what they came to see as a world family lifted all of life—even Mary's and Niel's physical limitations—to a different plane. Anna made it her business to see that Mary and Niel had what they needed. Both of them had repeated medical problems, involving surgery, leg braces, medications. Both of them, while being full of life and energy, had fearful physical disabilities to cope with, and they coped with great spirit.

Guests were included at the family meals with all the children. Day tells this story: "One time when Niel was not yet in first grade and still ate lunch at home, Mother had several lady guests at the lunch table. Niel ate hungrily and listened to the talk. It was not really a conversation, as one woman complained endlessly about all the bad things that mechanics, servants, family and friends had done to her. No one else could get a word in edgewise. Finally she drew breath and Niel looked at her with his huge blue eyes and said, 'Did you not know that when you point one finger at your neighbor, you point three back at yourself?' Then Mother and others could start her to think about a new way to live."

It occurred to the family that Niel needed a dog to be his special friend. Beryl Evans recalls, "I returned from the farmer's market one Saturday with an apparently healthy, short-haired brown and white puppy in a paper bag that had been found by a lady on the street. After inspection by Jack and Connie, it was presented to a delighted Niel. They became inseparable."

Niel declared, "Her name is Rumpus." Connie trained Rumpus to be a harmonious part of the household. "The first week we had Rumpus," Day remembers, "Mother kept her tied to herself day and night and taught her what to do, such as lying under the tall chest in the hall during meals. Mother said that if you make it clear to a dog what is appropriate, then you have a happy dog, as dogs love to please you." Later on, at one point, Rumpus dashed out into the street as the front door opened for someone, and was hit by a car. She was rushed to the vet and her life was saved, but for some days she had to be carried upstairs, and Beryl remembers Connie gently doing that.

Most of those who came to work, and especially those who came to stay at the family home, took care to respect it as just that, a family home in which they were privileged to be included. Some, like Mary Lou Merrill and Willard Hunter, became very dear to the family. Mary Lou is the only person who has mentioned that at this time in his life Jack had trouble with ulcers. She says that in the months she worked with the family she regularly brought Jack a glass of milk to help soothe his stomach.

Willard Hunter was working with Jack and others to cultivate their relationships with people in the government and in the Congress, "on the Hill." When he was drafted into the Army the family followed his progress closely. When he graduated from Officer Candidate School nearby they were all at the graduation. Connie spoke of Willard over the years with real affection. And when the day came soon after the war was over that Willard proposed to Mary Lou, the Elys took that as a family affair. The wedding took place at the Merrills' vacation home in Michigan; they were all there helping, and Mary and Niel were "flower persons."

The Ely's extended family also included Arthur and Ellen Lee Meigs. Arthur had married Ellen Lee Blackwell of Richmond, Virginia, a beautiful young woman who was a close friend of Connie's. One fall after the Mackinac conference, Ellen Lee came to help Connie with all the practical details at the house. As Day describes it, this was "a move on faith on Ellen Lee's part, as she had never done any housekeeping before, certainly not with ration stamps, for a household of twenty people. She and Arthur were always part of our family as long as we lived in Washington."

Over the years, Connie and Jack maintained a strong bond with Frank Buchman as a man they trusted and loved. They saw the way he interacted with people, the way he exercised leadership, the way he lived and worked by faith and prayer, and especially the very genuine way he cared for them as individuals. This was care, not control. Being people of immense wealth, they had to learn by experience that this man was not after their money; Buchman was a real friend, and as time went by they came to trust that his concern was for how they accepted God's demands on them, not his own.

One outcome was that, as the work grew and as the years went by, Connie and Jack gave to the work of MRA with extreme generosity. The federal tax laws provided that if for ten years one gave to charity a sum equal to 90 percent of one's income, and after ten years continued to do so, then from the eleventh year on one would not need to pay annual federal income taxes. For twenty-five years Jack and Connie complied with that law by their gifts of capital to MRA.[6]

In these growing-up years, Day and Florence noticed that their mother, Connie, a vigorous, active and keen-minded woman, was learning what it meant to live to see her husband fulfill his potential. This was not a thing to be taken lightly. Connie had the spirits, the energy, the quick mind—and the money—to be and do anything she wanted. Through the years, as in the early episode of who would drive the car, Connie moved from what she herself wanted to what her prayerful relationship to God told her was important for her *and* her husband. She bent over backwards to see that Jack was not reminded that their wealth was hers; and indeed, she had asked him to manage it, and he did so very well.

Beryl Evans had a glimpse into their relationship. "Once," she said, "when anticipating Jack's return from a trip, Connie said to me, 'I'm a woman of strong emotions. Need I say more?'"

Parenting skills did not seem to come naturally to Jack. "Dad was kind of stiff with us when we were young because he had really had no loving childhood," Day recalls. She remembers a startlingly welcome revelation when she was about twelve, in 1940. They were at Elyston, and Day had invited a friend from school to stay with them for two weeks. The girl's attitude to life turned out to be very different from her own: "After three or four days, she had gone to bed, and I was so upset about having ten more days of this that I wanted to cry. I went off to find Mother or Anna, and they were out somewhere. I wandered through the rooms and found my father in his den. To my intense surprise, his was a good shoulder to cry on. I can remember being so surprised. He took me on his lap—great big tall and skinny, five foot eight I was—and I cried on his shoulder and he mopped me up with one of his big handkerchiefs. I can still remember what a happy revelation that was."

There was not always perfect harmony, no matter how deep the commitment. Connie, according to Beryl Evans, had misgivings about her husband's preoccupation with photographs. Several people in the full-time work of MRA made a point of recording events and people in pictures. Jack saw that as a way he too could help, and he loved doing it. He was an artistic person with few outlets for this facet of his nature, except photography. He maintained good photographic equipment, and carried it with him much of the time. Connie would be frustrated sometimes with Jack taking pictures when she felt he should be giving his attention to the people instead of being preoccupied with photographing them.

Yet, Day and Florence have said they were able to watch the relationship between father and mother mellow and grow year by year, as they sought to live out, together, their individual commitment to God's will. One of the impressive and moving things about the Ely family was their unity of purpose. Father, Mother, Day, Florence, Mary, Niel: as time went on all six of them took "the race with time to remake men and nations" as their common and individual goal.

The Elys had a Christmas tradition that typified the way the family lived. After decorating their tree and the house, some boxes of decorations were left nearby, so that everyone who came in during the days before Christmas could add something to the tree. Everyone could feel included—guests, postman, delivery boys—anyone who came to the house.

. . . .

Notes

1. Irene Gates, *Any Hope, Doctor?* (London: Blandford Press, 1954).

2. See Garth Lean, *On the Tail of a Comet* (previously cited), and the MRA video *Pickle Hill.*

3. For a full account of Newton's remarkable friendship with Charles Lindbergh, see James Newton, *Uncommon Friends*, previously cited.

4. Alan Thornhill, Fellow and Chaplain of Hertford College, Oxford, priest of the Church of England, and long-time colleague of Dr. Buchman, wrote a number of plays, including *The Forgotten Factor*, which was performed in many languages on five continents.

5. As in most houses in America in the 1940s, there was no air conditioning at the Ely residence. Air conditioning came into widespread use only after World War II.

6. This provision of the federal tax law no longer obtains.

THE ELY HOME ∴ WASHINGTON

The comfort of Christ is in this place,
His liquid love o'erflowing.
The cleansing healing springs of grace
Pour out beyond our knowing.

Yes, heaven meets earth in homes like this,
In each heart CHRIST abided.
In life, in death, through pain and bliss
God's folk are undivided.

Gratefully
Peter

After one of his many visits in their home, Peter Howard wrote this poem for Jack and Connie

11

To Win a Peace

ALMOST A YEAR BEFORE THE FALL OF the Third Reich, MRA began to put into place its plan to participate in the rebuilding of Europe. The genesis of what happened in 1944 was a thought that came to Philippe Mottu, of Geneva, in the spring of 1942. "If Switzerland survives the war," was Mottu's thought, "we must put at Frank Buchman's disposal a place where the people of Europe, now divided by hatred, suffering and bitterness, can come together again. Caux is the place."

Jack and Connie Ely were involved intimately and fully in the story that follows. Jack's whole life had been a preparation for this. His upbringing, his connections, his wife's fortune, his training, all were used to help reshape Europe and influence the course of history. Although it is Jack's part that is emphasized here, in reality it was both of them, the combination of their lives together.

In the spring of 1944, Mottu, then with the Swiss Foreign Office at Berne, received a telegram from Buchman inviting him and his wife, Hélène, to the United States to confer on plans for when the war should be over. Mottu's boss, Swiss Foreign Minister Marcel Pilet-Golaz, said after he had read the telegram, "Why not?" The "why not" included the difficulty of traveling to the United States from the heart of Western Europe, in the grip of a ferocious war in which the U.S. was on one side and Germany and Italy were on the other, and all of France was occupied territory.

Adam von Trott, a German diplomat who was a dear friend of Mottu's, visited Mottu at his home a few days later. He undertook to get the Mottus, as neutral Swiss citizens, a safe conduct pass to Stuttgart, from whence they were able to fly to Spain and on to Lisbon. Alan Dulles, at that time head of American intelligence services in Europe, was headquartered in Bern, and he was able to help. When the Mottus stepped off the plane in Lisbon, Dulles' men met them and escorted them to the Pan American Clipper bound for New York.[1]

Von Trott's major motive in making arrangements for them was to enable Mottu to carry to the United States government a detailed description of the plot against Hitler, in which von Trott was a key player. He gave Mottu a full exposition of the identity of the planning group and of their strategy for Germany. Sadly, von Trott was rounded up after the plot failed a few weeks later, and was executed along with several hundred others. In aiding the Mottus, his life was used in the long run to forward the cause of healing the wounds of the war, even though he lost his life in the process.

Von Trott had given Mottu specific details of the assassination plot and who was involved in it because the plotters wanted President Roosevelt and the Allies to understand the dimension of the plan and the depth of dissatisfaction among key Germans with the Nazi regime. They wanted to sound out if there were any way this information could be used in the conduct of the war and to assist the plotters.

The Mottus arrived in the U.S. in mid-June, shortly after the Allied invasion of Normandy. Their first task was to go to Washington, where Jack and Connie received them into their home to use as a base from which to accomplish their mission. It was a busy time at the house, with the many people who came and were entertained there. It must have been stimulating for guests to be able to hear from Philippe and Hélène of their current experiences from the heart of Europe. While they were in Washington, nine-year-old Mary was admitted to the hospital for an operation. Sharing both these wartime experiences and intimate family crises served to bring Jack and Connie closer to the Mottus.

Philippe had meetings with the War Department and State Department, which he found frustrating because the United States government was not interested in the plot to assassinate Hitler. The U.S. apparently did not trust who in Germany might assume power if Hitler were eliminated. The mentality was that the Germans were all Nazis at heart; complete military defeat and unconditional surrender were the objectives of the Allies. Mottu's impression also was that President Roosevelt and his men did not think that the conspirators could destroy National Socialism from within, and that the Allies would need to destroy it from without.

Whether or not a thorough study of the information Mottu brought to Washington would have made a difference in the war's progress and in the post-war period, we will never know. The unsuccessful bomb plot took place on July 20.

The Mottus' next steps definitely did have a key effect on post-war Europe. They journeyed to the MRA center on Mackinac Island. There they spent several weeks conferring with Buchman and his key people, and studying what it would involve to set up a "Mackinac" in Europe.

The conference at Mackinac was in full swing. The quiet consultations about the future took place during an assembly that involved industrialists, labor leaders, people from the government, Americans—and Canadians—of all descriptions. Connie's diaries detail how she served on a cooking shift preparing meals for 600 people almost every day, and how the Elys were in the thick of the work of giving the perspective of Moral Re-Armament to countless individuals. They would do this over meals, or would give their convictions from the speakers' platform in the daily plenary sessions, or during walks in the beauty of the island and in other personal encounters. At the same time, she and Jack were back and forth between Mackinac and Washington, working to bring people to the island and to make sure people in the capital got the story of what was developing there.

That summer of 1944, Chicago was the site of both the Republican and Democratic national conventions. Jack Ely, Howard Davison and Brewster Bingham, all Yale men with connections to Republican Party leaders, were there for the GOP convention in late June. All three stayed at the Racquet Club. Jack wrote to Connie, "With a developing faculty of acquiring new friends, I picked up an amazing giant of a man, seven feet tall, in the waiting room. He turned out to be Prof. W. K. Winnsatt, of Yale, who teaches English to the Navy V-12s [a college-based program for training officers for the Navy in World War II], a fellow member with me of the Yale Elizabethan Club. He had an amazing fund of misinformation about MRA. We had luncheon with him. Howard and I found ourselves at this club the guests of Mr. Walter Palpke (your friend's hubby) who is head of the Container Co. . . .

"After almost a week in this perfect club, with the acme of service, a tennis court in the building where I beat Howard, and luscious steaks, and griddle cakes and sausages!, I'm moving down to the Stevens Hotel to be more in the thick of things."

In mid-July Jack was again in Chicago with others, for the Democratic National Convention; President Roosevelt was nominated for an unprecedented fourth term. As many "insiders" were aware, the crucial issue within the Democratic Party was the choice of a vice-presidential candidate; the President was seriously ailing, and it was more than likely that he would not live out his new term of office. Senator Harry Truman was nominated over a number of more prominent prospects.

Several years later Jack wrote to his friend Ray Purdy regarding Ray's constant thought for Harry Truman, who was now nearing the end of his first term in the White House. Jack cast back over their connection with Truman, which had begun during the time that *You Can Defend America* and *The Forgotten Factor* toured cities vital to the production of war materials. Senator Truman had made his first real impact in Washington by his detailed monitoring of federal spending on war production. Jack wrote to Ray Purdy that he was "more than ever convinced that he [Truman] would never be in his present position had it not been for the help he had from you and others during the years."

The letter reviewed some of the ways Purdy and others had worked with Truman: "Bill Jaeger, you will remember [an MRA colleague specializing in the labor movement] prepared the way for Truman's first talk to the United Auto Workers in Detroit, where he was given the opportunity to win the confidence of organized labor." At the 1940 Democratic Convention, Jack continued, Truman "was none too sanguine about his chances in the November [senatorial] election and told me at that time that he would rather have you as his campaign manager than anyone else in the country."

The war in Europe ended with the German surrender on May 7, 1945. As soon thereafter as they could, later in the summer, a delegation of Swiss, English, French and Dutch made the trip to Mackinac Island. Transatlantic transportation was swamped with demand, but the travelers managed it. Philippe Mottu, Robert Hahnloser, and Erich and Emily Peyer were among the group. These Swiss became the nucleus that made the acquisition of Caux possible. Hahnloser was an engineer from a wealthy and distinguished family; Peyer was a soldier and lawyer working with personnel in industry. At Mackinac they took time to think together with the others for the next steps for post-war Europe. From the assembly most of them went with Buchman and his team to California, where they were engaged in further work in the Los Angeles area.

By late July of 1946 there was a full-blown conference at the former Caux Palace, the newly acquired property of Moral Re-Armament, high on the mountainside above Lake Geneva. The sacrificial giving that had characterized the lives of Connie and Jack Ely for the past years was replicated by hundreds of Swiss and other Europeans. They emptied their pockets to make the purchase of Caux possible, and people from all over Europe spent thousands of man-hours working to put the place in order.

Jack spent at least part of that summer in Europe, in Caux and London. He returned by ship in mid-November.

In Buchman's mind, his team's astounding feat of acquiring and readying what they had christened "Mountain House" at Caux was no reason to dwell on their accomplishments. His eye was on the purpose. On his arrival at Caux, his first question was, "Where are the Germans?" That was a revolutionary question at the time, because the victims of German aggression had no desire to meet their former conquerors.

Many persons, groups, and forces played a role in the rebuilding of a new Europe that included a new Germany. Moral Re-Armament's key role in the reconciliation of France and Germany has been discussed by Edward N. Luttwak in *Religion, the Missing Dimension of Statecraft*.[2] Luttwak examines what happened in the five or six years following Buchman's question about the absent Germans. Jack, Connie, Day, and Florence were in Europe for much of that time, and Mary and Niel for one summer also.

From 1946 to 1950, 3,113 Germans and 1,983 French citizens took part in these MRA assemblies. Because of European politics, the acts of reconciliation that took place there between German and French are perhaps the most notable, but the healing of hurts between Germans and Dutch, Belgians, Norwegians, Danes, English and others were every bit as important. This was an extension of what Buchman's team, including Jack and Connie, had been doing all along: relating to individuals, their needs and aspirations, their hurts, their relationships, and helping them to get in touch with that spark of God in each one.

The outreach from Caux was tremendous. Italians came in large numbers. A breakthrough occurred in 1948, when the Occupation Forces allowed the first Japanese to come, a high-level delegation of the cream of that country's government, business, industry, and labor leaders. Soon all of Asia was represented at Caux, as was South America and a great cross section of Africa. Caux became a place where people could realistically conceive of a world without colonialism, without Communism, without hate and bitterness, without repression of any kind.

As this is written in the summer of 1997, we are celebrating fifty years since the United States embarked upon the Marshall Plan. It required a major shift in thinking for America to undertake to finance the rebuilding of war-torn Europe. Franklin Roosevelt's Secretary of the Treasury, Henry Morgenthau, had proposed that the Allies make of Germany an agrarian economy, devoid of industrial production. We can be thankful that that view did not prevail. Jack Ely was one who saw in that idea the clear signs of World War III. He fought vigorously for a positive attitude toward Germany's part in Europe's future, as did many others. In a world where one often says, "Don't we ever learn from history?" the attitude of the victors toward Germany after World War II, compared with the punitive attitude after World War I, is a striking example of a lesson learned.

In 1947, MRA designed and produced a musical pageant called *The Good Road*, which used some of the simple themes of *You Can Defend America* to point out how people could start with themselves. It went on to dramatize the spiritual heritage of our civilization and how in its roots we had the source of the good road for all mankind, East and West alike. Several dozen young Europeans were in the cast, along with Americans and Canadians.

The Good Road was designed for a world-wide audience; in America it had the effect of inspiring this country to be a creative part of the new postwar world, along with the other nations, and to influence Congress to enact the Marshall Plan which was under debate at that moment. *The Good Road* played in Washington, and brought into the theater hundreds of men and women of the Washington government establishment, as well as of the Congress.

Jack's correspondence brims over with the many facets of this battle in Washington. In one letter to Ray Purdy, in May 1947, he writes of visits with Governor Kim Sigler of Michigan and with a general who was a close associate of Generalissimo Chiang Kai-shek. He describes a private dinner at the Metropolitan Club, where Philip Marshall Brown was the host, which included Representative John Vorys of Ohio, Senator H. Alexander Smith of New Jersey, Benjamin Cohen of the State Department, General U.S. Grant III, and several others. "Cohen," Jack wrote to Purdy, "just back with Secretary of State George Marshall, spoke informally, off the record, and gave us a graphic picture of the difficulty of dealing with the top Soviet leadership. I have seldom heard such a clear exposition of Slavic psychology. Some of his thoughts, which showed a real comprehension of the war of ideas, I have incorporated into an article for *New World News*, [MRA's monthly publication].

"John Vorys, just returned from the inter-parliamentary conference at Cairo followed by a trip to Ankara and Athens, complemented Cohen's statements about the difficulty of reaching agreement with the Russians. John found that the Soviets checked any constructive action at Cairo by the obstructionist tactics of their Balkan satellites. I was asked to speak on the situation as I found it in Western Europe, and tried to give them a picture of the war of ideas as we have seen it developing. It gave me an opportunity to talk with Cohen later."

The war of ideas between Communism and Democracy for the hearts and minds of people everywhere was very real in those days. There is a general consensus today that the Marshall Plan was critical to shaping the post-war history of Western Europe, both through its investment of money and material, and through the psychological boost it offered to the war-torn nations.

This is precisely why Jack Ely belongs among the ranks of the "wise men" of this land. He never held a position of importance with the federal government or served in an official advisory capacity. Yet, in choosing to commit his life to God's direction, Jack was as surely focused on the destiny of the world as were any of the six individuals described as "wise men" in the book by Isaacson and Thomas.[3] While Averell Harriman, Charles ("Chip") Bohlen, Dean Acheson, John McCloy, George Kennan and Robert Lovett were creating policy, Jack and his friends were building the living reality, life after life, across Europe and America, creating the conditions that would enable policy to succeed.

Jack and Connie were not the only family members to commit their time to the world-remaking program of Moral Re-Armament in these post-war years. After Day graduated from National Cathedral School in 1946, she went with the family to Mackinac Island for the conference there. The teenage MRA play *The Drugstore Revolution* was being performed as part of the conference, and Day took part in it back-stage. In the fall the people of MRA took to the road again with several plays to tour Michigan and the East, including *The Drugstore Revolution*. Day listened to God daily as had become her habit, and felt it was clear she should go with the play. Her parents were in accord with her convictions, and Day spent her eighteenth year putting on the play and sharing her convictions with students all across the United States and Canada.

Jack's work was much facilitated when in March of 1947 Beryl Evans offered to be his secretary. Beryl had decided to give her full time to MRA without salary, as did all the full-time workers. She was a fine secretary and typist; the idea was that Jack could be even more effective in his work if someone were directly working with him, so he wouldn't need to type his own massive correspondence. Jack invested in one of the first electric typewriters, a move Day regards as stewardship of strength, since research has shown that pounding a manual typewriter eight hours a day is the equivalent of pushing a truck several miles! Beryl became part of the Ely family, and lived and worked closely with them for the next eight years.

Jack was also endeavoring, with Ken Twitchell and others, to bring selected Japanese delegates to the United States and to Mackinac and Caux to begin the healing process of the Asian side of World War II. This involved going through the Far Eastern Commission, a necessary bureaucracy because of the complexity of dealings between victor and vanquished nations. It took patience and strategy to achieve the results needed.

Some of this work Jack did from Osterville, on Cape Cod, in the summer of 1947. By telephone and letter he moved his part in this delicate process forward. Florence recalls Jack's telephone calls to Japan: "Father was hard of hearing so we had to turn off the radio and be absolutely quiet. If we were cooking a meal we couldn't let a pot scrape. The delegation was hand-picked, person by person. Father would say, 'General Sugita is going to come? Oh, that's fine!' All these people were three-dimensional to us before we ever met them."

In the summer of 1947, the Elys had taken Florence (sixteen), Mary (twelve), and Niel (eight) to Cape Cod for some serious outdoor exercise, swimming, and playing on the beach. Day was at Mackinac after her year with the *Drugstore Revolution*. She let her parents know that she planned to continue with the plays and people "on the road" in the fall, rather than attend Wellesley College, where she had been accepted. Jack journeyed from Cape Cod to Mackinac, and when it was time to return to the Cape, insisted that Day go with him. He told her he felt she was being guided by the flow of activity, and that he wanted her to get her own guidance from God about this decisive point.

On Cape Cod, with no bustling conference all geared to the activity of MRA, Day had her family around her and the sea and the beach. In her room, she wrote a list of the pros and cons of college and of moving with the play; what was useful, what was not. The lists weighed equally, and she could not get a sense of direction. "I flipped a coin," Day recalled. "It came out in favor of college. I went downstairs and said to my father. 'I'm going to college.' He said, 'What was your guidance?' I told him what had been going through my mind. He said, 'That won't do. I don't accept that. Find out what God wants you to do. That's what I want to back you up in doing.' He insisted that I get a sense of spiritual inner direction, whatever that might turn out to be—even though he hoped it would be college." In the end, Day matriculated at Wellesley in the fall of 1947.

While on Cape Cod, the family visited the Rev. Peter Marshall, who had recently been appointed Chaplain of the United States Senate, and his family, who were nearby. Marshall was as concerned as the Elys were about the development of the Cold War. And, Jack wrote to his friend Ray Purdy, "Today I took Niel to his first baseball game. We had a great time together, and I have just put a very tired little boy to bed. These days with the family have been priceless."

The Elys were in and out of Britain a good bit in 1946, 1947 and 1948. Britain was still experiencing food shortages and rationing. The Elys and others who knew the situation sent packages of food and clothing to their friends in Britain, and brought things with them when they traveled there.

The cost of the war to individuals is reflected in a letter from Jack to Buchman in October 1947. Jack wrote of the Earl of Selkirk, a friend of Archie Mackenzie's, who had come to the U.S. officially to work on aviation problems. "His suit is threadbare and his shoes are pitiful," Jack wrote. "They have been resoled so often there is nothing left. It is a heartbreaking experience to see him carry it off so well, a demonstration of Scotland's need and courage."

Jack went on in this letter to allude to the network of people in our government with whom he and his colleagues were in touch. "Maxwell Hamilton," he wrote, "has resigned as Minister to Finland and has just been appointed as Deputy for Secretary of State Marshall in the negotiation of a peace treaty for Japan, which it is thought will be undertaken by the end of this year. The Hamiltons are dining with us Friday evening and going to the theater."

The letter reveals Jack's understanding of the issues confronting members of Congress as they took steps to assume America's leadership in the post-war world. He writes:

> For a time this summer there was a feeling here in Washington, soon after the Marshall proposal was made, that America might save Europe by a policy of "economic penetration and political isolation." It was thought that dollars alone might turn the tide. But now it is realized that dollars spent under the Marshall proposal would in the long run be no more effective than those spent under UNRRA [United Nations Relief & Rehabilitation Agency]. They might be needed to avert disaster but must be supported by a firm political policy and backed by military might. The reason Congressmen are apprehensive today is that they are beginning to recognize the cost.

For moneys appropriated under the Marshall proposal will not mean any reduction in armament appropriations.

Another disquieting realization is that in Europe today no moderate government has a chance to survive. For a moderate government must by nature be a government based on compromise or coalition. The new pattern is a strongly centralized government. . . . France, if de Gaulle attempts to form a "strong" government, faces civil war. The Communists are so firmly entrenched there the recent elections should not fool us. The Ministry of Production has been controlled by the Communists; also the CGT [Confédération Générale de Travaille, France's major labor confederation] and to a large extent the Army, where patriotic graduates of St. Cyr [France's West Point] have been retired before their age limit because of their unwillingness to follow the party line.

All recent communications from the Pope have stressed the seriousness of the situation in Italy, where the confirmation of the peace treaty and the withdrawal of American and British troops places her at the mercy of Tito [the Communist ruler of neighboring Yugoslavia] and Togliatti [Italy's Communist Party chief] when and if orders are given in Moscow to take over the country.

You will find Washington sober and reflective, probably more open to our message than ever before.

Jack closed this letter to Buchman by saying that he and Connie would be coming to Cold Spring Harbor to vote and would stay with Mrs. Jennings, and would look in on him at Elyston (the Elys had loaned Elyston to Buchman for a stay when he arrived from Europe). The Elys maintained their residence in Cold Spring Harbor in order to be able to vote, as residents of Washington D.C. had no voting privileges at that time.

In the spring of 1948, the orthopedic surgeon who looked after both Mary and Niel held a conference with Jack and Connie. His concern was that the children, with their difficulties, did not get enough exercise to give them the physical development they needed. It was not possible for either of them to do enough normal activity because each of them had to go easy on their feet. So he suggested they go to a dude ranch where they could ride horseback, terrific overall exercise that did not strain their feet at all. The doctor recommended a ranch in Wyoming. Arrangements were made, and they asked Anna to spend the summer with Niel and Mary at the Dead Indian Ranch, in the Sunlight Valley near Cody. Connie went with them for the first month.

The ranch belonged to Paul and Allie Ritterbrown, who ran it with their two daughters and a couple of girls who did the cleaning and served the tables, plus a cook and a chore boy. The guests had to saddle and care for their own horses, and were out riding all day, every day, with a picnic lunch in their saddlebags. They rode up the mountains, through forests, great grassy meadows, and deep valleys.

In mid-August Connie, Jack, Florence and Day were in Caux. Big things were afoot, and Jack left Caux for the States soon after they got there, to mobilize a charter planeload of delegates from the U.S. At the same time, in early September, *The Good Road* with its large cast and its tons of scenery and lighting and sound and costumes, embarked for Europe on the S.S. *Aquitania*, whose lower decks were still configured as a troopship. The equipment was unloaded at Le Havre, which had not yet been rebuilt after the heavy fighting in Normandy.

In these days Jack and Connie, in addition to acting in the crowd scenes of *The Good Road* whenever they were with the show, played a special role. They represented what the place of capital could be when those who had it were open to commit their wealth, as well as their hearts and time, to a world vision under God's direction.

The Good Road was performed at Caux and then in the major cities of Switzerland. In early October about 250 people, from many nations, crossed the border and began a three-week visit to the principal cities of West Germany. The *Good Road* cast traveled in a fleet of Swiss buses with a Swiss tractor-trailer combination for the equipment and literature, plus 200 headsets for receiving the German translation of the show, which was performed in English. They performed in Munich, Stuttgart, Frankfurt, Essen, Dusseldorf. And then on to Holland and England.

This trip was an experience that none of those who took part in it would ever forget. The invitations to Germany had been issued by the recently activated state governments of the American and British zones of Allied occupation. The year before, Ken Twitchell and Jack Ely had paved the way for permission to enter the American sector of occupation through visits to the Secretary of State, General George Marshall and the Secretary of War, Robert Patterson. Marshall and Patterson had communicated their approval to General Lucius Clay, who headed the American occupation administration in Germany; other contacts had secured the approval of the British occupation zone.

As much as possible, German citizens had offered their homes to house the cast and crew. In one city, Jack and Connie found themselves the guests of a family who had just one room that had all four walls and the roof intact. That was the room they gave to the Elys; their hosts slept on cushions in the hallway, at the end of which was a wall blasted open by bombing and shielded from the weather by a flimsy curtain.

That fall of 1948 turned out to be a cold one. Traveling every few days to another city, Connie usually took the window seat on the bus so Jack could stretch his long legs into the aisle; the window by her shoulder was cold, and she got bursitis in that shoulder. Food for the group was scraped together by German host cities from the meager provisions of a blasted economy. Some meals were provided by the American and British occupation armies; but the German leaders were determined to do as much as they could, out of the sacrifice of their own people.

Jack had brought his camera equipment and took many photographs of the ruined cities and the bombed-out neighborhoods, and also of the crowd response to the show. He sent pictures home to America with detailed captions, to help Americans understand what was happening.

This brief visit stimulated a flood of applications among Germans to attend the next summer's conference at Caux—every German citizen had to be cleared by the occupying forces to leave the country. It also prompted more invitations from the various German cities for MRA to send people to work with them. The Germans wanted to expand their understanding of MRA and they wanted help in the reeducation of their populations after the fall of Nazism. Several dozen full-time workers responded to those invitations, people from England, America, Canada, France, Norway, Denmark, the Netherlands—their former enemies.

With the end of World War II had come the resurgence of the struggle between Capital and Labor, between those who owned the machinery of production and those who worked with their hands to make the machinery operate. This was true all over the world, where education and communication were making more and more people aware of what made society function. The spectacle of the Ely family—from Jack, the eldest at age fifty-three, to Niel, the youngest at eight—using all they had to build a new world, was a powerful one. Among the rubble of cities, among the dusty coal mines and the steel mills of Germany, and the mills, industrial plants and the docks of France, Britain, Holland and the Nordic countries, this work went on and was mirrored at Caux.

The Cold War today is history, but in those early post-war days it was a palpable reality. By late 1948, all of the Balkan countries had been swallowed up by the Soviet empire. The fall of Czechoslovakia was a particular shock to many in the West. It would be a mistake to give all the credit for Soviet expansion to the massive Red Army. Military force was one aspect of the Cold War, but there was also the aspect that Benjamin Cohen of the

State Department had discussed with Jack in the dinner conversation at the Metropolitan Club, as Moscow wielded its puppet states to achieve its aims in the diplomatic field.

Another aspect was revealed in the Ruhr Valley of West Germany in the postwar years; in the auto and textile plants of Paris and the north of France; in the heavy industry and chemical plants of Northern Italy; in the coal fields and docks of Great Britain. All across industrial Europe there was a daily pitched battle for control. The overlords of Moscow had set their sights on bringing those areas under the control of labor unions led by Moscow-trained men. And in each of those areas, men and women trained by Moral Re-Armament were giving equal personal sacrifice for democracy. Day after day and night after night, these committed workers would stay at the union meetings to the very end to be sure that anti-democracy forces could not control the votes, and to introduce instead of the class war, a mentality of "what's right, not who's right."

The Elys were an asset in this struggle. They were capitalists from America who were giving their lives to see change come in both Capital and Labor. Jack and Connie and their friends Bernard and Alice Hallward, and others from Britain and France, told how they had begun to apply the lessons of "It's not who's right but what's right," and "When man listens, God speaks." They shared their own experience of the simple truth that many of us are for democracy in our politics but are dictators in our own homes, and that if you want to see the world change, the place to start is with yourself. The Elys were seen to be as sacrificially committed as any Marxist.

This was strenuous work, especially in Germany, where the economy was under severe stress and there was not enough food for the population. Among those who responded most were doctrinaire Marxists who were challenged to live in their own lives what they wanted for labor and for their country, and to apply absolute moral standards to themselves as they would want to see them applied to the bosses. Many sincere ideological Marxists were intrigued by the thought that human nature needed to change in worker and capitalist alike, and that this was a far more fundamental and effective revolution than simply destroying capitalism. So many important Communist labor leaders in the Ruhr were captivated by these ideas that it is a matter of public record that the Communist party in that area had to be reorganized.

Ruhr miner and former Communist Party functionary Paul Kurowski became a friend of the Elys. He said, "I as a Communist wanted to destroy the capitalist society. Communists attach no value at all to this [the capitalist] class because they believe it is absolutely eaten up with materialism. That I no longer have that outlook is due to the ideology of Frank Buchman, who has taught us to unite all the positive forces together to fight for a new society. . . . Many revolutionary families like the Ely family have given me this conviction."

Jack Ely and his colleagues wanted to get this message to Washington: sincere Communists are being changed by the presence of what they see as an ideology superior to Communism, at work in the Ruhr, elsewhere in Europe, and in Britain.

Over this ideological struggle hung the mushroom cloud of nuclear warfare. Both the U.S. and the Soviet Union had the bomb. The president of the United States was shadowed day and night by a military officer carrying a briefcase, the key to letting that nuclear cloud loose over an adversary if we were provoked. Our heavy bombers circled our skies and oceans, twenty-four hours of every day, carrying the bomb, ready if necessary to head for a predesignated target in the Soviet Union. Air raid sirens were tested every Saturday at noon, all across America. The nightmare prospect of nuclear war was real for the leaders of this country and for many, many ordinary people.

One of the many Germans to come to Caux in those first years was Hans Heinrich von Herwarth. He had been in the German Foreign Service and had served in Moscow before the war, where he had made friends with American diplomats Chip Bohlen, George Kennan, and Charles Thayer; they called him "Jonny." While enjoying the privileged life of the diplomatic corps there, he was disturbed by what he saw developing both in the Soviet Union and at home in Germany. He began quietly to feed information to individuals among the diplomatic corps because he felt that they represented civilizing forces in a world in which both the Soviets and the Germans were losing their sense of humanity and decency. Von Herwarth began to cultivate a relationship of confidence with Chip Bohlen. These encounters were usually at the American dacha (country cottage), and often on horseback rides out away from everyone else.

In 1939, when World War II began, von Herwarth was in uniform, and became involved in the movement to replace Hitler. He survived the failed bomb plot against the Fuehrer on July 20, 1944, although many of the plotters did not. He was, by chance, exhausted, asleep at home. But the war was coming to a climax. Under the pressure of the Allies' attacks on all fronts, Germany began to cave in. As the National Socialist edifice was crumbling around him, Jonny happened to be spotted in Salzburg by an alert member of an incoming American army unit, his old Moscow friend Charlie Thayer. Charlie picked him up and took him along on his work as chief of the OSS, the Office of Strategic Services, for Austria.

As the war subsided and a semblance of government began to emerge in the German states, Jonny von Herwarth became State Secretary of the fledgling Bavarian state and in that position was invited to the assembly at Caux.

"At Caux we found a democracy that works," von Herwarth wrote, "and in the light of what we discovered there we had the courage to see ourselves and our country as we really are. We experienced profound personal and national remorse. Many of us who were anti-Nazi had made the mistake of blaming everything on Hitler. We learnt at Caux that we were responsible too. The absence of a positive ideology helped to bring Hitler to power. MRA had an enormous influence on Germany," he concluded. "It had a great influence on my life. 'What is right'—such an important concept. And teamwork. I saw and felt it at work."

In 1948, von Herwarth spent three months in America. He went first to New York. He became ill there because, after a Spartan existence in Germany, the rich food of New York affected him adversely. Then he went to the Ely home in Washington, from which he carried on discussions with the U.S. State Department. An impressive thing in the Ely home, he recounted, was the way the family interacted with their black servants, who were part of the family. And he was equally impressed by the way Mary and Niel lived; their physical limitations were obvious, but the spirit with which they and their family met them was remarkable.

In 1997 von Herwarth spoke about Jack Ely, in an interview held in Lisbon, Portugal. Jonny considered Jack Ely to be so well balanced—obviously convinced of what MRA was doing, yet with perspective. "He was one I really remember"" Jonny said. "When I close my eyes, he is before me." On a transatlantic call he told Day Ravenscroft, "Ihr Vater war für mich ein Vorbild" — "Your father was a model for me."

In 1950 von Herwarth became the first Ambassador of the new Federal Republic of Germany to Great Britain. Later on he was Ambassador to Rome. He had a distinguished career, and today, at 92, he is sharp of mind and of a great heart.[4]

. . . .

Notes

1. The Pan American Clipper was the hottest thing in transoceanic transportation at the time of the war. Flown by Pan American Airways, the Clipper, built by Boeing, was a four-engine flying boat, taking off and landing on water, with luxurious berths and meal service.

2 . Edward N. Luttwak, "Franco-German Reconciliation: the Overlooked Role of the Moral Re-Armament Movement," in Douglas Johnson and Cynthia Sampson, eds., *Religion, the Missing Dimension of Statecraft* (New York: Oxford University Press, 1994).

3 . See the author's preface about Jack Ely's place among his peers, and the book *The Wise Men* by Walter Isaacson and Evan Thomas (New York: Simon & Schuster, 1994).

4 . For the full story of von Herwarth's critical role in intelligence and peace-making before, during and after World War II, see Hans von Herwarth, *Against Two Evils* (New York: Rawson and Wade Publishers, 1981).

12

A Committed Family

I N THE FALL OF 1948, MARY ELY WAS approaching her thirteenth birthday. Her mother and father were in Europe, and their letters told of
families in Germany and France who lived in the ruins of those war-
torn countries. As Mary talked with Anna Hale about her birthday, suddenly she said, "I can't bear to have all my friends bring me presents I don't
need. I already have everything! But the girls in Germany and France don't
have food to eat or clothes to keep them warm. I want to do something for
them." So she decided to have a different kind of a birthday party.

Anna wrote about this in her autobiography. "She got her parents to
send her the names of thirteen girls who were in need, one for each of her
years. The next thing was to contact CARE to find out what kind of foods
to send and how to send it. Then Mary invited her friends to come to the
Ely home for her party, bringing no gifts for her but foods to be sent overseas. She enclosed a list of acceptable foods they could choose from. The
party meal, Mary explained, would be very simple because she wanted to
use the money to buy the right kind of boxes to pack the food in." Mary
asked her Grandmother Jennings, whom she knew would be sending her
something, to send money for the postage—which she did.

"When the day came," Anna wrote, "Mary's friends arrived, full of
excitement over such a different kind of birthday party, and carrying instead of beautifully wrapped gifts big brown paper bags full of dry and canned

goods. . . . I have never seen a birthday party that could rival this one for the joy, excitement and caring it generated. And there was even food left over, enough for two or three more boxes which could be packed later. It was a commentary on the contagious quality of Mary's spirit that her friends had been so generous."

In March of 1949, while Jack and Connie were working in Switzerland with the Mottus, Peyers and others, Buchman sent them a cable urging them to return to the United States. They flew home the next day. They found that Mrs. Jennings was in very poor health, and while they spent time working in and around Washington, they had the chance to spend much time with her and in concern for her. They had just a month with her. And then she died.

Buchman's cable to return home had been an intervention of the Holy Spirit. The funeral was at St. John's in Cold Spring Harbor, and Jean Brown Jennings was buried beside her husband in the wooded cemetery a few miles from the church. Mr. and Mrs. Henry Stimson were among her old friends who attended the funeral service. Of course it was an important family time. Buchman sent a cable to Connie about her mother. "I was very moved," Jack wrote Buchman, "by the kindness and generosity of Connie's brother and sister and husband. It has taken death to give me this rich and painful experience and to see the beam in my own eye. Brother Ollie was specially struck by your cable. Connie's faith and calmness and obedience to guidance have been a great challenge to me. With abiding love to you and to all our friends from us and the children, devotedly Jack."

Ollie inherited the Burrwood property. He decided not to keep it. Connie and Day helped sort out the things in the lovely house, and there was an estate sale in the fall of 1949. At the same time they moved all their furnishings from Elyston. Some of the things went to the house in Washington and some to help furnish other places used by MRA, such as the MRA headquarters in Los Angeles, known as "the Club." The Elys shipped nine barrels of china and glass and other valuables to Washington. Brooks took several trips with the Ely station wagon bringing loads of linens, silver and other furnishings, as well as plants for the garden.

During this period, Jack and Connie were intimately involved with the task of bringing Japanese delegates to Mackinac and to Caux. This was not easy to arrange, as permission had to be obtained from the State Department and from General Douglas MacArthur's headquarters in Tokyo. This process took a lot of high-level work in Washington, but it was done. A delegation of ten people came in 1948 and a larger group in 1949. Then a group of seventy-six government, business and labor people was picked for the following year, and a charter airplane booked.

But the cash was not in hand; the Japanese had raised the money, but the occupation authorities refused permission to export the Japanese yen. Jack was on the telephone with Basil Entwistle and Rowland Harker in Tokyo, many times, trying to work out the finances as well as the diplomatic permission. Jack and Connie decided to sell a number of valuable things from their home to contribute to this venture. Connie and Day took a collection of family treasures to New York, including a family heirloom that Connie had received from her Aunt Annie Burr Jennings, a cherished emerald (Connie's birthstone), and a number of silver pieces. Among these were vases that Connie's family had brought from Ireland in the eighteenth century and Florence's silver christening mug, which was a fine George II piece. They gave the cash from these sales and then contributed the balance that was needed to meet the cost of that chartered plane.

In the summer of 1949, after Florence had graduated from Madeira School, she went to Caux with her father at the MRA world assembly. Connie and the rest of the family were in the United States. Florence went to her father and told him that she had prayed and meditated on the next step for her life. She told him her conviction was to remain in Europe to work with Moral Re-Armament for the next year, rather than returning home to enter college, as might be expected—and as Jack certainly expected. Florence recalls that her father just turned his back on her. They stayed at Caux for the next three months, but their relationship remained distant. Florence says of that time, "I had a lot of growing to do. Father and I covered up the split between us so well, very few others knew about it. We would even be at the same table for the occasional meal, at someone's invitation. All very civilized."

Florence recalls this as a moment of learning one of the great lessons of the life of the Holy Spirit. "I went up into a meadow by myself, and I remember sorting it through," she said. "Dad had always been the center of my universe; I'd always tried to please him. When I was six I told him I was going to be a doctor because I knew that would please him. Be the first female brain surgeon.

"I can't judge Dad too harshly, because of his upbringing. If you look at the way Victorians were raised, it was considered really bad to praise your children at all. When I took my college entrance board exams, by mistake I did one in Latin instead of French. I came in first in the nation. Dad's comment was, 'You were probably the only one stupid enough to do it in Latin.' Never ever did Dad say to me, 'Good. I'm proud of you.' Dad was a perfectionist. He was never happy with himself.

"I think the mistake of having had a human at the center of my universe rather than God was the lesson I learned," Florence continues. "This is a life lesson that makes a permanent marriage possible. To live expecting no rights, but considering love as a gift to be cherished."

Jack probably knew from his own experience how valuable a college education might be for Florence. Connie asked Miss Madeira, the principal of Florence's high school, for advice on Florence's future education. Miss Madeira replied, "Don't worry—she will always go on learning."[1]

In the spring of 1950 Jack and Connie took Mary and Niel to New York for their spring vacation. Aunt Polly—Mrs. Oliver Gould Jennings—had them all to lunch for Jack's fifty-sixth birthday. Several parties ensued. And Ollie, Connie's brother, took them to the Roosevelt Grill, where Guy Lombardo's orchestra was the attraction. Jack had his first dance with his youngest daughter, who was blossoming as a young lady, and Connie and Niel danced too. Jeannette and Henry Taylor entertained them. And the four Elys went to the powerful musical drama *Lost in the Stars*, based on *Cry, the Beloved Country*, Alan Paton's book about South Africa.

Connie had inherited some $45,000 from her mother. She decided to give a third of it to Caux to use as the leadership saw fit, a third to help with the periodic payments for the purchase of MRA's center in Los Angeles, and a third to improve and maintain the house in Washington. She sent a check for $15,000 to Robert Hahnloser, who had shouldered the burden of maintaining and developing the physical plant at Caux. Very shortly after mailing it she learned that Hahnloser had died, at the age of forty-two, of a massive heart attack—a great loss to that work in Switzerland.

Although some of the Elys' traditional friends had distanced themselves because of Jack and Connie's work with Moral Re-Armament, they had gained a whole world of new friends, such as Robert and Dorli Hahnloser and countless others literally from every corner of the world. In the 1950's these friendships ripened as the weeks and months went by—in Caux, Mackinac, all across Europe, and then India, Pakistan and Ceylon (now Sri Lanka), the many countries of Africa, South America, Australia and New Zealand, Japan, the Philippines—a network of world citizens. Some of their old friends also helped in the Elys' new activities. Jack's financial advisor, groomsman and longtime friend Charlie Ames gave him a substantial check for Moral Re-Armament to help with what he was realizing to be an important effort for the country.

Bernard Hallward, one of the businessmen with whom Jack often worked, was a special friend. Bernard was a Canadian paper manufacturer who felt as much at home in the United States and Europe as Jack did. Both men were conversant with the history of Western civilization and with classical Latin and Greek literature. Their conversations tended to be sprinkled with references to Horace, Cicero, Pericles, Homer, or Herodotus, that would be over the heads of people lacking that background. Both men came from a world of privilege and illustrated what could happen when capitalists as well as workers accepted a change of heart.

Among the new friends the Elys made at Caux were an American business couple from Minnesota, Ralph and Theone Beal. One day Theone reacted negatively to something she had heard at the assembly, and wanted to go home. At that point Connie and Jack invited the Beals to go with them from Caux to the top of the mountain, the Rochers de Naye, by the mountain railway, and have tea. They had a marvelous afternoon. Somehow the time together brought Caux and the work of MRA into perspective for Theone. From then on, Jack and Connie took the Beals under their wing, and the two couples remained friends for life. Jack and Ralph were similar in many ways—both were independent men with a responsible place in the world, and shared a commitment to put what they learned through MRA to work in the world around them.

In June of 1950 the family was on Cape Cod—Connie, Jack, Mary and Niel, with Anna. Anita Ritter, their neighbor in Washington and fast becoming one of Connie's best friends, was nearby. Early in July Connie, Mary, Day, Niel and Anna sailed on the *Queen Mary* to Southampton, England. The crossing was an adventure. The family had no reservations, so they sat and waited on the pier, on steamer trunks full of table linens, bed linens, and clothing from Gar's Burrwood estate, which they were taking to friends in Europe. One by one, five places were found. Day was the last to get a berth and had to enter by the crew gangplank, as the passenger gangplank had already been removed.

At Southampton they were met by Florence, who had spent the previous year working with MRA in England. They stayed a few days in London. Reggie Hale, one of the Englishmen who had been drafted into the American Army and who had been in and out of the Ely home for many years, gave them a whirlwind tour of London. He showed them the Tower, a performance by the Horse Guards, all his favorite sights, in thanks for all they had done for him in America.

Then they flew with Florence to Geneva. Connie took Niel to the top of the mountain above Caux, the Rochers de Naye. She said in her diary, "Niel walked miles!" In early August Jack flew, with Beryl Evans, to join them at Caux. The family took Niel to see Interlaken, where a man played the alphorn, to Niel's delight; then a glorious drive over the Susten Pass to Lenzerheide and St. Gallen and then via Zurich back to Caux.

The time in Switzerland was a joy for Niel. Connie, Anna and Niel had a place to stay halfway down the mountain in Glion. They could go down to Lake Geneva to swim, or take naps, and come up to Caux on occasion. Eleven-year-old Niel was invited to work backstage with the stage crew that summer. The men made sure he had something to do, so he could feel that he had a part in the production of plays. Meanwhile Mary, who had great natural musical talent, sang with the international chorus; Florence served in the dining room, and Day in the kitchen.

While the Elys were at Caux, they met the members of the high-level Japanese delegation whose trip they had played a major part in financing. The delegation included the mayors of Hiroshima and Nagasaki, the governors of seven prefectures, representatives of the Diet (the Japanese parliament) hand-picked by the Prime Minister, members of some of the great families like the Mitsuis, Sumitomos and Sohmas, and the former Ambassador to Washington, Kensuke Horinouchi. Mayor Hamai of Hiroshima[2] gave Jack a camphor-wood cross from a giant tree growing near the epicenter of the atomic bomb, a tree that was the symbol of the city.

The Japanese had flown first to the world assembly at Caux and then were taken to see the changes happening in Germany, France and England. On their return journey they visited Washington, where the key delegates stayed at the Ely home. A delegation spokesman, representing Japan's Prime Minister, was invited to address the U.S. Senate. His statement, a bare four years after Japan's surrender to the United States and her allies, brought a standing ovation in the Senate chamber. A day or two later the Japanese were received on the floor of the House of Representatives, and another delegate, representing the Japanese parliament, apologized for the "tragic trouble that we have caused to the people of the United States." He also was given a standing ovation.

Early in September of 1950, Connie and Niel flew to New York for another operation. He came home about ten days later, to find Day, Florence and Mary there to greet him. And by early October he was in school. Connie's diaries log every appointment Niel had with a doctor or a school counselor. It was constant. Although Niel strove to be, and was, a normal boy with many interests, he was also a boy with countless health problems.

He had an interrupted school life and could not play sports in any regular manner. All this he bore with a great heart. Some years later, Connie talked about her children and particularly about Niel, and what his life surrounded by people committed to God had meant to him.

"Our boy loved everybody," Connie said, "and felt everyone had the possibility of being his friend. Didn't matter whether he spoke their language or not. He welcomed them all. By this time he had been over to the center of Moral Re-Armament in Switzerland at Caux and he had stood in the lobby and watched Frank welcome different nationalities, and he just developed this tremendous love for people, and people responded.

"Eleven German miners came [to Washington], and lost their interpreter on the way. They had been referred to us by a friend of Frank's in the Ruhr, and so had our address on a piece of paper. They showed this to a taxi driver and they drew up at our front door. They spoke no English. Florence spoke a little German. She asked them please to come in and immediately fixed tea. We found that was the greatest icebreaker—to feed them immediately. After they had been there a little while, very difficult, our son came home from school. Florence went to meet him at the front door and told him that we had these German miners; they'd been sent to us by our friend Max Bladeck in Germany, the Ruhr miner with whom Niel had been great friends.[3]

"So Niel rushed upstairs to his room and put on his best clothes, in record time, and came down all slick and funny-looking, saying 'Guten Tag, Guten Tag,' which was all the German he knew. Then he beckoned to the miners and took them into the other room where we had a portrait of President Washington, and he pointed to it and said, 'Our Presidente'—I don't know why he had all these accents on these words—and put up one finger and said 'First.' And they understood perfectly. Their interpreter came in at this point, all embarrassed, and the miners put up their hands and told him to be quiet and told him in German what our son had been telling them. He was about ten or eleven."

Jack and Ray Purdy worked vigorously in the fall of 1950 to develop an opening with the airlines of the East Coast. A serious labor dispute had broken out between the pilots of National Airlines, which operated up and down the profitable Miami-New York corridor, and National's management. Through the action of MRA's labor-oriented people, and others like Ray, Jim Newton and Jack who took particular interest in management, private talks began to take place between key people on both sides. The solution of the dispute was national news, and caught the attention of the major carriers such as Pan American and Eastern, as well as of the Administration of the United States and the Congress.[4]

This all happened in the weeks before an MRA assembly that was scheduled to take place in early December at the Shoreham Hotel in Washington.

Developments such as these would whirl around the Ely home. A fascinating "cast of characters" that grew over time flowed in and out of the house. Congressmen Charles B. Deane of North Carolina and Charles Bennett of Florida were part of this. Stanley Hoar, an Englishman who was Loan Director for the International Bank for Reconstruction and Development (often called the World Bank) was another. Each had a family who came in and out of Washington. Jack and his team had an ongoing concern that these men and their families should grow in their faith and become better grounded in the Holy Spirit, whatever major events were afoot. Teas or coffees were often arranged for the ladies, or play-days for the children.

Connie pursued her conviction to spend some $15,000 of her inheritance to upgrade and improve the house. She recorded in her diary that after completion of the work, they served 700 meals in five days and entertained 300 people at tea in two days.

Ralph and Theone Beal's daughter Carol Ann, who later became Mrs. Gene Francis, wrote to Day about those days from her perspective as a young woman living in the home and doing secretarial work for Ray Purdy: "I never thought of '2419' as being a center. To me, it was always the Ely home, which was generously opened to be used for MRA.

"I was pretty green when I came there, and your mother undertook (as I saw it) the refining and educating of Carol Ann, among others. She treated us more like her own daughters than staff who were doing a job. I had a bad habit of glancing at papers that were on her desk in the upstairs sitting room, and once she chided me about this, saying it was bad manners and none of my business. Training that I needed and remembered. We used to sit up there after dinner, bringing our mending and listening to records—particularly I remember the recording of *Lost in the Stars*, which I have loved ever after.

"Your mother," Carol Ann continued, "used to keep a gallon jug of cider in the refrigerator in the pantry and let it 'sit' to ripen a bit, and then she'd give me a little glass to sip. I still remember how much I liked it. She was so gracious the time I broke one of the lovely Beleek cups while we were washing up—to my great horror and embarrassment." Connie strongly believed that people were more important than things.

In January 1951 the MRA people took their new musical, *Jotham Valley*, to Broadway, opening at the Coronet Theater. Although the play had a powerful message it needed a lot of work, and received little or no notice in the reviews. Jack and Connie had been brought up with Broadway theater. Jack wrote a long and thoughtful letter about it to Frank Buchman.

The letter is a model of Jack's relationship with Buchman. It was handwritten on small blue notepaper—the stationery of the Henry Taylors' apartment in New York, which Jeannette had offered for the Elys' use while they were in New York with the show.[5] Jack began with some words about their possessions. They had just put Elyston, at Cold Spring Harbor, on the market, and had sent some of its furnishings out to the MRA center in Los Angeles. "What a privilege it is," Jack wrote, "to have our possessions used in this way, to have them now in a bigger home which so many across the world have come to know and to love because of your vision and work! We are grateful for the lessons you have given so many of us in the joys of stewardship."

About *Jotham Valley*, Jack wrote: "The fears I shared with you in Washington as to the treatment the critics would give the play and the nearly empty houses would have seemed in part to have been justified; but what I didn't see was that in spite of such seeming failure it may be the weapon God wishes us to use at this time. . . . But certain lessons I believe we have learned. Firstly I feel that without compromising in any way we could have brought a more finished production to New York. It is now much better than when we started. . . . It may have been necessary for us to learn this the hard way. But I am not fully convinced. I think we need to profit more than we do from criticism of our productions. Secondly I think our plays, while and perhaps even after we have progressed further with them, can be used best in connection with assemblies like Caux and Washington . . .

"Thirdly I believe we might reappraise the great weapon we have in Leland [Holland][6] and the chorus—apart from the plays—for many times they might be sufficient to spearhead a task force. . . . Musical evenings have meant more to me personally and have given me a more comprehensive picture of the rising tide of our work than the plays."

Jack concluded this letter with mention of his old law partner Reed Dawson joining him for *Jotham Valley* one evening. Jack, Reed and another friend had formed the law office of Harris, Dawson & Ely for the years 1923-1926.

After the run at the Coronet Theater, *Jotham Valley* was taken out of New York and was worked on intensively, and returned to Broadway to the

48th Street Theater, where it drew larger audiences. This time, all the newspapers reviewed the show. They wrote of it as both Broadway theater, in which respect they mostly considered it less than professional except for leading man Leland Holland, and as an evening with a message.

Brooks Atkinson of the *New York Times*, the dean of Broadway critics, gave it a thorough review, concluding: "No doubt Broadway is not the most congenial environment for a morality play of this order. The standards for professional entertainment are too exacting. But Broadway would be as good a place as any other to listen to a serious and straightforward statement of a moral attitude toward other human beings and the world. When *Jotham Valley* has the courage of its convictions and dramatizes a moral situation, it is more moving than you are likely to imagine from this notice. Even Broadway has no defenses against simple goodness."

After *Jotham Valley* moved on from New York, Connie had minor surgery. In mid-March the Elys traveled to Jamaica for a short rest, and then to San Juan, Puerto Rico. There they stayed with Jack's cousin Kay and her husband Admiral Marshall Raymond Greer, who was in command of the Tenth Naval District and of America's interests in Caribbean waters.[7] The Elys then moved to Miami, where the plays were spearheading a follow-up of the work with the airlines and the team was beginning to explore the Latin American connection.

In a note from Jack to Buchman, Jack confesses, "I failed to act my age on the beach and pulled my Achilles tendon which for the next six weeks must be encased in plaster."

In June 1951 they attended Day's graduation from Wellesley College, where she took honors in Medieval studies. Soon afterwards Day went to work with MRA in France. At their last family meal, Niel turned to his sister and said, "If you're lonely, you must pray." Day asked, "Is that what you did at camp last summer?" Niel replied, "Yes, but it doesn't help to pray for yourself. You have to pray for somebody else."

The Elys sent Buchman a note for his birthday in which Connie wrote, "You have given us a sound home, many happy years and a chance to fight with you in the greatest revolution of all time. Our birthday gift this year is ten thousand blessings, with the symbols thereof, and the prayer God may give you ten thousand more happy, joyous days." She enclosed a check for $10,000.

Connie again wrote to Buchman: "Jack has had another flare-up of his ulcers. We don't know from what fear or worry. He has plenty of them as you know, and the girls and I are determined he shall become free. His relationships are all 'difficulties' for him (also as you know) and we hope to get the family ones straight at least and have a sounder basis for approaching the others. . . . [I] begin to understand his intensity and strong emotions but my job is to have such security and serenity I don't 'blow' too (as you know)! . . . We are everlastingly grateful for all you are, Frank, and for what changes come because of your obedience and we love you dearly because without you life would have long since become untenable, as a family together or in the world."

A young Englishman working with MRA, John Becker, spent some time in Washington between taking part in the chorus of *Jotham Valley* and the other plays. He described being at the Ely home, and in a quiet moment picking up their copy of *We*, the story Charles Lindbergh wrote of his pioneering solo flight across the Atlantic in 1927. The book so gripped him that he read it right through the night. The next day he went down to the Smithsonian Institution to see "The Spirit of St. Louis" hanging above the other exhibits in the Air and Space Museum. He told Jack about his fascination with the book and the flight and the little plane. Jack's reply was, "You better come to dinner tonight. Lindbergh will be here." John had the good fortune to meet Charles Lindbergh that night and several times thereafter.

In July 1951 Elyston was sold, and torn down.[8]

In August Connie needed a serious emergency operation. The family had a time of quiet meditation with her before she went into surgery. She wrote down, "Grateful I can trust the Lord, my Savior, not only for me but for the ones I love." Afterward the secretary in the surgeon's office said to her, "I can't get over how quickly you have gotten well. That comes of being a Christian." Connie answered, "Yes, and I can't get over all that God has done, because I had no frustration and no ambition and was willing to do whatever He guided." The secretary asked, "Couldn't you get some of these people to come to you instead of to a psychiatrist?"

Connie and Mary flew out to Dead Indian Ranch to join Day, Niel, Jack and Phil Rickert, who had driven out. Phil was one of four children of Van and Migs Rickert, friends in Washington, at whose home Jim and Ellie Newton had been married. These were wonderful days—full of riding, of snow in the high places, of deer hunting. Connie would really let go and enjoy these times. They stayed more than a month. When they came home in late September, Connie continued to ride, sometimes two or three times a week, in Rock Creek Park near their home.

Phil Rickert had some serious mental problems, and was in and out of a mental hospital. His own father, Van Dusen Rickert, had died in 1950. Jack and Niel and the family did their best to make the boy part of them and their enjoyment of life. Phil's younger brother Stephen recounted many years later that he was worried that he might have problems like Phil. He visited "Uncle Jack" Ely, his godfather, in his study at the Ely home, and told him he was worried that he had the same genes as Phil: "Uncle Jack simply said, 'Don't worry. You are not Phil, you are Steve.' It meant a lot to me." Sadly, Phil took his own life several years later.

Jack began to think of going to Latin America with several friends to lay groundwork for a delegation to attend an assembly of the hemisphere in Miami in January 1952. In his mind was his tour of the continent in 1914, and the promise he had felt for those countries all those years ago. In early December he flew to Peru with Eugene von Teuber, a staunch Roman Catholic member of a distinguished Austrian family, and Vincent Vercuski, a Roman Catholic of Polish descent who had a background in law enforcement and criminal investigation. They logged 14,000 miles in seventeen days, visiting high-level leaders in Peru, Chile, Argentina, Brazil, Venezuela, Costa Rica and Guatemala. Their report summarized: "Everywhere we were met with a lively and enthusiastic response which exceeded our fondest hopes. Our trip which opened up countries to the idea of uniting nations and the opportunity of a continent to take offensive action to win the millions everywhere was in contrast to the adventures of Balboa and Pizarro in the 16th Century."

Vince Vercuski later evaluated Jack's role: "Because of Jack's stature as a successful businessman in the U.S., he was warmly received by the business and government leaders of the countries we visited, thus opening many doors for the fulfillment of our mission."

Christmas 1951 was a happy time at the Ely home in Washington. Florence had come home that September from Caux. She had felt Niel needed help to keep his life moving—schoolwork, his physical difficulties, his reaching out to new friends, school friends, and life in general. So she had been tutoring him after school, every day. At the age of twelve, he was fascinated with electricity. Together they had engineered a physics experiment. It concerned the squirrels that he observed going up the screen door in Connie's upstairs porch, who would leap onto her bird feeder and help themselves to the birdseed. The experiment involved how much of an electric shock, depending on the squirrels' average weight, would be needed to warn them off but not to kill them.

When Jack returned home he found the next ten days free to spend time with his son. This proved to be some of the best times they had ever had together. "Everything seemed perfect," Jack wrote of that time. "The Christmas creche before the fireplace, under the Rembrandt Peale portrait of Washington. That room, as well as the rest of the house, was used as a headquarters of a world force, but it was also the place into which each afternoon at tea time a hungry small boy came bursting, throwing aside his schoolbooks, and saying 'Hi, everybody' as he greeted his mother, Rumpus (his dog), and the guests while appraising the sandwiches, cookies, and cakes. After dinner at the Christmas season we would often gather in this room before the creche, turning out all lights except the light which seemed to come from a hidden source, perhaps from a star, over the manger. Niel loved it all."

Niel had added two baseball players to the traditional creche.

"New Year's Eve," Jack continued, "Niel and I had a wonderful time making a home recording of an interview in which he pretended to be Admiral [Richard E.] Byrd and assigned me the role of a newspaper reporter. He allowed his imagination full scope. On his next polar expedition, the 'Admiral' said, he was going to use a helicopter, well-tested in Korea, instead of a dog team! When the interview was over, Niel reverted to imitating radio sound effects. He made the noises of a train pulling into a station so perfectly that I felt like reaching overhead for my bags and putting on my coat."

The next morning, New Year's Day 1952, Jack and Niel went out to breakfast with Ted Purdy, brother of Ray, and their young friend Phil Rickert. "Never had I felt more companionable with Niel," Jack wrote, "never had I loved him more, than as we drove along that crisp, sunny morning together. We understood each other." The four of them had a time of prayer and meditation together, and shared with each other their thoughts.

Then after breakfast, Niel, Connie, Florence and Mary went off to ride horseback in Rock Creek Park. Niel had wanted to spend his Christmas money and planned who should ride each horse. He called the little stable down in the park near Massachusetts Avenue and booked the horses by name, with appropriate saddles. While they were cantering, as they usually did, Niel's horse fell, and he was thrown against a bank beside the path. He remounted and they rode back to a telephone. Jack drove out immediately. The others rode on, with Niel's horse. Father and son drove home together.

That afternoon Niel began to experience pain. Florence read Longfellow's "Hiawatha" to him, hoping the cadence would ease the waves of pain. In the evening their physician had him taken to the hospital in an ambulance. Niel asked his mother, who rode with him, if they could "have the sirens." They did. There was surgery, and blood transfusions. He suffered some, and he prayed that Jesus would help him bear the pain. He visited with his family and with the nurses. On the third of January he slipped away out of this life. Florence remembers that the last look he gave his parents was full of a mature love.

The passing of this twelve-year-old boy triggered a flood of expressions of affection for him, of gratitude for his life, of a richer understanding, through his life and death, of what it was all about, of the Almighty's provision for individuals as well as for the world. Some seventy telegrams poured in for his funeral. Young men working with MRA who had become his friends—and Brooks Onley, who had often carried him when he couldn't walk—were his pall bearers, in the service at St. John's Church Lafayette Square. People from Congress and the government with whom Jack had been working attended the service. Raymond Zimmerman, of the Economic Cooperation Administration, said afterwards, "This plumbs depths I have never known."

Day Ely was in Caux at this time, as was Anna Hale. With their friends they held a memorial service for Niel. Another service was held in Miami by the cast of *Jotham Valley*, and one in Los Angeles.

When Niel's estate was settled, Day gave the portion that came to her to help MRA buy a home to be the local center for the work in France.

The family collected the many things that were said about him, and their own thoughts on his life, into a book, *Niel's Legacy*, which was printed privately. It is available still.[9] What moved many people even more than his death was the sense of the triumph of God in every adversity, and even in deep sorrow, that the family shared with their friends. Nathaniel Jennings Ely was buried in Arlington National Cemetery, on a slope overlooking the heart of the city, the first of the family of Albert Heman Ely Jr., Lieutenant (Junior Grade), United States Navy, to be placed there. The cemetery superintendent said, "Who was this boy? The whole world loved him."

It is quite a measure of Jack Ely that he went through the death of his only son, the last Ely male in his branch of the family, and one of the deepest sorrows of his life in the midst of the national and international work of building a new thinking in the world. And not with a stony heart, but with an open one.

A few weeks later, the Ely family and the house on Massachusetts Avenue were in the thick of a visit by a team of men and women from Europe who had come to support the upcoming assembly in Miami. Jack wrote to Buchman, who was at Caux, outlining the impact that men such as the Ruhr coal miners (former leaders of the Communist Party there), were having on men in Congress. He told of Joe Martin, Speaker of the House of Representatives, Richard Arens, chief of staff of the Senate Internal Security (McCarran) Committee, and Donald Dawson, Assistant to President Truman. "It was perhaps a pinnacle moment in our work in Washington over the years," Jack wrote. He told of Brooks and himself taking two of Buchman's close friends to see Niel's grave at Arlington. "Sometime we want you to go there with us, as it is a perfect spot. We have been broken open by the experience, but have found in our sorrow also intense joy and freedom. Connie and the girls join me in dearest love to you. Faithfully ever, Jack."

At the end of January 1952 Richard Arens convened a meeting at Washington's Statler Hotel for government officials and others to hear from Jack Ely and his associates their concepts of international security. Present were several members of Arens' staff at the Senate Internal Security Committee, Congressman Charles Bennett of Florida, and representatives of the State and Justice departments, the Displaced Persons Commission, the Immigration and Naturalization Service, the Organization of American States of the Pan American Union, and the American Legion.

Also attending were a newsman from the American Federation of Labor and Raymond Zimmerman of the Economic Cooperation Administration. They heard Peter Howard, former political writer for *The Daily Express* of London and one of MRA's most effective thinkers and speakers, and others from Britain, Ireland, Norway, and Australia who shared their experience and convictions.

"Dick Arens was particularly concerned," Jack wrote Buchman, "as to whether we had any specific proposals for their further cooperation with MRA. I took up the question and suggested several detailed points. My final point was for government to assist, in ways that will occur to them as this program develops, in the national positive awakening of America.

"After the meeting Zimmerman said to Peter Howard, 'This evening will have more far-reaching effects than you can ever imagine.'"

What impressed many in Washington was that in recent weeks Dick Arens had changed greatly. He had been holding the McCarran Act, which had strict definitions of who was admissible to the United States and who should be excluded as a security risk, as a stone wall to prevent the entry of many people who might otherwise be helpful to America's exchange programs and the success of the Marshall Plan. Arens had become much more cooperative, and his interest in former Communists working with MRA was opening doors and windows in the minds of people in government.

Among Jack's and Connie's closest friends in Washington was Anita Bell Ritter. Anita, the thirteenth child of a poor Southern schoolteacher, was a gracious and beautiful woman. Her husband, W.M. Ritter, owned a large mining and lumbering company in the Appalachians. "W.M.," as he was known, was a gruff man. Anita and Connie spent a good bit of effort on how Anita could do the most for her husband. Back in 1941, W.M. had invited Jack and some of his friends to introduce the wartime handbook, *You Can Defend America*, to McClure, Virginia, in the mountains in the extreme western part of the state where Virginia, Kentucky and Tennessee come together. McClure was the site of one of Ritter's major lumber camps.

Jack had written to Buchman at that time, "This trip has demonstrated the possibility of Labor and Management working together harmoniously and loyally. Anita's husband has put together an organization which, I believe, is unique in American business. And the secret lies in the fact that its officers are 'on the road,' know their men, and have grown up with the company. Their loyalty to that old 'scalawag' back in Washington is astonishing." Executives and foremen had held a meeting to decide how to get *You Can Defend America* to that part of the country. Jack had been impressed.

One of the things Connie loved about Anita was her laugh. Like Connie, she could let go and laugh a real, whole-hearted belly laugh. There was no affectation in this, she was just being herself.

In May of 1952 W.M. died. The Elys supported Anita and went through the whole process with her. Buchman asked Jack and Connie to represent him at the funeral in Hughesville, Pennsylvania, Ritter's hometown. They placed an arrangement of pink carnations from Buchman near the casket. Ray Purdy's wife, Elsa, who was possessed of a gorgeous and well-trained voice, sang at the service. On the drive from Washington Jack had written a poem for W.M.:

> *A Pioneer of Industry is riding home today,*
> *The country better for his life, his friends*
> *saddened but glad*
> *That after years of battle now he'll hear*
> *our dear Lord say:*
> *"Well done, you've held the vision true I*
> *gave you as a lad."*

Others whom Jack and Connie saw quite frequently were Justice Harold Burton and his wife. Justice Burton had served in the Senate from Ohio at the time *You Can Defend America* had been published, and had asked Jack for fifty copies for use in his office. He was appointed an Associate Justice of the United States Supreme Court in 1945, and kept in close touch with what the Elys were doing. Typical of the social affairs to which Jack and Connie were regularly invited was a reception the Burtons gave in the spring of 1952. It gave the Elys the opportunity to visit with President and Mrs. Harry Truman, Vice President Alben Barkley, Chief Justice Fred Vinson, Senators Alexander Wiley and John Stennis and their wives, Eric Johnston, President of the Motion Picture Association of America, and Mrs. Steelman.

By midsummer of 1952 Jack could write from Washington to Buchman, "The consensus on the Hill is that there is little likelihood of war in Europe now. The Soviets seem to feel to wait until the election, and that the Democrats are a better bet for them than the Republicans." Yet B-52 bombers carrying atomic payloads were in wide and ever-changing holding patterns in the air non-stop as they had been for several years.

American congressmen, by and large, were new to the world of international politics. Yet there were gatherings of international parliamentarians yearly, and meetings in Strasbourg for the emerging European parliament, and American participation was more than welcome at such affairs. MRA's people moved in and out of these meetings with ease and had a wide network of connections.

Many in the U.S. Congress began to value their help. One request came from Rep. Edward Cox of Georgia, the joint chairman, with Senator Theodore Francis Green of Rhode Island, of a congressional delegation to the Council of Europe. Cox wanted to present the message of MRA as the hope of European unity; he asked Jack to help him prepare his speech for the Council, and to advise him on whom to see in France, Germany and Austria.

In the fall of 1952, Buchman set off for Asia with several hundred of his people, including Jack, Connie, Day and Florence, in response to invitations from leaders in Ceylon, India and Pakistan. He took with him five of the current theater productions, including *Jotham Valley*. As the plane flew low over the plantations surrounding Colombo, the sight of elephants working to clear a field was a symbol that this would be an adventure!

Accounts of this trip, which took seven months, are found in the references cited for this book. In city after city the newspapers trumpeted the story. The group stayed in the homes of people of all types. It was person-to-person diplomacy at its best. And almost from the beginning, this event was attacked from Moscow, by radio and in the Leftist press.

In Colombo, Jack and Connie stayed with a family who took them sightseeing. They came to a river where men were working with elephants. The host asked if Jack would like to ride one. Jack was in his washable, lightweight nylon suit; he said yes. The elephant had just come out of the river and was soaking wet. Jack was helped up onto the elephant's neck and had a ride. When he got off, of course his trousers were all wet, but since they were nylon they did not wrinkle. Day comments that her father was among the first to wear a nylon suit and delighted in explaining the virtues of this new technology.

The hosts then took the Elys to see Lion Rock, the Temple of the Footprint, and to Kandy. At Citadel Rock, their hosts invited them to go up the steep trail. Connie prayed, because although she did not want to go (she had severe acrophobia, fear of heights) she also did not want to insult their hosts; she went, made the climb in good shape, and felt again that God had enabled her to do what she had feared to do.

In New Delhi, the President of India gave a reception for Buchman and his party, outdoors in the lovely gardens of the presidential palace. Day and Florence and their mother were listening and watching and being served tea by impressive attendants in starched turbans—but where was Jack? As Day tells it, "A little movement drew my attention to the facade of the palace. There was Dad, climbing out an upstairs window onto a narrow ledge with his camera!" Jack got a superb bird's-eye photo that was used in many newspapers.

The family also remembers Jack at a luncheon at the ashram of Mahatma Gandhi, who had been killed by an assassin in 1948. The party was seated on the ground, according to Indian custom, with a large banana leaf in front of each person on which food was placed—to be eaten with one's fingers. Jack's legs were very long, and he had to sit with his feet on each side of his banana leaf and his knees up around his ears, like a grasshopper.

Jack wrote to his friend Ray Purdy: "Calcutta with its six teeming millions is a key to Asia. The Communists know it. When our young people speak in the schools and colleges they have to fight every inch of the way. The head of one of the student bodies, who had organized the opposition to us, is now well on his way to being changed.

"I do not believe," the letter went on, "we will ever win here if we think other than for the good of India. I should like to see severe disciplinary action taken against any American who ever again uses the expression, 'We are doing this in our enlightened self-interest.' What reaction do you think it sets up in an intelligent, cultured, group of people like the leaders of India? It is thinking along materialistic lines and plays directly into the hands of our friends to the North who are adroit and quick to drive home at every opportunity their contention, which I do not believe to be true, that America is not interested in the Asians as people but as pawns in the great game of world dominance."

The crowd response to the plays, and the individual response in meetings and encounters large and small, was overwhelming. Indians came in numbers to the assemblies at Caux and Mackinac, and not long after this the Indians interested in MRA created their own conference center in Panchgani, near Mumbai (Bombay), which today continues to serve as a conference place for all of Asia.

Jack concluded that letter with a mention of being with Buchman and a few others in Darjeeling, north of Calcutta, for a little break. "Some of us were up at 3:30 a.m. to go up Tiger Hill where we saw the full moon set and then a rainbow dawn and the sunrise on Mt. Everest. It was one of the great moments of my life. I am not able to express what it meant to me except to say that we must not allow ourselves or others to damage further the perfect world which God has given us. Poverty, misery, hunger, unemployment and other evils must have no part in it. MRA properly applied can give to every nation food and jobs and an idea that satisfies. . . . Many of us with Frank gave ourselves again in full commitment to this greatest of all revolutions. We have the promise of Easter! . . . An Easter hug to Mary and the joy of the Risen Lord to each of you."

Ray and Elsa Purdy were living at the Ely home in Washington during this time, and Ray wrote often, giving news of the household and of the reaction in Washington to the news coming from the venture into India. "Mary has been a joy," he wrote in March 1953, "constantly on the give with a facility of understanding and hospitality which makes many feel at home. With these she couples the delightful spontaneous acting her age. . . . We had the Ambassador of Ceylon to dinner with Mary next to him."

While the group was in India, Joseph Stalin died.

The group moved on to Pakistan, to Kashmir, where Jack got exquisite photos of the blue lake, pink roses, orange marigolds, sparkling fountains and the Himalayan snow peaks. From there the group moved to Europe. Florence stayed on the Indian subcontinent, while Jack, Connie, and Day accompanied Buchman to Germany.

. . . .

NOTES

1. Florence has never let the lack of college prevent her from a passionate pursuit of learning and from sharing that knowledge and the excitement of discovery. The Desert Center in Scottsdale that she founded hosts thousands of school children each year for a hands-on experience of desert flora and fauna. And Florence has earned her cap and gown: in 1996 she was awarded the honorary degree of Doctor of Humane Letters by Arizona State University for her work on behalf of education.

2. Mayor Hamai and his wife were both affected by the bomb; Mrs. Hamai had to wear a wig to Caux, because her hair was falling out from the effects of radioactivity.

3. Max Bladeck, like his friend Paul Kurowski, was a coal miner and a seasoned Marxist dialectician, twenty-seven years with the Communist Party. When he and Kurowski became convinced of the revolution MRA meant for them, they were expelled from the Party. Peter Howard details this story in *The World Rebuilt* (New York: Duell Sloan & Pierce, 1951).

4. See *The World Rebuilt*.

5. Henry Calhoun Taylor (1894-1971) had a successful career in the textile industry and was president of his own company, Taylor Pinkham & Co., Inc. He served on the board of directors of several corporations, including the Roosevelt Hospital in New York and the Yale Commission on the Library. He also distinguished himself in deep-water yachting: he had a 72-foot yawl, *Baruna*, built for ocean-going racing. He entered *Baruna* in the New York-to-Bermuda race, Class A, in 1938, 1940, 1948, 1950 and 1952, winning in 1938, 1940 and 1948.

Henry had become interested in a book written in 1627 by Captain John Smith, seafarer and at one time governor of the colony of Virginia. Smith wrote in *A Sea Grammar* about the books he would advise any sea captain to take with him. Henry collected a first edition of each of these books and went on to collect other early specimens of the art of seafaring as well as maps and charts. He presented them all, 410 items, "The Henry C. Taylor Collection," to the Yale University Library, together with a small volume describing the collection, dated 1971, the year of his death. In the introduction is the final phrase that ties Henry to his brother-in-law, Jack Ely, in spirit: "that combination of knowledge and daring which has enabled men to 'move mountains.'"

6. Leland Holland, who played the leading role in *Jotham Valley* and subsequent productions, had a superb baritone voice.

7. Kay was the daughter of Elinor Merchant French, Maud Ely's sister.

8. Over the years, since Connie's brother Oliver Jennings disposed of Burrwood, the estate has gradually been redeveloped. The Jennings' big house became the Industrial Home for the Blind; it was torn down in 1994. By 1995 the whole estate, with the wrought-iron gates still bearing the "WJ" logo, was being reconfigured into a series of gracious homes; the stable, a mile from the main house, now houses the maintenance center and town offices of the town of Lloyd's Neck.

9. To obtain a copy of *Niel's Legacy*, contact Mrs. Day Ely Ravenscroft at this publisher's address.

Niel's Legacy

by Sarah Eustis Moore, January 1952

Now Niel is whole again, and lithe and strong,

And where he goes he runs. And everywhere

He will find friends, and sun and laughter. There

Each moment like an early morning song—

His time of day. There he can do no wrong;

No loneliness, no fear, no pain to bear,

His heart made new, and God's full love to share.

This is your triumph, Niel, this is where you belong.

It is God's dazzling gift, this heart of change

He intends each of us to find, to go

Deep into joy and pain until we see

Beyond them to Himself; it is not strange

God's own Son suffered that we all might know.

And finding Him now we claim Niel's legacy.

13

Building Blocks of a
New Age

Aᶠᵗᵉʳ ᵃ ᵛᶦᵍᵒʳᵒᵘˢ ˢᵘᵐᵐᵉʳ ᵃᵗ Cᴀᵁˣ, Jack and Connie found themselves spending the fall and winter, 1953-54, moving back and forth
across Western Europe to follow up on people who had been to Caux
and others whom they had met along the way—the building blocks of a
new Europe. They had bought a Mercedes 220 (bigger than the 220 of the
1980s and '90s), an extremely comfortable car and admirably suited to their
purposes. The Elys put over 11,000 miles on the car that winter. Connie's
diary shows them in Naples, Rome, Florence, Portofino, Genoa, Monte
Carlo, Paris, back to Lausanne, by ferry to Dover, back to Caux, down
again to Montecatini for Christmas in northern Italy with Frank Buchman
and a group of his friends, and their daughter Day.

This was a crucial time for Western Europe. Jack and Connie wrote
home often to Beryl Evans, whom they loved and trusted greatly. Following are excerpts from their letters of March through May of 1954. From
Firminy, an industrial city near Lyon, in eastern France:

"In Firminy we found that although 85% of the people are said to be
Communists, yet only three civil burials [as compared to church burials]
were held last year. The Church, often discredited and attacked, still has its

Connie and Jack at breakfast while traveling

Switzerland, 1954: Jack and his faithful Mercedes at a mountain pass

Caux-sur-Montreux in the winter. In the background are the Dents du Midi

Florence (top) with some of her friends in the Caux kitchen, 1950

Mary (center rear) in the chorus at Caux, 1950

The Castle of Chillon

Jack as "Mr. Diehard" in The Good Road, *Britain, 1949*

Niel swimming in Lake Geneva, 1950

Among the Ely's close friends in Europe were Robert Tilge of France, above left, head of the national manufacturers' association, and Irene and Victor Laure from the docks of Marseilles

Jack took these pictures while traveling with MRA teams in Europe after World War II. Left, a colleague talking with Communist workers in Torviscosa, Italy. Below, Germany in 1946. Jack said of this photo, "There are ruins not only in the streets but in the hearts of men."

Camphor wood cross given to Jack and Connie by Mayor Hamai of Hiroshima, 1950

Ambassador and Mrs. Kensuke Horinouchi at Elyston in 1940, on their way home to Japan. The Horinouchis and Elys were friends for fifty years.

Jack with Takasumi Mitsui of Japan, a friend from 1935 until his death in 1986

With grateful appreciation from the Japanese Delegation to the World Assembly for Moral Re-Armament, Caux, Switzerland June-August, 1950

Signed photo of Japanese delegation to Caux, 1950, presented to Jack and Connie in gratitude for making the trip possible

New Delhi, 1952: Jack climbed onto the ledge of President Prasad's palace to take this shot of the President's reception for Frank Buchman and his team

Doë and Peter Howard, 1955

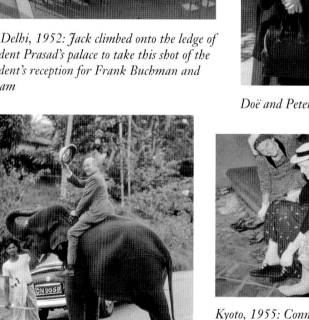

Ceylon (Sri Lanka), 1955

Kyoto, 1955: Connie (left) and friends preparing to enter tea-ceremony house

Costa Rica, 1951: Jack (right) and Eugene von Teuber (second from left) with President Jose Figueres, known as the "George Washington" of his country, and Mrs. Figueres

Left, Connie with Max Bladeck, former Communist mineworker from Germany; right, Bladeck's colleague Paul Kurowski

The von Herwarths at the gate of their castle in Bavaria, 1986

Cairo, 1955: The "Statesman's Mission" of The Vanishing Island *received by Prime Minister Gamal Abdel Nasser*

From the Elys 1959 journey, clockwise from top: Jack in West Africa; crucifix in the Eglise de Ste. Anne in Brazzaville, Congo. Jack's special pilgrimage of faith included a visit to this shrine and that of Fatima in Portugal; John and Joy Amata and their children with the three Colwells in Lagos, Nigeria; South Africans Nico Ferreira and P.Q. Vundla

The view from Connie's bedroom in Scottsdale, Arizona; to the east, the McDowell mountains

The Jennings sisters in September 1964; Jeanette Jennings Taylor and Connie, photographed by Jack

Connie, aged 85, preparing to snorkel in Hawaii

hold when it comes to the things that matter. If we live straight and bring change on the level of the four standards [absolute honesty, purity, unselfishness and love], people in and out of the Church will see things more clearly. We still have to do in France what we did in Germany. We must win the Marxists. . . . The Communist leader, who was distributing pamphlets against us outside the theatre, was challenged to go in and see the play. 'You haven't the courage to go in,' said Jorgen [one of the international team]. 'Courage,' the man roared, 'why I fought the Nazis with my bare hands.' 'That may be,' answered Jorgen, 'but you haven't the courage to go in there, and what's more you haven't the courage to be honest with your wife.' It was a good stroke. The man sobered down and said, 'You had better come to my office tomorrow. I'd like to talk things over with you.'

"Connie and I saw quite a bit of Monsieur Blain, Chief Research Engineer of the Acieries de Firminy [steel company]. He wrote, 'I have found a completely new climate in my family life . . . joy . . . and I ask your forgiveness for my skepticism which has acted as a brake on your enthusiasm.'

"I want to share some 'approaching 60' thoughts," Jack continued. "First, I'm grateful for my family and that we all may be part of the greater world family. Second, I feel I have been far too soft and sentimental . . . and I've succumbed to temptations, to bury myself in books and daydream of far off places I'd prefer to be, rather than giving myself fully to our tremendous job of saving this country. A leading industrialist gives us two years! Third, I *have* changed quite a bit—it may not be visible to my friends but I feel closer to God—and I am looking forward to ever more glorious years. . . . It is a beautiful, warm, spring-like day and the sun is streaming in the window of our room in the Palace Hotel, Livorno, as we look out at the blue waters of the Tyrrhenian Sea. A perfect spot. This historic seaport once served the Florence of the Medicis; now it has its commercial port (Communist controlled) and its American port (supplying the U. S. Forces in Austria)."

That afternoon Jack and Connie stood beside the Tyrrhenian while a colleague took the photograph that the family used at the time of Connie's funeral twenty-seven years later, and that is now reproduced on the cover of this book.

From another letter: "The remainder of my birthday . . . was spent in continuing our work to assemble the casts for the plays at Torviscosa [textile mills near Trieste]. We called on the Savi family, dockers, in Livorno. Elvas Savi plays "Mac" in *The Forgotten Factor*. His mother pointed out the real hardship it was for the family to have their only bread-winner miss any work on the docks, but they all realize the importance of our work and Elvas agreed to go to Torviscosa. . . .

"I am writing this a little over a week later—what a week—in a hotel at Udine (get out your maps, it is near Trieste), an arcaded town with old palazzos, a mingling of the old and new, friendly and clean, where Connie and I are staying during the campaign at Torviscosa. We motor back and forth, some 40 kilometers from Udine to Torviscosa. In the distance are the mountains, something like Kashmir with their snows, and halfway between the two places we go through a story-book town called Palmanova with medieval walls and breastworks, a moat around its hexagonal fortifications, narrow gates with portcullises, and crammed with soldiers who live within the town in new barracks. It is like going through a full-size section of a toy store.

"Torviscosa itself is a vast, ultra-modern, cellulose plant built on the main highway between Venice and Trieste. It is a huge plant, part of the Marinotti industrial empire. The Communists are so amazed at the difference between the reality of MRA and what they had been poisoned to expect that yesterday they voted *against* holding an anti-MRA demonstration! The Management said (1) the workers won't come to the play, (2) the workers certainly won't come if it rains, and (3) the workers positively won't come on Sunday afternoon if it's good weather because they go to the football games or on outings in the country. Well—the big theatre was completely filled for the first show, hundreds standing, with an overflow of more hundreds outside which was addressed by our speakers. . . . The second night it poured, a regular cloudburst, and the crowd was bigger than ever. The third afternoon was a glorious day, almost lyrical with Spring, and the crowd was overwhelming. The Management . . . are 'punch drunk.' The Mayor is delighted. The local priests say we can't leave. It is a major win."

The Elys and a few others visited Venice, where they had a number of contacts. Among the group were Cecil Broadhurst, the author of *Jotham Valley*, and his wife Mary Jane, daughter of the Elys' old friends Nort and Mary Brotherton. They were all staying in a hotel, which looked out upon the Grand Canal, when Cece came down with the flu. When the others planned to move on, the Broadhursts decided to stay there and recuperate.

Mary Jane loves to tell the story of how Connie and Jack burst into their hotel room and announced, "We're staying to look after you!" The next morning, Mary Jane says, "Connie and Jack knocked on the door saying 'Anyone want to go for a gondola ride?' I went out that door so fast! Cece was very happy. He had some books, and a nice view, and could sleep.

We went out and rode gondolas—not only in the Grand Canal, but we went up all these side canals where the balconies hang right over the water and people have their washing out, and their flowers. Connie and Jack were such wonderful hosts. They enjoyed themselves so much, enjoying having other people enjoy it. One of the happiest times I've ever had."

One day in the spring of 1954, Connie was seeking guidance as to whether the Elys might need to go home soon. Jack needed to see Charlie Ames, his financial advisor, and had not attended a meeting of the Burrwood Corporation in two years—he was responsible for Connie's part of that sizeable investment trust. The thought she wrote down was, "If we do return to the U.S., don't go in the expectation that you are capable or able to answer the needs or to do incredible things. The extent of our usefulness is always the same. Never attempt to judge how great or how little is our contribution; nor where we may be better used; but ask only where does God want us to be?"

Connie was also thinking about her daughter Florence, who had been two years in India and Pakistan and had lost considerable weight. Connie wrote further: "Jack has felt a bit frustrated this winter and needed the Lord a lot because he wanted to go to Africa, was invited to Brazil, had guidance to go to Japan, and spent the winter in Italy!"

The Elys worked together across three continents: In 1953-54 Florence was in India, Jack and Connie in Italy, France and Switzerland, and Day in Stockholm. Mary was at home in Washington, attending the Madeira School from which she graduated in 1953, and was then at Caux and in England. Florence wrote to Day in Stockholm to look after the Bhavnani family of Bombay, friends of Prime Minister Nehru who were coming to Stockholm.

Day prepared a curry meal for them. As they ate it, they asked where she had learned to make a curry like that; she told them about the Indian lady at Caux from whom she had learned to cook Indian food: "Oh, she's my aunt," Mrs. Bhavnani said. Then Day informed Mary and Beryl that the Bhavnanis were coming to Washington, and asked that they coordinate their schedule with the Indian ambassador to be sure the Bhavnanis had a meaningful and exciting visit.

Jack had many personal contacts with press people, including Charles Merz, editor of the *New York Times* and David Lawrence, editor of *U.S. News and World Report*. "Dear David," he wrote from Milan, in answer to a question on why he found the magazine disappointing. He quoted a twelve-year-old boy he had talked to in his travels: "This magazine makes America sound right all the time," the boy had said. "This attitude of conscious rectitude, of superiority," Jack wrote, "burns up the Asians and Africans. I heard a man say 'We will fight Communism if you will give us a bigger idea for which to fight. But we will not fight Soviet materialism just to defend American materialism.' An Italian industrialist told me that our economic aid has been ten times more effective in Italy where MRA has been at work." He ended the letter, "With gratitude and affection, Jack."

In September 1954, Jack and Connie returned to the United States on the S.S. *Saturnia*, and soon after arriving were at Mackinac Island. Connie's diary notes that Mary McLeod Bethune attended the conference there, and that Connie had most of her meals with Mrs. Bethune.

In February 1955, the Elys entertained Mary McLeod Bethune and some of her associates from Bethune-Cookman College, at their Washington home. To see her was always an event. She was in her eightieth year. She had said to Connie, the first time she had visited them, that this was the first white home in which she had been offered an armchair that had padded arms. A black woman of quality, she was used to being snubbed by whites who presumed that black skin would stain or leave an odor on their fine upholstery. Mrs. Bethune died a few weeks later. Jack and Connie journeyed to Daytona for her funeral.

In 1955 on Mackinac Island a remarkable musical play was produced, *The Vanishing Island*. Written by Peter Howard, it caught the essence of the Cold War—a regimented, militant force of organized materialism versus an indulgent, easy-going, me-first mass of disorganized materialism. And it portrayed an answering force of vigorous, whole-hearted people, honest, humble, willing to start with themselves, with a passion to change the world. By the first of June this play, with its cast of a hundred, started on a round-the-world journey. It was called a "Statesmen's Mission," because traveling with it much of the time were men like Ole Bjørn Kraft, former Foreign Minister of Denmark, Theodore Oberlander, Minister for Refugees of the Federal Republic of Germany, Tunisian cabinet minister Mohammad Masmoudi, and Charlie Deane of the U. S. Congress.

Along with the statesmen, and taking various parts, were a phalanx of people including Jack and some of his counterparts in many countries, and their "opposite numbers" from the working men and women who wanted to promote the idea of the play. The Mission visited Hawaii, Japan, Taiwan, the Philippines, Thailand, Burma, Sri Lanka, India, Pakistan, Iran, Iraq, Egypt, Kenya, Turkey, and Switzerland. Small groups also made brief appearances in high-risk Korea and Vietnam.

Mary Ely had spent the previous two years at Aston Bury, a lovely English country house, where she was looking after the four-year-old daughter of one of the full-time MRA couples. At the end of the summer of 1956 she left Aston Bury by train to journey to Caux to meet her mother and father who were arriving with the *Vanishing Island* party. The morning her train pulled into Basle at the Swiss border, she woke with fierce abdominal pains. They telephoned ahead to Dr. Margaret Burton, who knew Mary well, and who was at Caux. The advice was to leave the train at Lausanne and check into a clinic whose specialty was appendicitis. The doctors removed her appendix, which turned out to be healthy, and were mystified by the large amount of blood in her abdominal cavity but closed up the incision. When Mary emerged from the anesthesia, she found she was sharing a room with Beryl Evans. Beryl had come to Caux, and had needed to have her appendix removed.

Day had come from Sweden to Caux, and was heading a cooking shift for the assembly that was taking place there. Day drove down to Lausanne every day for ten days after her shift. She found that Mary not only was not any better after the surgery but was vomiting and becoming weaker: "I told the people at the clinic that something was wrong. They didn't think so. In order to get Mary out of that clinic, we had to pay the full charges. The week before, I had received my annual income check from inherited investments. That Sunday there was a desperate plea for funds for an MRA program in which I was greatly interested. To my surprise, I had guidance to give only about a third of the money. I asked God if that wasn't a mistake but the same amount came very clearly. As a result, when I wanted to remove Mary from the clinic, I had the money to do so."

In the Caux infirmary, Mary continued to vomit after every drink. Day sat with her all night. Suddenly Paul Campbell, Frank Buchman's doctor, appeared in the infirmary and said Frank had awakened him, saying he was sure that Mary was seriously ill. Paul checked Mary's history and condition, and ordered an ambulance to take her to the world-famous Nestlé clinic in Lausanne. Meanwhile Jack and Connie, who had been in Egypt and were now en route to Kenya with *The Vanishing Island*, got a phone call about Mary. They immediately flew to Switzerland from the Khartoum refueling stop.

In the Nestlé clinic, X-rays showed that Mary's esophagus was fully closed above her stomach and she hadn't been able to absorb any nourishment since the appendectomy. The doctors operated and found that a dried lump of blood was pressing on the esophagus. They removed it and recommended that she discover its cause when she was stronger. Now that she could swallow, Mary began to get better.

Mary and Connie went to stay at St. Moritz. The idea was that at a higher altitude your body worked to produce more oxygen-carrying red blood cells and Mary's anemia would improve. Jack joined the European tour of *The Vanishing Island* and Day stayed on at Caux to close up after the conference.

Mary and Connie had a happy and relaxed time in St. Moritz. Taking daily walks through the village, Day later reported, "Mary got a lot of wolf whistles from the guys. She exuded sex appeal. She said to Mum, 'I think I need to claim something from God in my heart so that I don't draw those wolf whistles.' They prayed about it together. On their next walk, there were no whistles. Mary said to Mum, 'He sure took me up quickly, more quickly than I expected!'"

Gradually Mary improved. She and Connie stayed at St. Moritz until Christmas, when along with Jack and Day they joined Frank Buchman and a few others at the Hotel Bella Vista in Montecatini, where Buchman was invited as an off-season guest of the owner. Day recalls singing Christmas carols around the candle-lit Christmas tree.

Dr. Buchman had a custom of giving Christmas or birthday presents to those around him. Usually it was a fine little embroidered hanky for the women and a handkerchief for the men, often products of St. Gallen, in Switzerland, the home of his ancestors. This Christmas Jack and Morris Martin, Buchman's executive assistant, produced poems that were read aloud as Buchman presented his gift to each person in his party at the Bella Vista.

Jack enlisted one of the Italian-speakers in the party and took Connie, Mary and Day in their car to see his favorite places in and around Firenze; especially the convent of San Marco with its frescoes by Fra Angelico, all the places he had written about in 1911. Connie and Mary bought prints of their favorite paintings. Connie chose Fra Angelico's *Transfiguration*: she remembered a vivid experience when she had given her life to God in 1930, of seeing that scene before her. Mary chose the "*Noli me tangere*," Jesus saying to Mary Magdalene in the garden, "Don't touch me."

After Christmas the Elys drove over the Apennines to join the *Vanishing Island* cast and crew. "The drive was one of our rare times to be just Elys together," Day says. "Mary had realized over the beautiful Christmas season that there were parts of her life of which she was ashamed that she had never told to the family. So she took this private occasion to do so. They were sins of omission or thoughts, I believe, but they were important to her as being divisive and she wanted to live united. Father wanted to assure her that he accepted her and loved her under all circumstances and said something that she took as belittling her convictions. She was very angry, feeling she was not being taken seriously. The road was narrow and mountainous and the traffic was heavy. We had a long time together and talked through all sorts of things."

In Milan, Buchman and his party, including the Elys, were special guests of Archbishop Montini—later Pope Paul VI—at the New Year's Day High Mass in the Milan Cathedral. "We were seated in the very front of the nave," Day recounts. "The marble floor was icy, the air was icy. We were all shivering. Mother always tried to take care of her friends and family. She taught all sitting near her, and we passed it on, to take three deep breaths and hold the last one. Strangely, it did make us feel warmer. Then she showed us that if the person behind you will lean forward and put their mouth near your coat between the shoulder blades and breathe long warm breaths, it really makes you feel wonderfully warmed. We did this very discreetly as we waited two and a half hours for the Mass to begin. Once Cardinal Montini started chanting the beautiful Mass with music by St. Ambrose, we forgot our frozen toes."

In Milan, the Elys had been assigned rooms in the city's best hotel, the Principe e Savoie. Soon after New Year's, Connie was invited to visit the wife of the leader of the Christian chemical workers' union. Their one-room apartment was home to the union leader and his wife, his sister and her husband, and his parents, plus two children. The very next day, the city council of the Milan suburb of Sesto San Giovanni invited an international group, including the Elys, to speak about building a peaceful and just world—"Sesto" had a particularly un-peaceful history. The hatred between different classes had been so acute that during the confusion of 1945, the workers had thrown several managers alive into the blast furnaces.

When Connie spoke, she told the mayor and city council: "Yesterday I was visiting new friends in their apartment—one room for three generations totaling ten people, no indoor plumbing and very little food. This morning in my comfortable hotel room I thought about that visit and I could not eat my breakfast. Then God said to me, 'If one rich lady gives up one roll and coffee, it will not feed anyone; but if that same lady commits her life and all she has to changing the world, it will feed many people.' So I have decided to make that commitment." She sat down. The mayor stood up and answered, "If God can change rich people, then I don't have to shoot them."

Early in 1956, an invitation came from Chancellor Konrad Adenauer of West Germany to bring *The Vanishing Island* and an international task force to Bonn and Berlin. Berlin was a divided city. The Allies and West Germany held the western part, which was over a hundred miles inside East Germany, and the Soviets were trying to force the Allies out of West Berlin. The blockade of Berlin by the Soviet Union and the Allies' spectacular airlift to supply the city had occurred in 1948-49, and the Berlin wall would go up in 1961.

Adenauer's invitation said in part, "In this age of confusion we need in Europe, and especially in divided Germany, an ideology that brings clarity and represents a moral force in the shaping of international relations as well as in our own national life."

And so Jack and Day and the whole group were off to Berlin. Crowds filled the theater for *The Vanishing Island*. As the politically divided city had a unified subway system, many East Germans were able to attend. So eager were the crowds for this message that parallel presentations were held in nearby halls for those who could not get into the theater. Day and Barbara Riffe, daughter of a U.S. labor leader, would go from hall to hall telling how their parents, from different backgrounds, were friends working together to change the world.

The Elys and those with them were strongly advised to leave behind their address books, birthday date books, and any documentation with lists of people who could be put in danger if the lists got into the wrong hands. Kidnappings were not uncommon in West Berlin, with people disappearing and being spirited across into East Berlin and East Germany. Day pictured her father, so aristocratic in appearance, being kidnapped, or herself. She memorized parts of the Bible for inner support in case she should wind up in a Soviet prison.

After the visit to Berlin, Jack returned to the Ruhr area where the work went on at full tilt. Ray Purdy Jr., by now a graduate of Princeton, was working there with many others. He wrote to his father from Gelsenkirchen, heart of the coal industry, "Jack Ely is an absolute ball of fire. Boy, he is giving the industrialists and everyone else a challenge they won't soon forget." What Jack was saying in meetings with coal and steel executives, and in speeches in public and in man-to-man conversations, is typified by this segment of a letter he wrote from the Ruhr to his old friend Charlie Ames:

"Unless we capitalists are willing to put ideology before profits, careers and comforts, and to live a constructive answer to Communism, we may make our fortunes but we will lose our countries. Why should all the revolutionaries come from the Left? Why not revolutionaries, as well, from the Right and Center who are above race, class, party and personal success?"

Jack wrote from Germany to Congressman Charlie Deane at Easter 1956, "This may be the gravest year in recorded history." On the round-the-world trip earlier, he wrote, he and Connie had talked with many leaders: "All are convinced of the seriousness of the situation. Most would agree that it was put concisely by Whittaker Chambers when he asked 'Is civilization as we know it to be completely destroyed or completely changed? It is our fate to live upon that turning point in history.' Of the countries we have visited none has given me more anxiety than the United States."

Shortly after Easter, Mary sailed home with Dr. Irene Gates and some others, aboard the S.S. *Andrea Doria* (the last voyage before the ship burned and sank at sea). Florence was in Africa; Jack, Connie and Day decided their place was to remain in Europe. They went on to Holland with *The Vanishing Island*, and then to England and Scotland. By August they were at Caux once more, and in the fall returned to the United States. After accompanying *The Vanishing Island* in a tour of Michigan cities, Connie noted in her diary that she, Jack, Day and Mary had returned to Washington by train. "Tea," she noted, "in the garden of 2419!"

Buchman wrote to Connie at Christmas time, thanking her "for real live honest to goodness Pennsylvania food of the very best quality. Apple butter and scrapple, maple syrup and buckwheat flour and all the goodies." As he had grown older and more feeble, she had taken to sending him packages of the kind of food he had had as a boy in Pennsylvania Dutch country, and other things she knew he found especially tasty.

From home she replied to Buchman: "Just a line to say my guidance was, 1957 a year of unparalleled riches. Then Alice Hallward and I had guidance together and my guidance was to give 1/10 of available capital, i.e. $250,000—what a joy to have Emily Hammond [Mrs. John Henry Hammond] overshadow my bit! My decision was made with all the facts of capital and income on the table with Elsa and Ray Purdy and Min and Ken Twitchell and Jack and Day. This has been a freeing experience. I had often checked with others the amount of a gift but never had *all* the cards on the table." She added that the Ambassador from Vietnam had been at their home, and that when he said "good night," he spoke with vehemence and said, "Every time I come here I go away so much richer!"

There followed many weeks of activity around the Detroit area. Jack and Connie met a flamboyant character named John Earl McQueen, and his wife Patty. McQueen owned a tugboat service down-river from Detroit on the Canadian shore. His flagship was the tug *Atomic*, which was famous on the river and the adjoining Great Lakes. There were annual tugboat races, and *Atomic* was almost a sure thing to take the top prize. McQueen also drank a quart of whiskey a night, as he had done for thirty-five years.

His times with the MRA plays and friends like Jack and Connie had their effect, however, and his first major decision was to go on the wagon. Knowing that this can be an extremely tricky state for a man, the Elys invited the McQueens to visit them in Washington and then drove them up to Dellwood to enjoy a visit with the MRA people there, including Mary Ely, and then to Mackinac Island. There were cruises on the Detroit River in the *Atomic* and many happy times. Sadly, a few months later Earl McQueen died. The Elys attended his funeral and gave as much support to Patty McQueen as they could.

One of Jack's most interesting friends in Washington was John V. Riffe, who had been a labor organizer with the Congress of Industrial Organizations (the CIO) and was among the union's top leaders. John and his wife Rose had a transforming experience of God at a time when their life was coming apart, and they were an active part of the MRA team with the Elys and others. In the 1950s John was working to bring the "divided house" of labor together, to effect a reunion of the American Federation of Labor and the CIO.[1]

John Riffe's daughter Barbara is emphatic about what her father felt about the Elys and their home. "Dad felt the house was a place he could bring people, and he would say to them 'Here is a man who could be sitting at the Union Club right now, reading his paper, not bothering with anybody, and ordering another highball, and here he is making himself available to me and my friends.' His friends, of course, meant the hierarchy of the labor movement in America. The Elys showed there really was a classless society. I think my Dad felt that every day he went there: 'It is true, and it happens right in front of me.'"

One Saturday John invited Jack out to his house to meet his new pastor at his local Presbyterian church. John was in very poor health, but was in superb spirits. That afternoon was a life-changing time for the pastor. He talked with John and Jack about things in his life that needed to be different. The following day the men attended his church service. He began his sermon with "He who confesses his transgression will obtain mercy," and went on to share his determination "to become a Christian." He told of how he had begun to steal his sermons from a book, and with that his devotional life had gone to pot. He saw that if the cross of Christ were to be alive to him it would be necessary to right the wrongs he had done to God and to his parishioners. He asked them to find it in their hearts to forgive him and went on to relate the need of change in his own life to the world's need of change.

"As we left the church," Jack wrote to Buchman, "one man turned to a friend and asked to borrow a handkerchief. 'For ten years I have been to church and this is the first time I have ever needed one.' A lawyer said, 'You struck home today. I have longed to hear a preacher whom I felt I could trust. I feel I can be absolutely honest with you now. My family needs help. We want to see you and find out where we go from here.'"

The Ely's guest book records the visit to their home, in mid-1957, of Dr. Martin Luther King, Jr., of Montgomery, Alabama, with his father and a group of his colleagues, including the Rev. Ralph Abernathy and Toussaint Hill. Earlier that year, Jack had gotten to know G. Lake Imes, who had been personal secretary to Booker T. Washington. When Imes died some time later, a chair that Dr. Washington had given to Imes was left to Jack in Imes's will, and is now at Florence Ely Nelson's home.

At Mackinac an unusual new theatrical production was developed around the life story of Mary McLeod Bethune. Mrs. Bethune had had a life-changing experience at one of the MRA assemblies at the Shoreham Hotel in Washington, at which the daughter of former slave-owners had apologized to her for her attitude of superiority and indifference toward her race, and it had touched Mrs. Bethune deeply. She had said at that time, "To be a part of this great uniting force of our age is the crowning experience of my life."

The musical play based on her life story—and on the wider vision she had experienced at that meeting at the Shoreham—was called *The Crowning Experience*. It featured the marvelous voice and personality of Muriel Smith, an African-American woman of tremendous vitality who had created the title role of *Carmen Jones* on Broadway and had sung the title role in the opera *Carmen* at Covent Garden in Britain. The play became an extraordinary vehicle in our nation, which was beginning to feel the power of the civil rights movement.[2]

As this new play was developing, the Ely family gathered some of their friends to consider what their own next moves should be. Mary had the thought that she should do what had been recommended when she had been so ill in Lausanne—to find out what had brought her so close to death at that time. She checked into the University Hospital in Ann Arbor, Michigan, under the care of Dr. Arthur Allen. Art Allen's wife was a daughter of Norton and Mary Brotherton, whose other daughter, Mary Jane, was married to Cece Broadhurst. That whole family was seeking to keep God at the center, which made the Elys feel safer about Mary's care.

At this time *The Crowning Experience* opened for a run in Detroit, forty miles east of Ann Arbor. In the cast of the play were a number of children from African-American families of the Detroit area. Mary had become a good friend of several of them and was looking forward to finishing her time in the hospital and traveling with them—this would be her first experience of being "on the road" with a play.

Mary had grown and matured a great deal, from a teenager who enjoyed every bit of male admiration to a young woman of twenty-two whose life was given to Christ, and who knew in detail what that commitment meant. At home her schoolbooks had had the names of boys written all over them. One boy lived behind the house on Massachusetts Avenue, and they had often walked the dog together. She had loved dancing classes, and would dance until her deformed feet would bleed. Now her life was focused, with a strong and straightforward faith that sustained her and that was a gift to everyone around her. Her likes and relationships were held up to the light of what she believed Jesus Christ wanted her to do. Furthermore, she lived in the heart of a world family.

The days in the hospital were tough for Mary and baffling for Dr. Allen and his associates. She had much pain, and was given a lot of painkillers, which kept her in a stupor much of the time. An Englishman named Oliver Corderoy was staying in Detroit, working with the MRA program. He knew the Ely family was going through a very hard time; sometimes Mary felt better, often she felt worse. One night Corderoy and Jarvis Harriman drove out to Ann Arbor to have dinner with the family. Corderoy told the Elys about his mother, who had faced terrible pain in the last stages of bone cancer. Although she was an atheist, she had prayed with her son and daughter to be spared the pain, and it had happened. Mrs. Corderoy had received a vital sense of God's loving care for her and complete freedom from fear. As a result, she had not needed powerful painkillers, even on the last day of her life.

Day says, "Oliver suggested that even if Mary could not pray with us, we could together claim his mother's fearlessness and trust in God's loving plan for Mary, and it might affect her spirit. So in the hospital corridor we prayed together for this gift. Next time Mary woke up, she was clear of mind and did not need any more of the major drugs. This was a great gift to us, to have her with us those last days. Every letter in her travel-desk was answered, every button sewed on, every note in her quiet time book fulfilled. Even a nice cloth for her Aunt JJ embroidered in red, JJ's favorite color."

Jack's diary for January 24th, 1958: "Soon after midnight we were called as Mary was in shock. Art Allen was there and fought hard to bring her back. Three blood transfusions." Day stayed by her, with Art, while Jack and Connie went for some breakfast. Day said, "All at once Mary looked up and raised her arms like a baby being picked up by her mother, said 'Whoops—here I go!' and was gone." Jack's diary concludes, "Our beloved Mary was with Niel. There followed a victorious day."

. . . .

NOTES

1. Through the efforts of John Riffe and others, the historic merger of the AFL and CIO was formalized in 1955.

2. For more on the impact of *The Crowning Experience*, see Garth Lean, *Frank Buchman: A Life* (London: Constable, 1985) pages 498 ff.

Certainly

Ellie Forde Newton wrote this poem in 1958, after Mary Ely's death at age twenty-three. Mary had worked frequently as a switchboard operator at Moral Re-Armament conferences.

"Certainly!"
We heard her voice come through the telephone
And in that word she made her faith our own.
"Certainly!"
Meant yes, that she would do it; it was fun,
And beyond the shadow of a doubt it could be done!

"Certainly!"
She gave her whole life to us in the word.
Much more than Mary's loved and loving voice we heard;
We heard the echo of the eternal deed,
When she said "Certainly" to God, for all in need;
When youth and wealth she did not hoard nor heed,
But gave it all to cure the world of greed.
We heard God's answer to an age of doubt;
We heard faith putting duty dull to rout;
We heard a note of gentle jubilee
Whenever Mary answered "Certainly."

So frail the life, so dauntless in its gift,
Holding a world an Atlas could not lift,
Because each time without a moment's loss,
"Certainly!"
She said to Christ when He said: "Share My Cross."

Mary, your voice all down the future years
The world will hear in answer to its fears,
Laughing and loving, that unfaltering "Yes,"
To challenge gently, heal, and win and bless,
And those who best have known and miss your voice,
With you today confirm that valiant choice:
Say "Yes" to God who asks that men may be
Faith-born—aye, Mary, we will do it,
"Certainly!"

14

Elder Statesman

I T IS IMPOSSIBLE TO GAUGE THE DEPTH of the loss of a second child to the Ely family. Jack's diary: "Such sorrow, such rejoicing. Put away all 'if only' thoughts and know that Mary went straight into God's hands and that God loves us."

The Elys had given Dr. Allen permission for an autopsy, as this had been a case with complications reaching over Mary's whole life. The autopsy revealed an enormous scar on her aorta from her earlier crisis in Lausanne. "It must have been the hand of God that saved her then," Dr. Allen told the family. The autopsy essentially confirmed Dr. Allen's diagnosis and methods, which was important to him as some of his colleagues had been quite critical of the medical decisions he had made.

In the hospital, Mary had arranged to send a gold bracelet to her friend Helen Hunter, who was engaged to Frank McGee. Their wedding took place in Atlanta just a day or two before Mary's funeral. Afterwards, Helen McGee sent her bouquet to Washington for Mary's casket. Day recalls, "We put the pure white wedding bouquet over Mary's heart as she was a bride of Christ, by choice pure as the driven snow these last years."

The next day Jack wrote, "Easter for Mary! She is risen. Sing out my heart, but it is very hard. Think of tomorrow, Day says, 'as Mary's wedding day.' So many came, it seemed from everywhere!" and he listed the names of many friends. "A glorious Mary-planned and God-led day," Jack's diary reads. "Mary, Mary what you gave us! The service at St. John's at 11 a.m. was triumphant. The sun shone through the diadem of daffodils on the casket as Mary left the church. Ninety-seven of Mary's friends at lunch [including] Ambassador Gunawardene [of Sri Lanka]. A rich time, also, at dinner."

Florence was thousands of miles away in South Africa. She and her friends there held a memorial service for Mary, which included the family of William Nkomo, a founder of the African National Congress Youth League, singing the Twenty-third Psalm in the Xhosa language. Florence remembers, "It was all clicks and harmony, simply beautiful. I thought how much Mary would have enjoyed that."

Asked whether she had considered coming home for Mary's funeral, Florence said that circumstances made that impossible: "And also, it wasn't the Ely way. Our unity as a family was in our common commitment to God, not on being physically together." Later when she met her family in Switzerland and learned how they had all prayed at Mary's bedside and accepted her pain, Florence suffered deeply at having missed that time. "I went off by myself and had it out with God," she recounts. "I told Him that I was never again going to be apart from my family. He said to me, 'If you pray now, I can put it back and it will count and it will help your sister.' It became so real to me that time and distance are only human ideas and do not matter to God. That has removed from me any dread of not 'being there' at a particular moment."

Mary was buried in Arlington beside her brother. Once again there was the sense of a world family reaching out to support and sustain them. Once again the sense that in the midst of life there is death, and in the presence of death there is full and overflowing life. Jack designed Mary's gravestone, with the verse from Paul's first letter to the Corinthians, "Thanks be to God, who gives us the victory through our lord Jesus Christ." When Mary's affairs were settled, the family gave her whole estate to MRA.

And life went on. Connie, Jack and Day made family visits in New York that they found very comforting after Mary's death. Jack attended a Yale Class of 1915 dinner and a Burrwood Corporation meeting, Connie a Foxcroft reunion. They went out to Cold Spring Harbor to see Lyman and Ruth Bleecker, who had been such good friends at St. John's Church there, and to catch a glimpse of Burrwood.

The Elys then went to Atlanta to participate in the showings of *The Crowning Experience*. According to Frances Woolford, daughter of one of the first families of white Atlanta, the work spearheaded by *The Crowning*

Experience was a turning point for that city. In the heat of the civil rights movement, that mighty upheaval in "business as usual" that was shaking the South, the presence of this multiracial company with their heart-moving musical drama of change in racial attitudes, healing and forgiveness helped to bring Atlanta into the modern age without violence. *The Crowning Experience* and other MRA plays pushed for and achieved integration of the theaters where they played.

That summer and fall the Elys spent some weeks on Mackinac Island where, in addition to holding an assembly, MRA was shooting a film of *The Crowning Experience*. There was a death in the group making the film: In November, Lina Kurowski of Germany passed away, and was buried in the little Protestant cemetery in the center of the island. Her husband Paul had been a dialectical tactician for the Communist Party, and was one of those who had grasped the essence of the world revolution for which Moral Re-Armament was calling. As a result, Paul and Lina had found a real change in their lives. The Kurowskis and the Elys had traveled around the world together with *The Vanishing Island*, and had shared the fellowship of a new way of life in which capitalists and Communists found a common goal. Paul Kurowski had comforted the Elys when first Niel, and then Mary, died; now the Elys supported him.

In the fall of 1958 Day Ely moved on to work in London, and Florence went to Los Angeles. New Years Day 1959 found Jack and Connie with Florence and some of her friends at the annual Rose Parade in Pasadena. Jack and Connie drove from there to Tucson, where Buchman welcomed them in his new home there. A few days later Jack had a dizzy spell and pain in his left arm. Dr. Paul Campbell, who spent much of his time looking after Buchman as his personal physician, recommended Jack go home to be with his own doctor.

They returned to Washington by train and within three weeks Jack was feeling more like himself again. They attended the wedding of Jane Case, daughter of Senator and Mrs. Francis Case of South Dakota. The bridegroom was about to be posted to Thailand with the International Cooperation Agency. The next evening the Cases came to the Ely house for a quiet family supper, and Jack showed his slides of Thailand. Mrs. Case was especially pleased because she had no real idea of the country her only child was about to live in. In describing the evening in a letter to Buchman, Jack said of Senator Case, "He may be the best informed member of Congress on Germany."

Life in Washington was full for the Elys. They had many good friends, including Douglas Cornell, Executive Director of the National Academy of Sciences, and his wife Priscilla and their children. They also visited with Douglas Mayberry, the new young rector of St. John's Church, and his wife. Jack saw his friends: General Lyman Lemnitzer, who was expected to become the next Chief of Staff of the Army; Ellsworth Bunker, Yale 1915 and now Ambassador to India; and Richard Arens of the Senate Internal Security Committee.

Edith Staton had become Connie's close friend in the 1950s. Her husband, Admiral Adolphus "Dolph" Staton, was retired. Edith was a Blair. Her family had built the Blair House on Pennsylvania Avenue across from the White House in the time of President Andrew Jackson. Blair House is now the President's guesthouse. Edith had been born there in a third floor bedroom. When Dolph Staton was bedridden and dying, Connie and Jack would drive out to the Staton home in Chevy Chase; Connie and Edith would take a walk and Jack would visit with Dolph.

In March 1959 Priscilla Cornell died, leaving four children of school and college age. She had battled cancer for several years. During her illness she had welcomed visits from Connie, who was a relaxed person and no stranger to suffering. Both women were rooted in their faith. They would set up a card table at the foot of Priscilla's bed and Connie would bring people to visit.

Jack had more heart warnings, serious enough for Day to fly home from England.

In May they took "a darling wee house" at West Falmouth, on Cape Cod, where they were joined by Day and Florence. It was too early in the spring for the social set, so there was time for a real rest, for walking and for watching the birds, woodchucks, rabbits, and an occasional skunk. They drove to Newport and toured "The Breakers," where Jack showed his family the bedroom where he had stayed when visiting the Vanderbilt family in earlier days. Jack bought Connie a lovely bronze doorknocker on one outing, and on another a blue pottery platter. He was allowed to go to church on Sunday, and as usual he made friends with the minister. Day recalls that she, Florence and Connie took turns reading aloud to Jack and each other, while those not reading worked on two pieces of needlepoint embroidery that Connie had bought in Paris on her honeymoon and had not had time to finish.

Buchman sent word that Brooks Onley, who was by now a part of the cast of *The Crowning Experience* and was at Mackinac for the filming, had also had heart trouble. Brooks was getting the best of care and was doing as well as could be expected.

During the six weeks in Falmouth, Jack had time for reflection. He wrote to Buchman: "If we do not possess more moral backbone as a result of our religious practice we need to ask ourselves if we have really penetrated to the heart of the Christian faith. I am finding here that tension—which has played such a part in my illness—comes from wishing to do things in my way, from ambition, from pride, from fear of being wrong and fear of what others may say or think. . . . If I could be sure God would direct I could relax and let him. Just as a child places his hand in his father's to cross the street! I think that's it. I am really beginning to have that childlike faith."

A grand adventure began to take shape in the Elys' minds during the weeks of quiet on Cape Cod and later at Mackinac where they spent some time. According to Day, Jack had always wanted to circumnavigate the globe in the Southern Hemisphere. And Jack had received personal invitations to visit several of the emerging nations of Africa, from jurists whom he had met at Caux and on the *Vanishing Island* tour. Florence, who accompanied her parents on the trip, puts the invitation in perspective:

"These countries were becoming independent nations for the very first time. They had been tribal entities, then colonial offices had divided them into countries and had ruled them. Now, in 1959, they were facing a totally new situation. Many of the leaders had been at Caux, and over meals with Father and hearing him speak, had come to value his brain and worth and his love of constitutional law. He had the economic and legal background to talk to these men. So these chief justices decided to invite him to their countries."

On the twenty-third of September, 1959, Jack, Connie and Florence flew from New York to Lisbon. Day remained in Washington, to "hold the fort," looking after the staff and managing the finances, as the house would continue to operate with various guest hosts during the Elys' extended absence. Connie's instructions to Day were clear: "You must pay the bills promptly because you don't know how close the vendor figures his budget. Pay on time."

The Elys left Washington with the assumption that they would be away for eighteen months. Their plan was to spend a few days in Portugal seeing Lisbon, but especially Fatima, which had for years been a quiet but major thrust of Jack's prayer life. The Virgin's appearance at Fatima in 1917 had called for people to repent of their sins and to pray for the conversion of Russia. Then on to Caux for a couple of weeks, where they would plan in detail for a trip to Africa. Connie wrote in a note to Buchman, "Personally, Frank, I've never felt more inadequate and with less know-how. Guidance is the only sure signpost and absolute standards are what I decide daily to live and fight for. I'll never give up and I'll never withdraw any more. I see my nature and God is changing it. Gratefully, affectionately and faithfully yours, Connie Ely."

After five weeks at Caux they flew down to Rome, where they visited with Nigel Hazeltine, an advisor on African affairs to the United Nations Food and Agriculture Organization. Hazeltine was very pessimistic; he felt that the West had not more than two and a half years to save Africa from Communism. The Communist strategy, he said, was to set up one-party governments, to penetrate economically and culturally, to set African against African as they had already done in the Belgian Congo and in the Cameroons, and to set black against white—and in the confusion to seize power. He advised the Elys that the only real solution in Africa would come not through Europeans or Americans but through Africans like those he had met at Caux, Africans who had an ideology.

The next weeks were a whirlwind of movement. The Elys flew from Rome on November 15, to Dakar, Senegal, on the west cost of Africa, and immediately found themselves at a frontier of the Cold War. At the airport were larger-than-life pictures of Mao Zedong, Florence reports: "We had not realized that Communist China was virtually running Senegal. They had set up a one-party government and had penetrated economically. It was scary."

On to Monrovia, Liberia. The Elys spent about ten days there, traveling the length and breadth of the country "in rackety trucks over incredible roads," Florence says: "It was an orientation time, and Mother and Father began to realize the diversity of the continent." They met the president and vice president of Liberia, and visited the iron-ore mines in the interior, run by Swedish engineers.

They also had to acclimatize to cultural differences. For Jack, to whom punctuality was an essential courtesy, the more relaxed African attitude toward Western clock-time and meal times meant a somewhat difficult adjustment. Florence realized that her father's health depended on getting the right food at the proper time, and undertook to see that his needs were met, cooking in her bedroom if necessary.

The family traveled by car to Accra, Ghana, where they stayed for about ten days with the chief justice, one of the jurists who had invited Jack to the continent. He and his wife were a gracious couple, in whom the Elys saw poignantly one of the key troubles in these new African nations. The previous chief justice, an Englishman, had built a gorgeous house for himself, which the African chief justice and his family had inherited. For the Africans, it was all artificial. The huge house and the limousine had been designed to bribe the European civil servants to stay in this hot climate. "Just think," Florence reminisced, "if that man had been able to push through the new government the change he felt was needed. They wouldn't have spent the next years aping the white man, would have been far less corruptible, would have had their own self-respect and wouldn't have developed a champagne taste. Within eighteen months Prime Minister Kwame Nkrumah had put the chief justice in jail. He died there."

From Accra, Connie wrote to Buchman, "Jack has given matchlessly and in spite of unusual conditions! His ideology has been consistent and powerful and very winning. His apology for U.S. [arrogance] and a sentence or two of what we need goes deep every time. He does feel less lively but he does not indulge his weariness."

The Elys moved on to Lagos, Nigeria, where again they met with the chief justice. They had excellent contacts through their link with Nigeria's first president, Nnamdi Azikiwe, whom they had hosted when he represented his country in Washington. The journey continued, to Ibadan, to Brazzaville, (Congo), where Jack particularly wanted to see the Black Crucifix, then to Leopoldville (now Kinshasa, in the Democratic Republic of the Congo), and by air to Johannesburg, South Africa.

Mostly the Elys were the guests of friends they had made in the cast of the all-African play *Freedom*, written at Caux by men and women from all parts of the continent. They worked a great deal with John Amata of Nigeria, who portrayed a young revolutionary leader in that play. Their days were busy with many people, yet their schedule was loose enough for Jack's moderate supply of strength.

Florence wrote to Buchman: "Dad seems older, slower, but also far closer to God. He reads people and their needs and potentials far more than before. . . . The academic solutions begin to seem flimsy to him, with the change in human nature and God control the only answer. He talks a lot about his youth, things we have never heard. And about his parents. And the brothers who died. And about the early days with you. We understand now what 'I have been wonderfully led' [a favorite phrase of Buchman's] means. Whatever the future holds, I feel he is living his destiny."

She further wrote, "Dad has just come upstairs after a four-hour fight with John Amata for Onumara Egwonoke of the Floating Staffs Union [of

Lagos, Nigeria]. Dad's fight for people and nations has been inspired. There is a bigness-wideness and depth that moves people into God's space."

They arrived in South Africa, where the descendants of the Dutch and English settlers were still in control. Here Nico Ferreira, a young Dutch South African, became an indispensable colleague. Jack went with him to visit the ministers of defense, finance, and economic affairs, also the deputy speaker of the Parliament, the leader of the opposition, and a number of others in Parliament.

The Elys lived in a small apartment in the Cape Town suburb of Vishoek, which they used to host people of all races—black, Indian, white. They found themselves interpreting for South Africa's white leadership what they had experienced in West Africa and what they saw as the ideological struggle for Africa. Jack's colored slides of the people and the places where they had been were used to illustrate the hope for fresh and creative life taking root in the new African nations. Florence commented, "For these South African leaders to talk with someone who had actually lived in the homes of cabinet ministers of these new countries, and talked with them off the cuff, meant a tremendous amount. It broke some of the isolation barriers."

The practical running of the household and preparation of these meals fell largely to Florence, who also typed Jack's numerous letters and drove her parents in her 1956 Chevrolet. She was joined in these tasks by Ann Laidlaw, a young Englishwoman from the Isle of Jersey. "We were the 'chefertary,'" Florence says, "chef, chauffeur, secretary." Nico Ferreira also helped in many practical ways and taught them how to select and prepare the local fish. "I can still preserve fish in salt," Florence recounts, "because that's what the 'voertrekkers'—the early Dutch pioneers—used to do."

Jack and Connie got to know P.Q. Vundla, a black South African who had been on the cutting edge of the hate between blacks and whites. He had been to Caux, and had experienced a profound change in his life through God's healing and guiding power, which reflected in a fresh attitude to white South Africans. Vundla was a truly big man, a great man. The absence of hate in his face, his voice, his bearing was a perfect match for Jack, and he attended many of these evenings in the little apartment in Cape Town. For many of their guests this was the first time they had ever shaken the hand of a black man.

"We have met men of every shade of political viewpoint," Jack wrote Buchman from Cape Town. "Some hold opinions which seem as cruel and warped as certain parts of the Karroo where it has not really rained for seven years. Others are as rank and tangled in their thinking as the sub-tropical forests we found around Port St. John's. Still others see the situation as clearly as we have viewed the glorious rolling country of the Transkei marked by its green pastures and native rondaval huts."

On this trip there was time to enjoy the beauty of Africa, to swim in the ocean and enjoy some leisure, but it was a trip with a purpose. Florence made sure her father had the diet he needed. "Dad liked hot milk in his coffee in the morning," Florence says. "He couldn't stand to have skim on his milk. I had to strain it through a handkerchief. And of course if you don't drink it immediately, skim forms on it again. Sometimes, I'd have to strain it through three handkerchiefs." Then there was Jack's everlasting passion for picture-taking. In Florence's words: "We drove five thousand miles—three thousand of them backwards, to get the right pictures!"

In mid-March they flew to Lorenço Marques in Mozambique and on to what was then called Rhodesia, now Zimbabwe, then Zambia, Kenya and Uganda, and a boat trip on the Nile, photographing hippopotamus and crocodile. They stayed in East Africa until the middle of May. Jack spent some days in bed, but he was mostly able to take part in everything, though at a slower pace. These visits were greatly enhanced by two couples who thought of every detail: Vere and Madi James in Nairobi, and Bill and Gwen McIntosh in Kampala.

On to Mauritius, the Cocos Islands, and to Perth, in western Australia. "Dad loved doing these 'Guinness Book of Records' kinds of flights," Florence said. "We took the longest over-ocean commercial flight, in this case from Mauritius to the Cocos Islands, two tiny little dots with a huge airstrip on one of them." These were the pre-jet age days of the much more limited DC 6 and Lockheed Constellation propeller airplanes.

They spent the whole of the summer—winter in the Southern Hemisphere—in Australia, enjoying rich times with friends old and new. Buchman had asked them to introduce the new film of *The Crowning Experience* in Australia, and they found themselves orchestrating film premieres in the main cities: Melbourne, Adelaide, Canberra, Sidney, Perth. In each case the premiere was a black-tie affair attended by the governor of that province, representing Her Majesty the Queen. In Canberra the "August winter" weather was very chilly and the houses built for keeping cool, so Jack got the flu. They warmed up and had a real rest up north at the Great Barrier Reef, on the beach at Dunk Island. Then on to Brisbane and Tasmania.

In October, they flew to New Zealand—Christchurch, Wellington,

Auckland. Connie, always a country person at heart, loved the visits with sheep ranchers and Maori friends and particularly remembered boiling their breakfast eggs in a hot spring with the Harawira family.

At the end of October they sailed on a Matson line ship to Pago Pago and Honolulu. They were met at the dock in Honolulu by Bill Alexander, who had served with Jack on the *Yale Daily News*, and his wife Alice. Bill was a sugar consultant from a pioneering family in the American history of the Islands. He arranged for Jack to speak at the Yale Club, which in turn led to Jack's addressing two senior classes at the prestigious Punahou School. Walter Dillingham, a "grand old man" of the American community, entertained the Elys at dinner on his patio with Hawaiian singers and ukeleles. He and others whom they saw had been involved in the *Vanishing Island* visit to Hawaii in 1955. Jack was also asked to speak at Kamehameha High School.

At Punahou Jack met a young teacher who was a fellow Yale graduate and, like Jack, a member of Wolf's Head. He visited with Jack and they had a very serious talk. The next night he appeared at the Elys' door in utter distress. He had been surfboarding with his best friend, and his board had hit his friend in the head so hard it split open the young man's skull and killed him. The young teacher stayed there with the Ely family, while Florence taught his classes for three days.

Jack, Connie and Florence arrived in Los Angeles on the twenty-third of November, 1960. The Elys had made friends and touched people's hearts on three continents, and Jack had done what he had long wanted to accomplish—circumnavigated the globe below the equator.

15

Requiem

O N NEW YEAR'S DAY, 1961, at home in Washington, the Elys attended St. John's Church for communion, and had a small luncheon party at the house. In the evening they went to Senator and Mrs. Case's home for dinner.

That January brought television to the Ely house for the first time. The family rented a set so they could all watch John F. Kennedy's inauguration, which was of special interest because of the new First Lady's connection to the family through Connie's cousin Hugh D. Auchincloss. Day wept—not, she avers, because Kennedy was a Democrat, but rather because of the disjunction she perceived between his beautiful inaugural speech and what she had heard of his character.

January also brought a difficult and unfortunate event in connection with the work to which Connie and Jack had so fully given their hearts and heads and treasure. They had but recently returned home after their world tour that had lasted over a year. During that time away they had entrusted their home to guest hosts so it could continue to be used as an embassy for the work of Moral Re-Armament. Now some of those in MRA, who had begun to regard their use of this home as a right rather than as the generous gift it was, took it into their heads to ask the Ely parents to leave; in short, to get out of the way. The reason given was that Jack's health limited the use of the house.

At about five in the afternoon of a day late in January, Connie, Jack and Florence piled into their car, with a suitcase each, and headed south, in a snow storm, leaving Day at the house. They drove into Virginia and stopped at a motel; the next day, Day brought them some forgotten items, and they headed down to Richmond. They checked into the John Marshall Hotel, where Jack registered a fever of 100.2 degrees.

Until a genuine apology was given to Connie several years after Jack had died, Connie would always say they were asked to leave so that Jack could be in a warm climate and have adequate rest, which was impossible at the Washington house. This was true, but they had left immediately, embarrassed and feeling ostracized from their own home. To the family, Day says, nothing could soften the abruptness of their departure.

In Richmond Connie saw several of their close friends the next day, while Jack stuck close to his bed. By the third day Jack's fever was gone. In easy stages they drove on south, with stops at Jekyll Island, Charleston, Savannah, Daytona Beach, Palm Beach, Fort Myers Beach and finally on to Sarasota. They settled into the Mitty Beach Hotel for a longer stay. Florence took the train back to Washington.

At each stage of the trip they visited with some of their oldest friends. Connie and Jack were careful not to let this unexpected virtual expulsion become a point of division; they were far too devoted to the work and fellowship of MRA to let themselves be used to divide people.

The Elys stayed in Sarasota and later at Longboat Key until the last week in April. Much rest, Jack not being well; days of as much walking and swimming and sun as they wanted, with good friends to see as they wished. Ray and Elsa Purdy spent many hours with them, as did Alan and Kay Limburg.

Later Day flew to join her parents, and they drove north by easy stages. In Georgia they were warned of a speed trap, and slowed down. As they came down a hill, they observed a wheel and tire going down the hill ahead of them; then as they applied the brakes, the car sank on one side. It was their own rear wheel, broken right off the axle, passing them! They had to stop, of course. Jack was trying to get home for an appointment, so he took a taxi to the nearest airport and flew to Washington. Connie and Day stayed "in a little motel, dark under the pine trees, waiting for the work on the car to be done."

In late May of 1961 Jack, Connie and Florence flew to Switzerland to join Frank Buchman at Caux. There Connie worked again, as she had on many previous occasions, to arrange the seating for special guests at

Buchman's table. "Frank's table" might accommodate twenty people, and was always seated carefully to produce congenial or effective conversations. Years earlier at Caux Buchman had asked Connie to plan the seating, as he had not always been pleased with the arrangements made by others. From then on, whenever Connie was there with Buchman, he wanted her to seat his table. He evidently valued her no-nonsense approach and shrewd sense of people and protocol, as well as her honesty. This summer of 1961, Frank sometimes came to the table, but often he was too weak to be there and someone else would host the table in his absence. The Elys dined there often.

Buchman and two or three of his closest friends and aides went from Caux to Freudenstadt, a charming town in Germany's Black Forest where in 1938 he had had his first concrete thought of the program of Moral Re-Armament. Early in the morning of the eighth of August one of their friends came to the Elys' room at Caux to tell them that Frank Buchman had died in the night.

The conference at Caux was stunned. A number of people had come to regard Buchman as indispensable to the work of MRA and could not visualize its continuance without him, while others, like the Elys, understood Buchman as a tool of God—as they themselves were committed to be—and understood MRA as God's creation. They did not feel that this work had come to an end, and they were sure that God would continue to guide those who listened to him.

Three days later a special train took a large group from Caux to Freudenstadt, where they attended a service in the central church and a memorial meeting at the Kursaal. Hundreds from all over Germany and Europe met to pay tribute to this extraordinary life which had meant so much for Europe; then the special train took them back to Caux.

A few days later several hundred flew on a special airplane from Geneva via Paris to New York, and went from there by bus to Allentown, Pennsylvania, Buchman's home town. Again, hundreds came to that funeral service from all over the Western Hemisphere. As Buchman would have wished, all were served a good Pennsylvania Dutch meal. Connie wrote in her diary, "Glorious day."

To carry on this work without Buchman required a huge leap of the imagination, a leap in faith. It was an opportunity for the entire fellowship to learn that God comes first, not any person, no matter how beloved. Five days later another charter plane took the Elys and most of the MRA leadership back to Caux. From there they brought a demonstration of MRA's message to Holland, then across Switzerland, and back to Germany—to Freudenstadt in the south, to Tübingen and the Ruhr, whose coal miners had served as an honor guard for Buchman on many occasions. Jack spoke frequently at these public meetings. Then he and Connie flew to London, where Day and Florence joined them. More large meetings and demonstrations.

Jack, Connie and a considerable group then flew to New York and on to Rio de Janeiro. The work had burgeoned across South America since Jack's trip in 1951. They spent Christmas in Rio, and then on to São Paulo. Early in 1962 a Japanese play came to Brazil, where there were many citizens of Japanese descent. Japanese students, whose trip to Mackinac the Elys had helped to finance, had written *The Tiger* to give their convictions for a new world. It played throughout Brazil, with huge crowds in attendance. The Elys spent three months with this campaign.

Kirsten Andersen Larsen, a young Danish woman working as a secretary to the leaders of the campaign in Brazil, recalls Connie's caring concern for individuals. Late one night Kirsten and another young woman returned to their hotel from the central post office, where they had gone to send out a press release via telex machine. They found Connie waiting for them in the lobby. Kirsten recalls, "Connie got up and said, 'I just wanted to be sure you girls returned safely—let's go and have a cappuccino.' It gave me such a warm feeling to know that someone cared like that." On another occasion, Kirsten was asked to fly from Brazil to South Africa and join a team there, but had no idea how to pay for a ticket. "Connie came up to me at breakfast and said, 'Jack and I have just ordered your ticket to Johannesburg.' I think I burst into tears of gratitude, but then Connie said, 'By the way, you can't go there without any money,' and she handed me $50, an enormous amount in those days."

In mid-April the Elys were back in the United States. After several busy weeks at home, they drove by stages to Oklahoma, where they stayed with Mr. and Mrs. Streeter Flynn, another couple from the Yale Class of 1915. Joel McCrea and his wife Frances Dee, one of the Hollywood couples who had become sincerely interested in what God was doing through MRA, joined them there in a campaign across the "Sooner" state with plays, meetings, and personal work. Jack had good and bad days, and concern about his heart, but was in the thick of the activity.

When they returned to Washington, Dr. Snyder took a good look at Jack. "It's more serious than we thought," was his considered verdict. "You need extreme quiet. You are fortunate to get home." Connie recorded that

Jack felt himself a sick man and knew that his days were numbered.

The Elys' close friends, Philippe and Hélène Mottu of Switzerland, visited Washington with three of their four children. Jack and Connie arranged for them to see the sights, and personally took them to Mt. Vernon. Then the four Elys drove at a modest pace to Mackinac Island. Along the way they stopped at Elyria, Ohio, to photograph locations of historic interest to the Ely family.

The Elys had rented a house at Mackinac, a comfortable cottage called "Bonnie Doon," where Jack could be close to the action yet away from the hustle and bustle. He stayed in the cottage much of the time, and people visited him. He walked with Day or Florence or Connie, but they had to cut down the visitors when Jack overdid it. He was helped in his wheelchair to attend a board meeting of Moral Re-Armament, Inc., of which he was a director.

Jack wrote from Mackinac to Peter Howard, who had assumed a position of leadership in MRA since Buchman's death:

> It is God's plan for me to rejoice in the peace and quiet of this beloved island and not to be swept into unguided activity. There'll be time for everything. Don't rush God!
>
> "If your brother hath ought against thee"—and how many of our South American brothers have—"first be reconciled to him before making your gift." Isn't this the basis of what U.S. policy should be towards Latin America? Why not view our motives and our acts through their eyes. If we did we would see our need to change, to drop our self-righteousness, to have done with our superiority and arrogance and as fellow workers with them in humility and brotherhood take on our common task of remaking this hemisphere . . .
>
> I am tired of reading about Assemblies meeting to frame an answer. The answer was given us close on 2000 years ago and proclaimed by Frank for modern man. Our task is not to frame, but to take it out of its frame and live it militantly. Basically it means each of us taking the beam out of his own eye. When we do that we'll have enough building material to construct a new world. But God must be the architect.

In mid-September 1962 the Elys drove back to Washington by easy stages. When Jack made these trips back and forth from Washington to Mackinac Island, he would quite often stop to see the Merchant family in Rochester, or visit Syracuse, where John Merchant's family lived for many years.

In December 1962 Jack's cousin George Merchant died. He had been something of a drifter, and an alcoholic; he had been a coal salesman near the end of his life. George's mother was distraught because she did not know how to pay for the burial. She was Jack's aunt Grace, widow of Maud's brother Gerald, and her husband had left her with very little money. When Jack heard about her need he told her, "Send the bill to me." Later, it turned out that the coal supplier had commission money due George, which paid for the funeral.

Over the years, Jack took thought and care for his Aunt Grace. She, like Jack's and Connie's families, traced her line back to the earliest days of the English in America—in her case, to Stephen Hopkins, the indentured servant of Elder Brewster of the Massachusetts Bay Colony. Jack's cousin John Merchant recalls that his mother and Jack were close and fond of each other. He also recalls that after Jack died, Connie kept up the relationship for the rest of Grace's life.

In late 1962, despite the usual bustle of activity in the home, Jack managed to lead a relatively quiet life. One innovation he enjoyed was a television set with a remote control! He got out to Yale Club lunches from time to time, and to the Newcomers Club, which he had joined when he first moved to Washington and loved to attend whenever he was in town. He and Connie kept track of the Riffe family, the Rickerts, the Cornells, the Statons, Admiral DeWitt Hamberger and his wife Tincy, and the new rector at St. John's Church, Dr. Harper. In early December he spent a week in the hospital.

The man who meant the most to Jack as a companion and friend in these months was Arthur Meigs. Arthur was a quiet man, some fifteen years younger than Jack. He, with his wife Ellen Lee and their two children, lived a short distance away, near the Washington National Cathedral. Sometimes Connie served Jack and Arthur a quiet lunch in Jack's study. They would talk for hours.

A vivid testimony to the strength of Jack's inner life is found in his worn copy of *Just for Today*, poems collected by Miles Phillimore, a friend and colleague from England. Jack jotted down notes, from his own thoughts, on every page of this little booklet. "There is no *room* for me in my own *house!*" Prayers: "*O Jesus*, make us to be *masters of ourselves* that we may be *servants of all!*" and quotations: "This is the Lord's doing, and it is marvelous in our eyes." Connie had the notes typed out, from this thin pamphlet of 40 pages, and the notes filled seventeen single-spaced typewritten sheets. "'No heart is pure that is not passionate.' —Frank [Buchman]." The hymn lines "Let the healing streams abound; make and keep me pure within" are underlined in the book, and this added: "Frank's strength. He calls them

'The greatest words written in the English language.'"

Jack went to New York with Day to attend the Burrwood meetings at the City Bank, whose trust officers were custodians of the corporation. The meetings involved presentations by experts in various aspects of investment and economic trends, national and global, and also involved first-class food, which both Jack and Day enjoyed. At this time, the Burrwood meetings involved the three children of Walter Jennings and their common interest: Oliver ("Uncle Ollie"); Henry Taylor, Connie's brother-in-law, representing Jeannette's interest; and Jack, Day assisting him, representing Connie's. The experts at these meetings didn't take Ollie seriously, as he was somewhat diffident and did not present himself forcefully. When Ollie finally died in 1968, any questions as to his financial ability were squashed by the revelation that he had more than tripled his inheritance through judicious investment decisions.

Jack had kept in moderate touch with The Hill School over the years. He had planned on Niel going there, and when Niel died his interest in the school waned somewhat. He usually gave a nominal sum ($10, for instance) to Hill requests for alumni support, except for $100 given in 1958 for a drive for the endowment fund. He had recommended to The Hill that the son of his cousin Kay Greer and her husband Admiral Marshall Greer be considered, and the young man was accepted.[1]

Jack had gone back to The Hill for his fortieth reunion, taking Florence with him. In May of 1961 he attended his class's fiftieth reunion. In thanking the school for the weekend he quoted the words engraved in the chapel, "Stand fast in the faith. Quit you like men," as a timely challenge, personally and nationally. His last letter from The Hill was a thank-you note for "your fine gift of $5 to the Forefront Challenge Campaign, which has now topped $3,050,000 of a goal of $4,000,000." Truly Jack was carefully directing his money into one burning focus to affect world history and not every fine cause.

Jack's touches with Yale were more lively. He had edited the class yearbook and served as class secretary for twenty-five years. But again, any gifts to Yale were nominal. He had attended a number of Class of 1915 reunions and meetings, and of course kept in touch with his Yale friends all his life.

In November 1962 Jack wrote Peter Howard with news from Washington: "There has been a continuing stream of visitors coming through '2419'. They seem far more open to ideology than our guests of former years. A number are on the way to change. . . . The whole household . . . is finding a new zest for the battle and we truly live in the expectancy of miracles.

"Connie has given several strategic luncheons, one for Janet Dulles, widow of John Foster Dulles [President Eisenhower's Secretary of State], and another for Representative Marguerite Stitt Church [Republican from Chicago].

"Connie and I went to a luncheon at the Sulgrave Club, [and] sat at a table with General and Mrs. Omar Bradley." Jack listed a number of other dignitaries from the United States and abroad he had met at the luncheon, and continued:

"For some time I have been overtired. My heart has responded well to treatment so the doctors . . . think my fatigue, which truly is not spiritual, is due to a cause which surgery can cure. They recommend an operation. . . . The choice is my own to make. I have had guidance with the family and think it is right to go to the hospital on Monday November 26 [unless] you have any check against it."

Howard wrote back from Osaka, Japan:

"My dear old Jack,[2] your letter to me . . . was the greatest joy. I am concerned about your health and if you feel that this operation, of which I can guess the nature, will help, I should have it by all means. Send me a cable when you go into hospital and we will pray you along to fullest recovery.

"I do not want to weary you with long letters. I only want you to know that you and Connie and your family and the way you are marvellously taking up the right battle in Washington, fills me with greatest joy. I look forward to seeing you again soon. Meanwhile, all the Howards send their love to you."

Jack had the operation at the end of November. Peter Howard and Paul Campbell wired him from Tokyo, "GREAT PEACE HAVE THEY WHO LOVE THY LAW AND NOTHING SHALL OFFEND THEM YOU WILL BE MARVELLOUSLY SUSTAINED LOVE." Jack was back at home in a week.

Jack wrote in March of 1963 to Peter Howard who was then in London: "A joyous Easter to all. I may be a bit ahead of time but our crocuses are up, the forsythia out, the willows a'greening along the Potomac, and a feeling of resurrection abounds."

This correspondence with Peter Howard meant a great deal to Jack. Peter's letters to Jack were encouraging, warm-hearted, the words of a genuine friend.[3]

Peter Howard had written a new play, *Music at Midnight*, which portrayed a fictional situation similar to the 1956 uprising in Hungary. In March of 1963 the Elys traveled to Cincinnati to see it. The play toured the country, performed by a professional cast. Florence was by then a member of the stagehands' union so she could work backstage as the dresser for the star, British actress Nora Swinburne, who wanted someone with a faith in her "corner."

From Cincinnati the Elys drove in leisurely fashion to Rockingham, North Carolina, to attend the wedding of one of Congressman Charles Deane's daughters. Day recalls that at this event her picture-taking father, enraptured with photo opportunities among the dogwoods and azaleas, practically superseded the hired professional photographer.

Peter Howard, who was expending his life relentlessly to develop fresh momentum for MRA following Buchman's death, also created a musical, *Space is so Startling*—again with Leland Holland as the lead singer. Florence went to Atlanta to join the company and help the show move through the country. Peter wrote to Jack: "[*Space is so Startling*] is a darned good musical and cuts in with a zip and bite that out-matches even *The Vanishing Island*. It will at the same time be a severe challenge to America because, although it is unquestionably anti-Communist in the right sense, it is also anti-materialist in the right sense in terms of the Western powers. It does present with much joy and a considerable degree of laughter and tears, the majesty of God's answer."

Sam Shoemaker, who had meant so much to Jack in the 1930s, died in the fall of 1963. And in November, John Fitzgerald Kennedy, the thirty-fifth president of the United States, was assassinated on the streets of Dallas.

Jack's diary for 1963 noted that he was putting his putting his papers in order so that they would be useful after he was gone.[4]

On Christmas day Jack and Connie were quietly at home. They celebrated with a game of backgammon. A few days after Christmas Jack and Connie flew south and spent a month at Winter Park, Florida. There was an assortment of old friends nearby. Jack suffered frequently from heart congestion, and it was evident that he was not well. But on January 22, 1964, Connie noted in her diary, "Pa gave me a white azalea—just beautiful."

At the end of July, Florence who was at Mackinac and Jerry Nelson, a dynamic entrepreneur and builder who had been a student leader at the University of California at Los Angeles, telephoned Jack and Connie to announce their engagement. Florence found it exciting that all four of Jerry's grandparents were born in Norway, and has always kept up the Norwegian connection. The Elys drove to Mackinac to be there with them. Jerry had been involved in construction, on the east end of the island, of a new center to replace MRA's use of the old Island House. The new buildings were bustling with life. A film was being made of *Music at Midnight*, renamed *Decision at Midnight* because of a copyright problem. After hosting an elegant engagement party for the happy pair and getting acquainted with their new in-laws, Jack and Connie quietly returned by car to the East Coast.

They left Mackinac Island and drove to Nort and Mary Brotherton's home in Ann Arbor for the night. They had known the Brothertons since the 1930s in New York. The Ely car developed trouble; they could not get it to shift into reverse. They put the car into a service garage, where a mechanic worked on it all night. In the meantime they had a "quiet, sleepy day," according to Connie's diary. They saw Flo Allen, the Brothertons' daughter, whose husband Art had been Mary's primary physician when she died there six years before, and Marge Eadie, whose husband was a public health physician. The Elys took Nort and Mary to the dining room of the Student Union at the University of Michigan for dinner.

In the morning they were able to leave Ann Arbor and drive to Westfield, Ohio. There they visited the church retirement home where Aunt Grace Merchant lived, and took her to lunch. By easy stages they proceeded to New Haven and booked into what Connie described as a charming Holiday House. The next day was Sunday, and they went to Trinity Episcopal Church on the Green, and had lunch with friends at the Taft Hotel.

The next day they drove to New London, took the ferry to Long Island, and arrived in Jack's old stamping ground, Southampton. They stayed at the Irving House.

It was like old times. Swimming, lunch at the Shinnecock Club, old friends, tennis, visiting the site of Fort Hill, which had recently burned to the ground. Jack was short of breath, but he watched tennis and even played a little. On Friday they drove over to Cold Spring Harbor for tea with Connie's sister Jeannette, and then returned to Southampton. Jack had further signs of heart trouble, and was in bed by 6:00 p.m. The next day, Saturday, they called a Dr. Diefenbach, who gave Jack a shot of diuretic medicine. He told Connie that Jack's heart had been tired for a long time. They stayed quiet all day. Florence phoned in the evening—it was good to talk to her. And Jack slept well that night.

On Sunday they were up and went to church, then a rest and to watch tennis, and to bed. Two more quiet days. Monday it was too rainy to swim but they drove along the beach. Tuesday was lovely; they had a glorious swim, and Jack took photos. On Wednesday they drove as far as Princeton, with a stop at Jones Beach, and booked into the Holiday Inn. Thursday they drove on to Washington and home.

Dr. Snyder saw Jack the next morning, and sent him to a specialist, Dr. Gustafson. Digitalis was prescribed, and Jack began taking it steadily. Day and Florence arrived to be with them.

On Monday Jack was taken to Doctors Hospital by ambulance. The family kept close tabs on Jack's condition at the hospital. Connie would go usually twice a day, and Florence or Day would visit in between. At first Jack was on oxygen continuously, but by the third day his breathing was enough better that he did not need it all the time.

He needed help with his meals. "Pa seems so weak," Connie noted on Tuesday, September 15, and "Pa very sick" the next day.

Meanwhile one of the preoccupations at their home was the preparation for the wedding of Florence and Jerry Nelson. They were planning to have the reception on the lawn, with a caterer and tents and all the trappings. Jack urged them to go ahead with all the plans.

Connie did not feel that the hospital staff was responsive enough to Jack's needs. She found that his oxygen had run out one day, and that the staff had not noticed it. At this time there were quite a few professional nurses working full-time with MRA, so Connie asked for help.

On Saturday that week Barbara Beal, daughter of Ralph and Theone Beal and a registered nurse with her degree from Stanford University, came to help in the hospital, as did another young nurse, Barbara Seymour of Louisville, Kentucky. From that time, one of the two Barbaras was always with Jack. They shared a room at the Ely home, but were never there at the same time. Barbara Beal took the day shift in the hospital room and Barbara Seymour the night shift. Being with Jack in these last days meant a lot to both of them.

Barbara Beal's recollections are clear. "It was congestive heart failure," she says, "the long-term result of rheumatic fever as a child [probably the incident he had at the Hill School]. When Jack was young, the medical profession didn't know that rheumatic fever was the result of streptococcus. Today strep infections are treated before they affect the kidneys and other vital organs. But strep residing in the tissues for long years slowly causes damage to the tissues. And then someday you get something like a heart murmur because the heart valves are damaged."

She noted that Jack was not at all demanding: "His breeding always came through, even to apologizing if you had to do very personal things. He accepted everything with grace. Because he couldn't do it for himself—like going to the bathroom. He was above such things as embarrassment or distaste. He would apologize because he didn't want to be a nuisance. It was a feeling, 'you're taking care of me because I can't take care of myself and we're in this thing together.' It was acceptance."

Barbara Seymour remembers, "He was a good patient, very polite, a nice person—but he didn't want to lie there quietly! He wasn't supposed to get out of bed, which just drove him crazy. I would go out to bring a tray or something, and there he would be, wadding up Kleenex and trying to shoot baskets. He obeyed the order to stay in bed but he was not happy about it. And he had gotten quite scared when the oxygen had run out, which was why we were there."

Jack was very much the gentleman; if someone were to visit him, even in his weakness he would arrange himself in his hospital bed properly, sitting up rather than lying back on the pillows.

Barbara Beal recounts further: "He was short of breath, and needed the oxygen. Mentally he was fine. We had some good conversations—about the world work of MRA, about my life, about my Dad's life. And once he talked about his brothers—Francis, the youngest, whom he had grown up with, and the little one who died almost at birth, and the one born after him who lived to be four. He did not have the energy to talk a lot. But he asked me if I knew how to sing. Yes, I did. Would I sing? He taught me some of his favorite hymns—he knew them by heart. They have become some of my favorites now. We'd sing them together, and when he got too winded I'd sing to him. The three that I remember: 'Ten thousand times ten thousand in sparkling raiment bright.' He knew all the verses. And the Navy Hymn, 'Eternal Father strong to save, whose arm hath bound the restless wave.' And 'For all the saints who from their labors rest.'

"I think he knew he wasn't going to survive this. He didn't talk about it much. But he did talk about life in the sense of eternity. He was comfortable talking about that."

"The night before he died," Barbara Seymour recalls, "I couldn't get him to go to sleep, and he didn't want to. Of course I didn't realize that that was what was happening, but I had experienced the same thing before, the night before a person dies. He talked for two or three hours, about his family; and that he was going to see Mary and Niel—especially Niel. The main thing he talked about was his father. I could see a mental picture:

'Dad took me into the White House with him,' a vivid memory. I didn't know the family well enough to ask some of the things he might have told me about, and I wanted him to be quiet. It was not a sense of fear in him, just a sense that he wanted to talk."

The end came just after one o'clock in the afternoon of September 28, 1964. Jack was seventy, three-score years and ten.

Barbara Beal was with him. "Connie had just left to go home for lunch," she recounts. "I fed him, because he was pretty weak. He ate his own bread but I fed him everything else. No idea this was the last time. Connie had some concerns; he was weak and complained of chest pains. I was just sitting with him there, talking, and he was just looking up, and all of a sudden his eyes went up like that and he was gone. Just like that.

"In those days a nurse, no matter how qualified, just observed, recorded and reported, but made no decisions. I called Connie, but she had not yet arrived home; I said 'Please tell her to come right back.' You don't tell a woman like Connie to turn around and come back unless you mean it. I wasn't used to telling someone like Connie what to do. So when she got my message, she knew.

"Then I got the staff; I knew there was no point in trying to resuscitate him, but you have to—so we tried. It was grotesque; he was gone. When Connie got there, I had him all straightened up and peaceful-looking."

Barbara Seymour was at lunch at the Ely home with the family, and Jerry and Florence were discussing plans for their wedding. Day was pinch-hitting at The Newcomers Club for her father who had been scheduled to make a talk. Then Barbara Beal called. Barbara Seymour went to the hospital with Connie: "We had a feeling—Connie was very stoic about it. Florence and Jerry must have come too. Jack was lying in bed, looking very peaceful. I had the sense he was there, comforting, saying 'It's all right; it's all right.' I haven't had that feeling too many times, but I did with him."

Sometime early in the fall, Jack and Connie had sent 731 copies of Peter Howard's latest book, *Design for Dedication*,[5] to their regular Christmas list, with a printed card saying:

Here—well ahead of time—is our Christmas gift.
It is a book for every season—particularly Christmas—
because it brings fresh hope to everyone.
We are sending it now so that you will have it before the election.
It contains information every American needs before he votes.

With our cordial greetings and very best wishes.
Mr. and Mrs. Albert H. Ely

The funeral service was held at St. John's Church, with the Rev. Mr. Harper, the rector, officiating. The Episcopal service for The Burial of the Dead was followed, with its quiet, reassuring sentences that were so familiar to Jack—the rector intoning, as he escorted the casket in through the church door and up the aisle to the chancel, "I am the resurrection and the life, saith the Lord; he that believeth in me, though he were dead, yet shall he live."

Muriel Smith, who had played the lead in *The Crowning Experience* and had often been a guest in the Ely home, sang "The Prayer of St. Francis" in Italian, in the setting composed by Seattle composer and family friend Herbert Allen.[6]

The congregation sang those favorite hymns that Jack and Barbara Beal had sung together in the hospital, "The Navy Hymn," "Ten Thousand Times Ten Thousand," and "For All The Saints."

Then the funeral cortege wound its way to that spot in Arlington National Cemetery where Niel and Mary had been buried, for the committal of Jack's coffin to the ground. A recording by Leland Holland, made a few hours earlier in the Ely living room, was played: "For The Risen," a great hymn that had been written at the end of World War II for the men and women of Moral Re-Armament who had given their lives in that war.

The whole crowd was invited to a time of remembrance that afternoon at the Ely home, and they packed into the living room and overflowed beyond into the halls. Jack's son-in-law-to-be, Jerry Nelson, with others of the men who had worked with Jack around the world, read messages from people in many lands who had cherished his friendship.

Wilbur Smith, the president of the Newcomers Club, wrote four handwritten pages: "He was one of those rare men who have engendered respect and admiration for the steadfastness of his convictions and his readiness to share them with all of us in the best possible sense. His compassion and courageous, forthright championship for the right and his pleasant manner won the genuine affection of all of us. . . . His influence upon us was great. It will continue to manifest itself tangibly and intangibly in our association and in our thinking and doing as individuals."

A message came from Peter and Doë Howard. Archie Mackenzie, now stationed in the British embassy in Rangoon, cabled, "Jack was the best of America. In God he trusted. Generous, farseeing, courageous." The leaders of Brazil who were working with MRA there, General and Mrs. Hugo

Bethlem and their colleagues, cabled, "We are at one with you at the start of this great soldier's new offensive." Rickard Tegstrom, the director of photography for *The Crowning Experience* film, cabled from Sweden. And messages came from Germany and Kenya.

Connie received this cable from Japan: "Your husband is the hinge on which the history of Japan has changed." It was signed by Japanese leaders who were on the 1950 plane for which the Elys had paid and by other distinguished families who had been their friends since 1935.

Among the names were those of two former cabinet ministers, Tokuyasu Fukuda (Minister of Defense) and Hisato Ichimada (Minister of Finance and Governor of the Bank of Japan); Conservative, Liberal and Socialist members of the Diet, including Jiro Hoshijima and Senator Shidzue Kato; six heads of major companies, including Kichizaemon Sumitomo and family, Taizo Ishikawa, president of Toshiba, and Shinji Sogo, governor of the national railways; leaders of the Seinendan (the rural youth organization); and the Sohma, Mitsui, Shirane, Horinouchi, Shibusawa, and Kabayama families—real family friends for thirty years.

Throughout the afternoon, Connie lived intimately into every moment, freely commenting on the people who spoke or the messages read. Speaking of the Japanese guests in the home and how welcome they had felt, Basil Entwistle said, "They took off their coats."

"And their shoes," Connie added.

. . . .

Notes

1. In 1991, Marshall Greer Jr. came to Connie Ely's interment at Arlington National Cemetery.

2. Peter Howard, born in 1908, was fourteen years younger than Jack.

3. Peter died unexpectedly in Peru about five months after Jack did; his widow, Doë, sent these letters when she learned that this biography was being written.

4. Jack's papers are the object of an extensive search. Connie noted in a letter written in the summer of 1968 that she was preparing Jack's papers to be given to Mackinac College, which had been founded in 1966 with Jack's great friend, Dr. S. Douglas Cornell, as President. The college, an exciting experiment in higher education, was forced to close its doors after four years for financial reasons. No one connected with Mackinac College has been able to throw any light on the whereabouts of Jack's papers.

5. Peter Howard, *Design for Dedication* (Chicago: Henry Regnery Company, 1964).

6. Herbert E. Allen went on to the be the musical director, for thirty years, of *Up With People*, which grew out of the work of Moral Re-Armament.

16

New Bloom in the Desert

FLORENCE AND JERRY HAD PLANNED to be married in October 1964, but when Jack died in late September they changed the date to November 21. "Father had made us promise that we would keep the plans for the wedding exactly as he had made them," Florence recalls. "It meant a great deal to him, it was pulling together all the threads of his life. He had invited his Yale friends, his old law cronies from New York—everyone was to be there." Over 300 came. Fifty-two people who had been part of the Elys' lives chipped in to give the bridal pair a set of china, "including taxi drivers," Florence says, "our dentist and oculist, a broad spectrum of people in Washington I'd known. It was incredibly generous."

Connie and Day spent Christmas in Arizona at the urging of Peter Howard, with whom Jerry and Florence were working closely. When they returned to Washington, Connie wanted to leave the Massachusetts Avenue house to the work of Moral Re-Armament and the growing "Up With People" program for young people. In deeding the house, she arranged that Brooks Onley and all the women (two Jackson sisters and Bertha Carter) who had been with her for twenty-four years would receive from her a pension as long as they lived.

"I don't think we could have had '2419' without Brooks," Connie said years later, "because he was really the pivot wheel. It was extraordinary what he did for us! He was one of the best friends I ever had. We used to laugh with each other because he always had to wear certain clothes for painting, certain clothes for driving, clothes for working in the house."

While Connie was casting about for the right situation—how to live as a widow after thirty-four years of marriage and family—her friend Carol Dunbar invited Connie and Day to share her three-story house for as long as they would like. Carol was a warm-hearted friend whose husband was with the government in Africa; they stayed with her for several months.

Finally Connie found a place that appealed to her, an apartment at 2126 Connecticut Avenue. The apartment had a large living room, which Connie wanted for entertaining, a good sized dining room, and three bedrooms—she wanted Jerry and Florence to feel at home there, and Day. She moved very little furniture from '2419'; rather, she left the house ready with its contents on loan. Instead, she bought some new pieces and brought some family pieces back from a house that MRA was closing, to which they had been loaned.

Connie's friend Frieda Lee helped with the decoration. The ample foyer was painted a gorgeous blue to match a beloved painting she had bought in 1921 in Spain, and she found the perfect Greek hand-made rug that reminded her of her good friend Doë Howard. Her style of living was going to be quite simple. She would make her own bed, serve her own meals, and be able to see her old friends as well as making new friends in the building. Connie was tired of organizing a large staff and wanted a relaxed household.

Wilhemina, the eldest of the Jackson sisters who had staffed the house on Massachusetts Avenue, was engaged to come in for a few days each week. She would do some cleaning and prepare dinners to keep in the refrigerator. This was enough for Wilhemina, who was semi-retired and wanted only a limited income to match her Social Security.

Connie had lived in the midst of the whirlwind for long enough. Now was the time to step out of the mainstream. She was greatly helped at this time, she later told her family, by a letter from a Dutch friend, Sophie de Bordes, who also had been widowed. "I discovered God had a whole new plan for me, myself," Sophie had written, "not just half of His plan for Jan [her husband] and me."

Soon came Day's engagement to Jackson P. ("Jack") Ravenscroft of Alabama, a financial manager and colleague in the work of Moral Re-Armament. Their wedding was held at St. John's Church, and they lingered at the church for an hour afterward greeting their guests. Connie's brother Ollie gave Day away, as he had Florence, and Connie's sister Jeannette brought the ancestral lace veil, which Connie and Florence had worn in their weddings. Connie gave a catered luncheon for about forty people at her apartment.

With her children involved in the work of Moral Re-Armament, and in particular with the building of Mackinac College on the MRA grounds at Mackinac Island, Connie bought the Pierce house on the island's main street. She spent several summers there, with ample room in the house to include others. Pierce House was the first home of her first grandchild, Nic Nelson, who was a great pleasure for Connie. Jerry Nelson was busy directing the construction program for the college, and Connie took an interest in all that was happening. She gave freely of her inheritance, as she had done for many years.

By 1970, Connie's focus shifted to Arizona, where both her children and their families now lived. The Ravenscrofts had moved to Tucson, where in February 1971 their daughter Virginia was born. She was Connie's third grandchild and only granddaughter. Virginia says today of her grandmother, "I think of a quiet but powerful presence. She had a grace and dignity that never wavered, despite the indignities that age eventually inflicts on all of us. There was something about her that made you want to stand up straighter, reach a little, and generally be a better human being."

Florence and Jerry had relocated to Scottsdale in 1969, when Mackinac College was preparing to close its doors, and had begun to develop land. They had started raising a family and were in the midst of a vigorous program of developing new communities in the burgeoning Sunbelt. Connie built a home close to theirs and took a lively interest in the three little Nelson boys, Nicolas, Tom, and JP. They were always welcome to drop in after school and visit with their grandmother, whom they called "Mormor," the Norwegian term for mother's mother. "Knowing there would be tea and cookies was one incentive for hungry boys," Florence says. "Every new merit badge, every victory—or failure—was shared with Mormor."

Connie also participated with the Nelsons in getting to know people in the community and the state. Florence remembers her mother helping her put on a highly successful dinner party for the governor of Arizona. The Nelsons had not yet built their house and were living in a small shack with no dining table. They served the dinner outdoors, on the flat trunk of the Town & Country Chrysler Connie had given them—covered with an ancestral lace tablecloth.

That year also Connie visited Japan with Florence and Jerry. The members who were still living of that 1950 Japanese delegation to Mackinac and Caux, which she had helped to finance, held a reception for Connie at the Mitsui Club in Tokyo. She was presented with a beautiful set of fine red lacquer that the group had purchased for her, and she, Florence and Jerry were given a private tour of Tokyo's world exposition. One of the 1950 delegates, Kichizaemon Sumitomo, spent five days hosting Connie, opening up his family's priceless collection of Chinese bronzes for her to see. He did this in gratitude for what Connie and Jack had done over the years to build a relationship with Japan.

In 1970 Jerry and Florence were looking for venture capital for their development north of Scottsdale. An investment group from Japan took a look at their land, with Jerry showing them the flow of water he had from hydrants connected to his wells. The head of the group, the president of the Sanwa Bank, came to dinner at the Nelson home with his men, and Jerry invited Connie to be there.

Florence tells of her mother entering the large living room at one end, "just as the president of the Sanwa Bank came through the front door. They saw each other, and they both burst into tears. He had been one of the delegates that Mum and Father had raised the money for in 1950. He knew that Father had died. He never expected to be able to find the widow and reiterate his thanks. He went over and took her in his arms and said 'I'm so sorry to hear about your husband's death.' Then he turned to the flanking twelve men behind him and let fly with a spate of Japanese. As they were leaving, the head of the trading company said to Jerry, 'I'm so sorry. We will sign the papers tomorrow.'"

Life in Arizona opened up a new realm of interest for Connie. She was fascinated by the Southwest and enjoyed getting to know its geology, flora and fauna. These were rich and happy years for Connie. Among her new friends were Walter Bohl, one of America's finest engravers, and his wife Annie. Connie bought one of Walter's steel engravings each year. The Bohls, an older couple, lived on a tiny dirt road in the McDowell Mountains. "They loved the Sunday paper," Florence recalls, "but they lived too far away to drive down to Scottsdale and get it. So every single Sunday after church Mother and I took the paper out to their house. We learned so much about the desert from Walter and Annie. They had a three-legged coyote they used to feed. They could tell us the habits of the birds, and told Mother what to feed them."

Connie made lasting friendships among the families that worked with Jerry and Florence. Four generations of the Treaccar family became close friends. "How she would rejoice that Troy Treaccar is entering Annapolis and is on the U.S. Olympic sailing team," Florence says. "The truly astounding thing to me was the way Mums made so many new friends, so quickly. Such deep friends. And so diverse."

Connie's sense of humor flourished. For her eightieth birthday, she said, "Well, if you're going to give me a big party let's have fireworks." Some 300 people, "all her 'close' friends," according to Florence, joined her and enjoyed major fireworks produced by a professional company. Another year she went hot-air ballooning on her birthday, and on yet another occasion went sail planing (gliding) with grandson Tom. Her outdoor adventures also included a rafting trip down the Colorado River at the age of seventy-two, two years above the normal cutoff age for whitewater rafting on that river.

Connie joined the Racquet Club and played tennis into her eighties. Her daughters remember that she was known for her diabolical placing of the ball. She rode horseback again, and biked. "She whizzed around the village in her golf cart with her poodle 'Pebbles' beside her," Florence says, "going down to the General Store to get her mail or calling on various neighbors." By car, she explored Arizona, taking her Mercedes off road when she felt like it. "She loved the chance to drive really fast on the freeway to Tucson," Florence recalls, "sometimes over 100 mph."

After Jack's death, Connie and her old friend Edith Staton spent a lot of time together. They had driven out to see Florence and Jerry in Scottsdale; after Connie moved there, Edith spent many winters with her. In the summer of 1995, when Edith was ninety-eight and still active in both private life and social service, she talked about her friendship with Connie. Connie's enthusiasm for the work of MRA had a lot to do with her devotion to Jack, Edith believed. "They really worked it out very well—using what they had for the glory of God."

For many years following Jack's death Connie traveled to Hawaii, at first renting an apartment on Oahu, and later on the Kona coast of the Big Island. While she still lived in Washington she took Tincy Hamberger to Hawaii in January to avoid the cold. Later, in Arizona, she took the family in July and August, to avoid the heat. In Hawaii she enjoyed being able to swim in salt water again, and went snorkeling with her grandchildren until she was eighty-six years old.

Connie maintained her interest in Foxcroft School until she died, and in the Episcopal Church. She could recite by heart the Communion service from the 1928 prayer book, and barely tolerated the 1976 revision.

She lived for more than a quarter century after Jack's death. She enjoyed seeing her grandchildren mature and make important choices for their lives. Virginia Ravenscroft started to learn Japanese at age thirteen, and when she was sixteen traveled to Japan by herself for her last year of high school. On that occasion Connie gave her, "with much love," an engraving of the Madonna by Fra Angelico to keep in her room.

As the years went by Connie became more and more frail, and then bedridden, and finally almost unable to speak. She never really lost her bearings, just became too weak to speak for the last four or five months. Day recalls, "With each new weakness Mother would show her anger and annoyance for a day or two. Then she seemed, each time, to sort out a new fresh relation to God so that she could again live in peace and acceptance. She was a blessing to me when I came from Tucson to sit beside her, as she was to all her Scottsdale friends."

"She may have lost a lot of her eyesight and hearing, but that didn't stop her from changing the lives of people, bringing God into them," Florence comments. Connie rejoiced to see that the faith in God that had meant so much to her continued on in the lives of her children and grandchildren. Florence remembers that the last photo of her mother with grandsons Nic and JP was taken when Nic came to tell her he was going to propose marriage to Kathryn and they were devoting their lives to witnessing for Christ in the inner city of Los Angeles.

Constance Jennings Ely died at home on May 15, 1991, the eve of her ninety-first birthday. Family and friends were around her bedside, including Jim Hunsberger and Ken Anderson, members of Jerry's construction crew whom she had known for decades. The family's boxer "Slicker," who had come into Connie's life after Pebbles had died, was present too. "Slicker was devoted to Mother, and she to him," Florence says. "I wouldn't have known that Mother had died except for Slicker's whimper."

The church in Scottsdale was packed for a service celebrating Connie's life. Later another service was held in Washington D.C. In a memorial booklet that Day and Florence put together, they wrote that one of their mother's greatest gifts was freedom from the fear of death. They copied hymns and Bible selections that Connie had written in the back of her prayer book, some under the heading, "Ideas to help planning my funeral, if I have one." One day, after Jack's death and Florence's marriage, Connie had written: "It will be a gay day, joining my Saviour (though I have so often failed him) and my husband and Niel and Mary, but I'll be sad and sorry to leave Day and the Nelsons."

"And Jack R." —this was added in different ink, after Jack Ravenscroft joined the family.

"And the Grandchildren." —this was also added later, in a third ink.

The family received hundreds of letters about Connie from around the world. Archie Mackenzie of the British Diplomatic Service wrote, "I owe a great deal to your Mother and Father. For three hectic years during World War II I lived with you all at 2419 and was wonderfully cared for, kept out of mischief, and met so many interesting people just by being there."

Sheila Hipps of Canada, a close friend of both Florence's and Day's, spoke for many: "I feel a bit bereft because she was like a second mother to me. . . . I not only miss your mother, I will feel the loss of all that she took with her—an era—the 'aristocracy of the spirit' which she exemplifies."

Migs Rickert of Washington wrote of how Connie "was always there for everybody. . . . She was such a good friend to me always and to my children. The night Van [Rickert] died, she and your father were on my doorstep in a half hour, even though it was nearly midnight."

And from Arizona friend Ann O'Brien: "I always will hold her in my memory as an example of how well a person can live as they age. I have a picture in my mind of her going [in a raft] down the Colorado River."

* * *

Shortly before Arthur Meigs died in 1996 he said, "Jack was one of the outstanding men of this country. Frank Buchman recognized him as such. Everybody I saw and met [in this work] had to face the cruelty of having your old friends leave you, because of the standards Frank focused. Jack went through this. Jack never, that I knew, had resentment against any of them—an Archie MacLeish or a Dean Acheson. They couldn't let him go, either. He was one of them. They couldn't resist his caring for them.

"It was Frank's vision that Jack responded to. Many of us didn't want to introduce our friends to Frank, but Jack did. Connie and Jack both felt humble that they could work with this force and with Frank."

"Jack fought for Frank to have MRA incorporated so as to have financial stability. He was always thinking of practical things like that. He'd get a conviction and would stick right with it. I think Frank respected that."

Congressman Charles Bennett, Democrat, of Jacksonville, Florida, had been in and out of the Ely home often after being elected to Congress in 1946. He spoke of the Elys: "Their frequent dinner parties and garden parties were devoted to spiritually uplifting conversations, good food, and quantities of well brewed English tea. It was an inspiration to know them and to see them put their vast fortune and background to support Frank Buchman in what he was trying to do. Jack Ely was a sweet-natured man who had strong convictions about world peace and about living a good moral life and being on the positive side. They dedicated themselves to trying to help mankind to a better level of life. That was inspiring to me.

"These people could have been spending every Saturday afternoon at the polo game; instead they're doing all kinds of things, working with members of Congress and international leaders. They—Jack and Connie—were a distinctive part of the conversation."

John Cotton Wood, a close associate of Frank Buchman who had been at the Ely home frequently all through the years, recalled: "Jack Ely was a distinguished citizen of Washington. He stood for excellence among the old permanent residents of Washington, the fine old families who didn't come and go with changes in the administration. He stood for excellence and quality among those people. That marked the Elys. He and Connie were friends, and hosts, and confidants to many of the leaders of the country, over a significant period of years."

Barbara von Teuber, daughter of labor leader John Riffe who had been so close to Jack and Connie, wrote after Connie's death:

> When my father became the Executive Vice president of the huge labor union, the CIO, we moved to Washington where he had his office just down the street from the White House. Your parents turned their "Embassy Row" home into a place where he could bring labor and management together on neutral ground to discuss solutions to their problems. . . .
>
> My father adored your "Ma." He once said that if Lenin had ever known anyone like Connie, he'd have become a carpenter! She had created a working model of the classless society in her own home. . . . It was a commitment to a selfless quality of life from which the Elys never departed.
>
> As I sat with your mother for the last time that lovely Spring day in May, I thanked her for all that she, your father Jack and the four children, Day, Florence, Mary and Niel have meant to us. To my utter delight, she squeezed my hand twice as though acknowledging what I had said. . . . Thank you for sharing her with us.

Archie Mackenzie said of Jack, "I think of him as a great provider, a little like Nicodemus in the Bible, a member of the establishment who broke with debilitating convention and stood for something new. That took courage. I think their gesture in making their home on Embassy Row available as a center for MRA made them harbingers of what is now fashionably known as 'Conflict Resolution' or 'Track Two Diplomacy.'"

Day Ravenscroft wrote this about the lives of her parents: "In 1930 they each decided to commit permanently to seek and follow the will of God. This decision produced a permanent change of direction for each of them. The new direction led to great achievements and to a constantly growing delightfulness of character in the eyes of those of us who lived with them.

"They were not saintly every day but they never turned back. They each kept going in the chosen, promised direction—some days faster, some days slower, but never quitting."

They were truly a matched pair.

Postscript

By Florence Ely Nelson

May this account of our antecedents mean as much to you as it does to us. I have had to come to grips with a fact of history—that there is no absolute right nor absolute wrong in memories. They are filtered through our emotions and our current knowledge and maturity, and even through wishful thinking.

For instance, I have had a revelation reading about my father, whom I thought I knew so well. My dark memories had overshadowed any other memories I may have had. I am relieved and rejoice at being given a different perspective, a different personality of my father. I regret that I did not evaluate our relationship while he was still living. I imagine he has a different view on it all now and my heart tells me that he understands and forgives.

This is true of many of the people and incidents in this book. My memories are valid and have aided in forming me into the person I am. Yet they are only part of the whole. It is hope-giving to realize that there is far more to each of us than any one person can perceive from the outside. More windows shed more light.

Please do not judge anyone in this book. Know that others probably have different memories of our family and its passage through life. We have tried not to be didactic ourselves. As time passes, moment to moment we each change and grow.

The delightful paternal Granny with whom I played backgammon, who told so many fascinating stories about railroading days, the spice business, and the foibles of those hanging on to youth, may well have been a difficult mother-in-law. Perhaps I am myself. But there was another side to Granny. She was a lover of America. Her penchant for Napoleon was not for what he represented historically. It was a fad to collect *something* in the "Roaring '20s"—the more offbeat, the better.

It is wondrous the way our family has been expanded and enriched by the marriages of my sister and myself. A new dimension came into it with Jackson Pittman Ravenscroft and the part his family played in the forming of our country. Jerry Nelson brought with him the rich heritage of his four Norwegian grandparents who came to America through Ellis Island. They contributed so much to the weaving of the fabric of our national life in Wisconsin, Minnesota and the early rough and tumble days of Hollywood and Los Angeles.

We are most truly an American family, with the concomitant responsibility.

We offer this, our history, to you thanks in great part to Jarvis Harriman's painstaking research. It is an irreplaceable legacy, offered to our friends and, most importantly, to our families. It is but the first chapter in a story that continues with our children and their children's children.

May it never end! We hope this will encourage each of you to explore your own story. May we all honestly embrace our own histories—our own realities—as we create tomorrow's history, the legacy of years to come.

Selected Bibliography

Extensive use was made of the telephone Information Service of the Tucson-Pima Library, who quoted to me from many of the encyclopedias cited here and from certain of the books cited.

The tapes of interviews are now with the publisher and when indexed will be deposited at Yale University Library.

A.H. Ely, 1917-1923. Vol. 1 of *Briefs and Opinions.* From the law offices of Kirlin, Woolsey, Campbell, Hickox & Keating, 27 William Street, New York.

Alexander, Irene K., *A History of the Incorporated Village of Lloyd Harbor 1926-1976.* Official publication of the Village of Lloyd Harbor. Huntington, Long Island: West Hills Printing, 1976.

B., Dick. *New Light on Alcoholism: The A.A. Legacy from Sam Shoemaker.* Corte Madera, CA: Good Book Publishing, 1994.

Biographical Directory of the U.S. Congress. Washington, D.C.: U.S. Government Printing Office, 1997.

Birmingham, Stephen. *Jacqueline Bouvier Kennedy Onassis.* New York: Grossett & Dunlap, 1978.

Brown, Philip Marshall. *The Venture of Belief.* New York: Fleming H. Revell, 1937.

Buchman, Frank N.D. *Remaking the World.* London, Blandford Press, 1961.

Charlotte Haxall Noland: 1883-1969. Middleburg, VA: Foxcroft School, 1971.

Clune, Henry W. *The Rochester I Know.* Garden City, Long Island: Doubleday, 1972.

Cold Spring Harbor Soundings. Cold Spring Harbor Village Improvement Society, 1953.

Constance Jennings Ely. Tucson, 1992. Printed by the family after her death.

Cooper, Jerry M., *The Militia and the National Guard in America since Colonial Times: a Research Guide.* New York: New York Public Library, JFE 93-11896.

"Creating Central Park 1857-1861." Vol. 3 of *The Papers of Frederick Law Olmsted.* Edited by Charles E. Beveridge and David Schuyler. Baltimore: The Johns Hopkins University Press, 1983.

Current Biography. New York: H.W. Wilson Co., 1955.

DeGregorio, William A. *Complete Book of Presidents*. New York, Dembner Books, 1989.

Dictionary of American Biography. New York: Charles Scribner's Sons, n.d.

Dictionary of American Naval Fighting Ships. Vol. V. Washington, D.C.: Office of the Chief of Naval Operations, U. S. Naval History Division, 1970.

Ely, Heman. *Nathaniel Ely and his Descendants*. Cleveland: Privately published by the author, 1885.

Ely Papers of Lorain County Historical Society, a Calendar, Index and Chronology. "Prepared under the direction of Robert S. Fletcher by Dorothy S. Payne, given to the LCHS from the estate of Mary L. Ely Moise, Oberlin, Ohio 1955." The papers include business transactions of Justin Ely from 1761, also of his father's and grandfather's business—buying, selling land in Massachusetts.

Ely, Reuben Pownall, Warren Smedley Ely and Daniel Brittain Ely. *Ely, Revell and Stacye Families who were among the founders of Trenton and Burlington in the Province of West Jersey 1678-1683 with the genealogy of the Ely descendants in America*. New York: Fleming H. Revell Co., 1910.

Elyria Historic Book Committee. *Elyria 175 – 1817-1992*. Elyria, OH: Heritage House, 1992.

Entwistle, Basis. *Japan's Decisive Decade: How a Determined Minority Changed the Nation's Course in the 1950s*. London: Grosvenor Books, 1985.

Grogan, William. *John Riffe of the Steelworkers: American Labor Statesman*. New York: Coward-McCann, 1959.

Hale, Anna Ward. *Autobiography*. Unpublished manuscript.

Hatcher, Harlan. *The Western Reserve: the Story of New Connecticut in Ohio*. New York: Bobbs-Merrill, 1949.

The Henry C. Taylor Collection. Compiled by John S. Kebabian. New Haven: Yale University Library, 1971.

Herwarth, Hans von. *Against Two Evils*. New York: Rawson, Wade Publishers, 1981.

Hidy, Ralph W., and Muriel E. Hidy. *History of Standard Oil Company (New Jersey): Pioneering in Big Business 1882-1911*. New York: Harper & Brothers, Business History Foundation, 1971.

Howard, Peter. *An Idea to Win the World*. London: Blandford Press, 1955.

———. *The World Rebuilt*. New York: Duell, Sloan & Pierce, 1951.

Humason, W.L. *From the Atlantic Surf to the Golden Gate*. Hartford, 1968.

Hutchinson, William Thomas. *The Bounty Lands of the American Revolution in Ohio*. Ph.D. diss., University of Chicago, 1927.

International Dictionary of Twentieth Century Biography. New York: New American Library, 1987.

Isaacson, Walter, and Evan Thomas. *The Wise Men*. New York: Simon & Schuster, 1994.

Kelley, Brooks Mather. *Yale, a History*. New Haven: Yale University Press, 1974.

Langer, William L. *An Encyclopedia of World History*. New York: Houghton Mifflin, 1940.

Lean, Garth. *Frank Buchman: A Life*. London: Constable, 1985. Published in the United States as *On the Tail of a Comet*. Colorado Springs: Helmers & Howard, 1988.

Lentilhon, Eugene. *The Lentilhons and their Kinsmen of Forez, France and the United States*. Paris: Eugene Lentilhon, 1931.

Lewis, Alfred Allan and Constance Woodworth. *Miss Elizabeth Arden*. New York: Coward, McCann & Geoghegan, 1972.

Limburg, Kay. *All Things Are Possible*. Santa Barbara: Kimberly Press, 1992.

Mathews, Alfred. *Ohio and Her Western Reserve*. New York: D. Appleton, 1902.

McCash, William Barton, and June Hall McCash. *The Jekyll Island Club: Southern Haven for America's Millionaires*. London: University of Georgia Press, 1989.

Mottu, Philippe. *The Story of Caux from La Belle Epoque to Moral Re-Armament*. London: Grosvenor Books, 1970.

National Cyclopaedia of American Biography. New York: James T. White, 1924.

Nevins, Allan. *John D. Rockefeller: The Heroic Age of American Enterprise*. 2 vols. New York: Charles Scribner's Sons, 1940. Autographed by Allan Nevins; on fly leaf, "OBJ from Mother, Xmas 1940."

Newton, James D. *Uncommon Friends*. New York: Harcourt Brace Jovanovich, 1987.

New York Times. April 16, 1912, Titanic story; February 7, 1951, page 37, "At The Theatre," by Brooks Atkinson; September 30, 1964, A.H. Ely obituary.

Niel's Legacy. Washington, D.C.: The Albert H. Ely Jr. Family, 1953.

Official Museum Directory 1994. New Providence, New Jersey: R.R. Bowker, Data Base Division of Reed Publishing, 1994.

Prominent Families of New York, being an account in biographical form of individuals and families distinguished as representatives of the social, professional and civic life of New York City. New York: The Historical Company, 1897.

"Recorders of American History since 1877." In *Encyclopedia of American Biography.* New York: The American Historical Company, 1974.

Rosenzweig, Roy, and Elizabeth Blackmar. *The Park and the People: a History of Central Park.* Ithaca: Cornell University Press, 1992.

Russell, Francis. *The Shadow of Blooming Grove: Warren G. Harding in His Times.* New York: McGraw-Hill, 1968.

Shuker, Nancy. "Elizabeth Arden." In *The American Dream,* edited by Silver Burdett. Englewood Cliffs, New Jersey: Silver Burdett Press (Simon & Schuster),1989.

Squadron A, A History of its First Fifty Years: 1889-1939. New York: Association of Ex-Members of Squadron A, 1939.

Strong, Arthur. *Preview of a New World: How Frank Buchman Helped His Country Move from Isolation To World leadership, 1939-1946.* Arvika, Sweden: Arthur Strong, 1994.

Twitchell, H. Kenaston. *Regeneration in the Ruhr: The Unknown Story of a Decisive Answer to Communism in Postwar Europe.* Princeton: Princeton University Press, 1982.

Twitchell, Hanford M. *Brownstone Saga.* New York: Exposition Press, 1973.

Washington Post. Obituary of Albert H. Ely Jr., Sept. 30, 1964.

Weeks, Lyman Horace, ed. *Prominent Families of New York.* New York: The Historical Company, 1897.

Welles, Albert. "Jennings." In *American Family Antiquity.* New York: Society Library, 1881.

Yale Class Books. Various editions. Classes of 1885, 1887, 1915.

Yale University, its History, Influence, Equipment and Characteristics. Edited by General Joshua L. Chamberlain. Boston: R. Herndon Company, 1900.

INDEX

About the Author

Jarvis Harriman is a New Englander by birth whose life was much shaped by the Depression and World War II, as well as by growing up in a clergyman's family. He is a graduate of Trinity College in Connecticut. After wartime military service he spent twenty-two years working without salary in the program of Moral Re-Armament in North America, Europe and Asia, in the fields of personal, racial and international relations.

In the 1970s and '80s Harriman was executive director of the Tucson Festival Society, celebrating the cultural heritage of that southwestern city's Indian, Spanish, Mexican and Pioneer American background. He is the author of *The Man from the Hills: a Biography of Leland D. Case*, published by Westerners International of Oklahoma City. He and his wife, the former Nancy Dole, live in Tucson, Arizona.